Fear of Success

Fear of Success

DAVID WARD TRESEMER

PLENUM PRESS · NEW YORK AND LONDON

Library of Congress Cataloging in Publication Data

Tresemer, David.
Fear of success.

Bibliography: p.
Includes index.
1. Success. 2. Fear. I. Title.
BF637.S8T65 158'.1 77-3369
ISBN 0-306-31012-0

A Division of Plenum Publishing Corporation
227 West 17th Street, New York, N.Y. 10011

Printed in the United States of America

Preface

Nought's had, all's spent,
Where our desire is got without content:
'Tis safer to be that which we destroy
Than by destruction dwell in doubtful joy.

So speaks Lady Macbeth upon the attainment of the aim of her ambition (act 3, scene 2). Is this expression of a fear of success the consequence of the highly competitive arena in which she is striving to achieve? Will this sentiment later lead to the avoidance of this or other forms of success? Does she fear success because she is a woman?

While the fear and avoidance of success are ideas that are not new to psychology or to human behavior, recent work by Matina Horner has excited great interest in the psychological measure of a personal disposition to avoid success and a behavioral measure of that avoidance. It is with this recent wave of research and writing that Part II of this book is concerned.

Great personal interest was stimulated in the "fear of success" concept. It is not only the hypochondriacs who find in the idea of a "fear of success" syndrome an explanation for the course of their lives. In Part I are presented the earlier forms which the concept of "fear of success" took, especially in psychoanalytic theory and personality theory, originating with Freud's discussion of "those wrecked by success," but citing some of the much older cultural traditions involving a fear and/or avoidance of success. Matina Horner's work is discussed in terms of the background from which she derived the term "fear of success" and which led her to the inference that women fear success. Current alternative formulations for the same phenomena in the social and behavioral sciences are offered to broaden the range of experiences and behavior suggested by a "fear" of "success." Chapter 2 sets the scene for the broadest questions concerning "fear of success": what is meant by "success?" Is there really a gender difference in this response? What are the psychological and behavioral dynamics behind a "fear of success?"

The last chapter of Part I explores the idea of a "fear of success" from a social psychological point of view, demonstrating how many current social psychological ideas or subfields use different words to describe similar phenomena. These are all integrated into a "theory of boundary-maintenance," a useful model for viewing an avoidance reaction to "success." The definition of "success" is again questioned, but no substitute is given: a negative reaction to what others call "success" implies a unique personal definition in every case.

Part II includes an introduction to the current techniques used to study "fear of success" and a review of research done to date. Based on the collected findings of over 150 pieces of recent research on "fear of success," statistical tests of some of the recurrent hypotheses in this field (e.g., Are There Gender Differences in Fear of Success?) are made on the aggregate data from all of these studies. Several studies are analyzed in greater detail, including Horner's original study.

In Part III, some of the newer approaches to "fear of success" are couched in the much older theories about the avoidance of success.

My intention has been to bring together perspectives from many different disciplines on the fear and avoidance of success. I have sought to ask again questions which have ceased to be asked. The lack of closure for these questions exists because in their general form they are still persistent and unsolved for all of social psychological inquiry into humankind. This area offers a very good case study in psychology for how the larger questions are addressed or ignored. The reader should not expect to "know all about 'fear of success'" after reading this book; I will have been successful if some very fundamental questions about motivation, psychological research, and the nature of the psyche in a social setting have resurfaced.

DAVID WARD TRESEMER

Acknowledgments

Conversations and correspondence with many people were instrumental to the completion of this work. I gratefully acknowledge the critical reading of early versions of Chapters 1 through 4 by Matina Horner, Stephen Cohen, and Shelley Taylor; parts of these chapters appeared in Tresemer (1974b). I am also grateful to Phyllis Katz and Virginia O'Leary for a critical reading of an early version of Chapter 5; parts of this chapter appeared in *Sex Roles: A Journal of Research* (Tresemer, 1976c). Catharine Stimpson reviewed an early version of the first section of Chapter 6, which then appeared in *Signs: Journal of Women in Culture and Society* (Tresemer, 1976b). I have benefitted very much from Joe Pleck's willingness to share insights and materials, from several very helpful talks with Dave Kenny, Robert Rosenthal, and Pierce Barker concerning some of the difficult methodological issues in Part II, and from the encouragement of Rosabeth Moss Kanter and Carol Tavris in the writing of my first piece in this area (Tresemer, 1974a). Many technical points were elucidated by communications with John Atkinson, Robert Birney, Donnah Canavan-Gumpert, Bruce Cobbold, Peter Gumpert, Judy Jordan, Sue Kaplan, David McClelland, Henry Murray, David Riesman, Phil Shaver, Alice Skinner, and Robert Weiss. Susan Fiske and Zoe Forbes helped arrange the use of computer facilities at a moment's notice. The cooperation of many other researchers in the area of "fear of success" was necessary; they took time to unearth details of their old studies that I needed for my secondary analyses. To all of these people I give my deepest thanks.

Most supportive of my effort, each in different and complementary ways, were David Riesman, Dick and Nancy Ninde, Jane Hollister, the Folks at Potter Park, and, most of all, Susan Sharrard. Without the encouragement of this group, and the provision of physical and psychic writing space, I could not have encountered the obstacles to the completion of this work successfully.

Contents

PART I

FEAR OF SUCCESS: FACTS AND THEORIES

CHAPTER 1

Fear of Success—The Traditional View

A pole vaulter routinely cleared 12′6″ in competition. Just as routinely, he failed to clear the next height of 13 feet. His teammates noted that he usually had more than 6 inches of clearance at 12′6″ and therefore reasoned that his inability to make 13 feet was "only mental." Thus they conspired to "help him." When his back was toward the take-off, they raised the bar from 12′6″ to 13 feet. Unaware of the bar's true height, the vaulter made a successful attempt.

A vaulter's first clearance of 13 feet is something of a milestone and traditionally calls for a minor celebration. Thus, as the athlete landed in the pit and the bar remained aloft, his teammates rushed toward him with cries of congratulations. When he realized his accomplishment, he was stunned. He left the area and never again vaulted. (Ryan, 1958b, pp. 131–132)

PSYCHOANALYTIC THEORIES

The paradoxical idea that people expect to suffer negative consequences as a result of a successful outcome and thus avoid it has taken many forms in modern psychology. Freud (1915) first described this phenomenon in a paper on character types frequently met with in psychoanalysis, in a section entitled "Those Wrecked By Success":

> So much the more surprising, indeed bewildering, must it appear when as a physician one makes the discovery that people occasionally fall ill precisely because a deeply-rooted and long cherished wish has come to fulfillment. (p. 324)

Schuster (1955) elaborated Freud's initial comments by describing the ways in which people subvert their own talents, and explained this behavior as "a fear of asserting one's self because of the possible consequences (punishment, retaliation, retribution, etc.)" (p. 416). Success is associated with defeating others: the successful person risks the collective wrath of his outdone rivals.

Fenichel (1945, p. 457) thought that for these people "success may mean the achievement of something unmerited or 'wrong,' bringing inferiority or guilt into the open," and attributed these feelings to the lingering of infantile guilt and of conflicts over dependence in childhood at the primary, undifferentiated oral stage (also Reich, 1960). Schuster, however, along with Freud and the current writers on the "success neurosis" or "success phobia" (Lorand, 1950, pp. 245–254; Portnoy, 1959; Arieti, 1959; Lief, 1967,[1], attributed this fear to the guilt associated with the Oedipal dilemma, and the deep-seated belief that the prohibitive threats of an all-powerful father (namely, the threat of castration) would be realized if the person ever asserted himself. In these and many other writings on neurotic avoidance of success, or neurotic anxiety in response to it, males are seen as the victims more frequently than females (Newman *et al.*, 1974; Perris and Espvall, 1973; Reik, 1941, p. 218). Interestingly, the dominant mythic pattern is downfall of the male after success which exceeds the father—not only in the case of Oedipus, but also in the

[1]MacKinnon and Michels (1971, p. 148) stress that the latter term is a misuse of the diagnostic category "phobia." In his comprehensive treatment on fears and phobias, Marks (1969) does not even mention success (or failure) as a fear or a phobia (nor does Fodor, 1974). Such disorders would probably be subsumed in his general category of social phobias, and indeed the cases he presents for that category often involve extreme anxiety in situations where rewards, competition, and performance standards are involved (material dealt with in Chapter 3). Although this kind of phobia is rare in general, the preponderance of women in this overall category (compared with agoraphobia and animal phobias) is at its lowest point: approximately a 60:40 ratio to men.

tales of Icarus, Phaeton, Herakles, and Prometheus. The extreme solution of the Oedipal dilemma, namely parricide, inexorably brings on the destruction of the murderer, well illustrated in Shakespeare's story of Macbeth. While the psychopathology of the pole vaulter in the example at the beginning of this chapter is not clearly Oedipal or otherwise, the sources cited in this chapter abound with case histories of a young man who enters a debilitating neurosis or attempts suicide at the very point when he has received an awaited promotion, or is about to take over his father's business.

Flugel (1945) likewise linked the fear of success to parental prohibitions experienced in early childhood. He went on to suggest that the internalization of these influences in the superego resulted in periodic experiences of guilt for trespassing into forbidden territory, and a consequent need to relieve it through punishment, reparation, confession, repression, rationalization, or projection. He termed this the Polycrates complex, feeling it had a precursor in the "fear of Hubris" (arrogance or "uppishness") among ancient Greeks.

This reference to Herodotus's histories is lost to the modern reader unfamiliar with the classics. Polycrates was a prosperous tyrant of Samos in the sixth century B.C., who, because of his unbroken string of successful economic and military exploits, received the following letter from the Egyptian king Amasis:

> It is indeed sweet to hear that a man, our friend and ally, flourishes. But with me thy great success does not bring pleasure, for I am convinced that the gods are jealous of thee. One should succeed in some things and fail in others, and pass one's life between success and failure. For I have never yet heard mention of anyone who, after being successful in everything, did not at last die completely miserable.

Polycrates decided to cast his favorite gold ring into the sea. Three days later, however, upon slicing open a prize fish presented to him as a gift, the ring was revealed in the fish's stomach. Polycrates' incredible successes continued, and he perished miserably, as foretold (as related by Herodotus around 450 B.C., in the version by King, 1929, p. 123).

Ovesey's (1962) helpful restatement of the concept challenged the unquestioned assumption in earlier writings that only males showed a fear of success. He did, however, grant that males in this culture were far more frequently in situations of competition and rivalry which might bring back the early intimidating parental situation. He also made it clear that, with both genders, it was a *symbolic* masculinity and phallic power which was identified with a public show of prowess and attainment of vocational success (Ovesey, 1956).

He additionally generalized the fear of incestuous sexuality supposed to be the root of a repudiation of success to a paranoid reaction to murderous wishes toward a tormenting parent of *either* gender, or even toward a sibling.[2] The strength of the murderous feelings is experienced as omnipotent and thus necessary to be repressed. The symbolically revealing accompaniments are erythrophobia (intense fear of blushing) or the conversion symptom of blushing, both manifesting fears of being "found out" or "caught *red*-handed" (cf. Abraham, 1922, p. 13). The link to symbolic (vs. real) masculinity meant that, for *both* men and women, inhibition of aggressive success-striving is experienced as castrating. From a psychoanalytic point of view, the common base for men and women of fear of exposure is in fear of castration, based on identification in *both* genders of their ideals and strengths with an "inner penis" (Jacobson, 1964, p. 114), and ultimately in the loss of the internalized "phallic mother" (Fliess, 1961, p. 349).

The aspect of fear of aggression is linked to the reemergence of guilt for Oedipal striving "to surpass the father and replace him with the mother" (Lorand, 1950) and anxiety over retaliation. The aspect of fear of autonomy is also related to the mother but in the form of separation anxiety, especially in relation to an immature, narcissistic mother who prevents the person's individuation via threats of abandonment and serves to maintain the omnipotent fantasy of dependency and union (Alexander, 1966; Brown, 1971; Engel, 1959; Halpern, 1964; Jung, 1943; Levinson, 1952; Perris and Espvall, 1973; Reik, 1941; Szekely, 1950; Tabachnick, 1964; Weinstein and Platt, 1969, 1973).

[2]For example, "the inability of an otherwise bright child to learn arithmetic, because to do so would have been to compare with an older sibling who was gifted in that particular direction. The self-imposed inhibition on his own intellectual activity protected him from some of the painful feelings arising from his jealous rivalry with his brother" (Brenner, 1955, p. 203).

While most cases document the rise and fall of a person who has attained success and then sabotaged that success or fled from it, Marie-Louise von Franz (1970) has presented an engaging and complete picture of one type of person who is unable to sever this attachment to the mother. Such a person is a *puer aeternus,* or eternal youth, who toys with the successes of the grown-ups but is afraid of them.[3]

In *Envy and Gratitude,* Melanie Klein (1957) has developed another explanation for what is here labeled as fear and avoidance of success, understood in terms of the infant's experience of the mother's breast. If this relationship is good, the lost prenatal unity with the mother is reexperienced and "the infant who was first inside the mother now has the mother inside himself" (p. 3). There is gratitude in the appreciation of goodness in self and others, and a place for love and generosity in later life. If the relationship with the breast is not good, the child experiences the breast as mean, grudging, and depriving. He or she develops an envy, "the angry feeling that another person possesses and enjoys something desirable" (p. 6); in this case that "something" is absolutely necessary for survival though the moral overtones to this sort of persecution come later. The result of a strong envy and impaired oral gratification is the desire to spoil that which one cannot have. In this way, Klein explains clients who devalue themselves and defile what is good in their lives, including the attempted reparations made in therapy. Such behavior begets guilt, with depressive, schizoid, or paranoid features.

Klein's early object relations approach is *pre*-Oedipal and need not contradict the other theories described here which trace the etiology of fear and avoidance of success to a later age. For all these theories, only the briefest summary is possible. The nuances of symptomatology and therapy are left for the discovery of the interested reader.

Further writings in the psychiatric literature have linked the phenomena of fear of success and success avoidance to masochism

[3]The *puer aeternus* type was effectively portrayed by Robert Redford in the recent film "The Great Waldo Pepper," including the typical fascination with fantasied or real mountain-climbing and flying, a flirtation with purposeful ascent without the commitment to stay there or to apply these energies to the other exigencies of life.

and self-injury (Reik, 1941), "moral masochism" (Flugel, 1945, p. 501f.), debilitating manic–depressive attacks (Arieti, 1959, p. 437), reactive depression (Seligman, 1973), and passivity, guilt, and shame. In nearly every case, the presenting symptom, or vehicle of the earlier difficulties, has been debilitating anxiety (Lief, 1967; Portnoy, 1959).

While the resources for the clinical view of "fear of success" may seem plentiful, they are mostly in the form of case reports of one or several persons, and have yet to be systematically related to the psychology of the average person.

The Case of Morphy

A fascinating psychoanalytic study of "fear of success" is presented by Ernest Jones, Freud's disciple and biographer, a capable psychoanalytic theorist in his own right. The case concerns Paul Morphy, an American born in New Orleans in 1847, who at the age of 21 had defeated at chess every expert in Europe and America. Jones' story is drawn from his own understanding of chess and from the accounts of Morphy's illustrious life.

The young Morphy began playing chess as a young boy with his uncle, whom he could soon beat regularly. His reputation spread, and he had soon met the most serious chess players in the United States, defeating each in turn. At the age of 20, he visited Europe, and defeated all the world's eminent players who would dare play with him, often with amazing displays of the highest development of foresight, calculation, and power of divining his opponent's intentions. His greatest achievements were truly spectacular: "Towards the end of his stay in Paris he defeated blindfolded the whole of the Versailles Chess Club playing in consulation" (Jones, 1951, p. 166). After winning all eight games, a tour-de-force which lasted ten hours, the crowd rioted through the streets and had to be subdued by the confused police. His achievement had positive consequences:

> Morphy became the lion of Parisian society, was entertained everywhere, politely allowed himself to be defeated at chess by duchesses and princesses, and finally left France in a blaze of glory, the culmination of which was a banquet at which his bust, made by a famous sculptor, was presented to him crowned with a laurel wreath. (Jones, 1951, p. 185)

His return to the United States was greeted with an even more fervent acclaim since

> it was widely felt that this was the first time in history in which an American had proved himself, not merely the equal, but the superior of any representative in his field drawn from the older countries, so that Morphy had added a cubit to the stature of American civilization. (Jones, 1951, p. 185)

After receiving many fine gifts in New York, Morphy proceeded to Boston, where a banquet was given in his honor at which were present Oliver Wendell Holmes, Longfellow, Lowell, Agassiz, and others.

> In a speech at this banquet Quincy made the witty remark: "Morphy is greater than Caesar, because he came and without seeing conquered." (Jones, 1951, p. 185)

He was afterwards presented with a golden crown.

After such success and recognition, what could happen? In Morphy's case, he returned to New Orleans, issued an open challenge to play chess against anyone in the world and, receiving no responses, gave up the game altogether. He tried to take on a law practice and failed; he tried several times to engage a woman and failed. His rejection of the game led to a revulsion for it as he found he could not escape his past associations with his brilliant successes. The revulsion turned to paranoia tinged with violence, then seclusion, introversion, and finally an early death.

Jones masterfully draws together the evidence in this case in terms of the symbolism of chess. He finds the game to be a supremely distilled enactment of symbolic murder, revealed in the overwhelming mastery on the one side versus the unescapable helplessness on the other. Morphy usually spent hours at a time gazing only at the board; those who played with him reported the eerie feeling of sweat welling out of their pores at the particular point in the game when he slowly raised his eyes to meet theirs. Even though the game might not be clearly resolved for several moves, opponents came to know this look meant they had lost. Jones explores Morphy's brilliance at the aim in chess of maiming one's opponent by "mating" or rendering helpless (castrating). And he found in Morphy's background sufficient material to understand the "killing of the king" as symbolic patricidal impulses stemming from repressed hostility toward his father. Morphy's breakdown occurred because the sublimation of chess had ceased to fulfill its defensive function; he broke under the strain of too much success which had diminished the distance between the unacceptable aim of the unconscious (patricide) and the real accomplishment (symbolic murder of many father-like opponents). Jones' analysis of Morphy's case is an engaging application of the theoretical principles presented earlier, bringing to life the psychodynamic ideas thought to be at the root of a neurotic conflict about success.

An Application to Sports

Similarly, the studies by Beisser (1967) and Ryan (1958a,b) overflow with dramatic illustrations of murderous aggression and guilt about its expression, all enacted on a symbolic level on the playing fields of modern-day sports. When an individual's or a team's violent wishes to beat the other coincides with an unfortunate event, the defenses against the symbolic aggression are shattered, and the victor of the moment collapses in guilt. Beisser (1967) describes several such incidents which resulted in upsets of favored teams in basketball. For example, "a team, seemingly on the way to victory, loses its spark under a cloud of depression when a member of the opposing team is injured" (p. 164). In tennis, he observed the action of conscience against such murderous thoughts in such powerful conflict that the player "unexplainably chokes or falters in the crucial moment" (p. 169).

A recent example is from a women's singles match in the $60,000 Tennis Week Open at the Orange Lawn Tennis Club in New Jersey:

> Cathy Beene said her problems began when she knew she could win. "The first game, I wasn't nervous." . . . "Then when I realized I could beat her, I got nervous." Miss Beene became so nervous that she served 11 double faults ("more than I've ever served in my life") and lost, 6–0, 6–2, to the 42-year-old Dr. Richards. (Amdur, 1976, p. 1.)

Beisser found, in addition, that victories in many sports are attributed by the victor to his or her captain, coach, or team as a way of avoiding responsibility for the successful aggression. Edinger (1972, p. 63) relates an ancient Mithraic custom of the same form to protect against dangerous inflation of the ego. A Roman soldier initiated into Mithraism always refused the crown or garland for military triumphs, saying, "It belongs to my god."

According to Ryan (1958a,b), the poor competitors—"those who falter at the moment of victory"—try to remain affable and friendly, rather than show outright hostility against a dehumanized foe. They are constantly searching for a magical routine or gimmick to assure them success, and concentrate on grandiose distant goals rather than imminent ones. Their performance in private practice is greatly superior to what they do in the actual game (cf. example at the beginning of this chapter); indeed, these athletes prefer to practice alone, and their potential is often fully realized only by coaches and teammates spying on their solitary workouts. Furthermore, they are quick to self-condemnation, verbally castigating themselves for even minor failures. Beisser (1967) and Ryan (1958a,b) analyze this kind of personality as crippled by a fear of aggression, based on the early learning that aggression leads to unhappiness through retaliation. They are unable to don the temporary clothes of seething hatred against their opponent, a preparation used by the successful athletes. While not explicitly linked to the Oedipal situation, these authors insist that these psychological issues are deeply rooted and extremely serious.

Other Conceptions

Numerous authors in other fields have suggested explanations for the phenomena of fearing and avoiding success without necessarily using this particular terminology. Harry Stack Sullivan (1953), for example, described the dynamics of performance decrement in terms of the sometimes disorganizing, sometimes redirecting, characteristics of felt anxiety:

> If you think in these [vector] terms, you will realize that anxiety—which complicates, by exact opposition, the manifestation of an integrating tendency in some particular direction—can mean only a *reduction* of, or a *reversal* of, the transformations of energy concerned in the action in the situation; that is, anxiety results in *less* activity toward the goal of satisfaction, or it results in activity *away* from the achievement of that goal. (p. 96)

Learning from such experiences of anxiety depends on the amount of anxiety. Too much anxiety is simply disorganizing while a moderate amount is organizing in that the individual can learn to minimize it by appropriate behavior. This was Sullivan's idea of the "anxiety gradient" from which new behavior is learned, especially in early life (see Finagrette, 1963, for similarities in Freudian theory, especially Freud, 1936). If the original behavior which provoked anxiety in others (and, in turn, in the self) happened to be something that could be called "success," this then explained success avoidance.

Using Sullivan's theoretical formulation, Marice Pappo (1972) devised a questionnaire measure of "fear of (academic) success" by assessing the presence of the following hallmarks of success avoidance: (a) self-doubt and negative self-evaluation, (b) a basically competitive orientation along with a preoccupation with the evaluative aspects of a situation, and (c) tendencies to repudiate personal competence and to engage in self-sabotage behaviors. As measured by her questionnaire, students high in fear of academic success did considerably worse than students low in this measure on a second abilities test after receiving information that they had succeeded on the first test. They also reported more tension and attributed their test score less to their own ability than did other students. There were no differences between men and women in the study.

Several approaches in experimental psychology also emphasize previous learning: "learned inhibition" (Harlow, 1959), learned escape and avoidance (Schoenfeld, 1950, pp. 82–95), and recently, "learned helplessness" (Seligman, 1973).

The Adlerian psychoanalytic tradition conceives of avoidance of success as another manifestation of effort to maintain a consistent self-conception. If a basic feeling of inferiority was learned early in life, stupidity can be used as a device for exemption from responsibility and success (Lowy, 1935; Credner, 1936).

In educational psychology, there is a large literature on the special education of "the exceptional child." Occasionally, a section is devoted to "the gifted child" (cf. Barbe, 1963; French, 1974; Witty, 1951; also Barbe and Renzulli, 1975, Burt, 1975, and Newland, 1976). The prominent effect, consistently confirmed, is that the gifted or bright people are more outgoing, sociable, independent, curious, and creative; a "fear of success" may lurk in the background crippling only a few to a great extent and holding others back a little. Several sources document the pretense of ignorance among the highly capable because of the feared deviance of too much success (e.g., Options in Education, 1976).

Two studies from educational psychology are worth mentioning here. In 1940, as part of Terman's huge longitudinal study of the gifted, three judges examined the records of 730 men over age 25 and rated each on success. Success here meant the extent to which the person "had made use of his superior intellectual ability, little weight being given to earned income" (Terman, 1954). The 150 men rated highest in success and the 150 rated lowest were compared on two hundred items of information. During the elementary school years, the "A" group and the "C" group were almost equally successful scholastically, and tested similarly for intelligence, at the 85th percentile level of Terman's highly selected Stanford students. By the end of high school, the C group had slumped in grades and achievement test scores, despite the greater involvement of the A group in extracurricular activities. Of the A group, 97% entered college and 90% graduated; the figures for the C group were 68% and 37%. By 1940, 80% of the A group and 67% of the C group had married; the divorce rate was twice as high for the C group.

Terman related these differences to family backgrounds: a greater number of the A group fathers and siblings were college graduates; a greater number of books were found in the homes of the A group; less than half as many A group parents had been divorced. Childhood ratings by parents and teachers showed them superior in prudence, self-confidence, perseverance, and desire to excel. Three sets of ratings made in 1940 by the young man, his wife, and parents agreed unanimously that the A group had a great deal more "persistence in the accomplishment of ends," "integration toward goals, as contrasted with drifting," "self-confidence," and "freedom from inferiority feelings."

Terman's initial orientation and likewise his conclusion was that the A group had a greater drive to achieve and better all-round mental and social adjustment due to sociocultural factors particularly dependent on the family setting. While Terman did not posit a "fear of success" for the C group, he did not collect the sort of information from which such a fear could be affirmed or denied. From an intrapsychic point of view, the question of why the men in the C group did not live up to their potential or find their success is not clear.

In a study of high school dropouts with high IQs (over 110), French (1975) found the males more frank, uninhibited, and happy-go-lucky, and also more assertive, independent, unconventional, and rebellious than those who persisted in high school. He did not link this to mental or familial instability, nor to fear or anxiety, but to an incompatibility between personality style and the demands of the institution. This point calls into question the specific definitions of success used by Terman's judges. French found that most intelligent females who dropped out of high school did so because of pregnancy or marriage; these tended to be shy and retiring. The remainder of the female dropouts were similar in character to the male dropouts.

It is important to note that the separate literatures brought together here are often closed systems. Fear and avoidance of success are understood only in terms of other concepts within that discipline. Thus, while several authors link the academic problems of "the child who won't" to parental narcissism and overcontrol, these analyses are not to be found in the educational literature but in the psychoanalytic literature (e.g., Newman *et al.*, 1974; Halpern, 1951).

Other conceptions of fear of success can be divided into (a) avoidance of an apparently successful endstate: e.g., Fromm's (1942) "fear of freedom,"[4] "fear of being superior" (Mead, 1949, p. 347), "fear of excessive good fortune" (Edinger, 1972, p. 32), "fear of giftedness" (French, 1974, p. 319), "fear of affluence" (Sisk, 1974), "fear of power" (Winter, 1973; Barzun, 1959, p. 75), and "need to lose" (Beisser, 1967, p. 158); (b) avoidance of ultimately negative consequences for success: fear of embarrassment (Holt, 1964, p. 37, 49), "fear of being thought inhuman" (Barzun, 1959, p. 70), fear of standing out (Coleman, 1961), fear of appearing unattractive (Holter, 1970, p. 175), "fear of conspicuousness, of public exposure of personal deficits, and of group disapproval" (Asch, 1956, p. 70; also Wolman, 1973), fear of loss of dependency or exposure of inadequacy (MacKinnon and Michels, 1971, p. 185), anxiety about the isolation from community resulting from the excessive individualism necessary for success (May, 1950, pp. 157ff.), and "price-cut fear" as a result of performance up to potential in a machine shop (Roy, 1952, p. 431); and (c) avoidance of qualities instrumental to attaining the

[4]The title of the British edition of his famous *Escape from Freedom* (1941).

desired goals: fear of competence, as evidenced by feelings of helplessness, inhibition of initiative, and an inferiority complex (Foote and Cottrell, 1955), "fear of competition" in politics (Rokkan and Valen, 1962), "fear of competition" in sports (Beisser, 1967; Ogilvie, 1970; Ryan, 1958a), "fear of competition" in business (Wolman, 1973), "fear of competitive situations" in the classroom (Scott, 1956), "fear of aggression" (Beisser, 1967, p. 158), and so on.

This accounting of all the forms of fear of success may seem one-sided—surely there is also pride and joy in achievement unsullied by tension and stress. Indeed, the positive relationship to accomplishment is usually predominant. There is not space enough to present the true balance of forces everpresent in any person, deed, or event, though it is attempted more systematically in Chapter 3. It must suffice to acknowledge that this balance exists as we concentrate on the oft ignored obstacles and negative forces that prevent attainment of goals.

The only quantitative social psychological research on negative responses to success images done before Matina Horner's research (see Part II) was by Haimowitz and Haimowitz (1958). They conducted a simple word association experiment where one hundred college freshmen produced approximately three thousand associations to five neutral and five "success" words (e.g., new car, best in class, a lovely marriage). Thirteen percent of the subjects responded with anxiety to the "success" words (scored as crossed-out or misspelled words, unpleasant or negative phrases, or complete blocking of any response) while only 4% did so to the neutral words.[5]

SOCIOLOGICAL AND ANTHROPOLOGICAL VIEWS

While the possibility that a person's achievement potential might be curtailed is disturbing to the personality psychologist, it is not surprising to the sociologist. Performance decrements and avoidance of conspicuously successful behavior are widely documented in sociology: e.g., "restriction of output" and social disapproval of rate-

[5]Gender differences were unspecified in the article, and were unfortunately lost with the original data (M. L. Haimowitz, personal communication, 1973).

busting among factory workers (Roethlisberger and Dickson, 1939; Roy, 1952, 1953; Blau, 1964). More on the sociological conceptions will be discussed in Chapter 3.

These phenomena are also commonly described in anthropology, including (with special definitions of success) "brother–sister avoidance," incest taboos, (Cohen, 1964), and intentional mistakes in intricate Navajo rugs. An example of adverse attitudes toward success-striving is offered by Ruth Benedict's (1934) description of the Zuni Indians:

> The ideal man in Zuni is a person of dignity and affability who has never tried to lead, and who has never called forth comment from his neighbors. . . . Even in contests of skill like their foot races, if a man wins habitually he is debarred from running. They are interested in a game that a number can play with even chances, and an outstanding runner spoils the game: they will have none of him. (p. 95)

It is interesting that the Zuni society without the conflicts of competitiveness for individual achievement also has no differences in status between the genders.

A widespread mythic form revealed by anthropological research is the hero or great man who has no earthly parents, such as Moses found among the bullrushes, or Christ conceived through parthenogenesis, or Herakles likewise conceived by God. There are many other examples from our own and other cultural traditions (cf. Rank, 1914). For these particularly important mythical and historical figures, the absence of a father (and sometimes a mother) means patricidal impulses need not be kept at bay since retribution is not a threat. One's full strength can be used for the task at hand and there are no limits on success. From another point of view, mammoth undertakings of a scope far greater than that known by the average human must be explained in terms of a unique parentage. For example, the existence and actions of Kamehameha, the Hawaiian chief who first united the warring island tribes, were justified by reference to his parentlessness, placing his accomplishment on an altogether different plane from goals available to normal humans (Wenkam, 1970).

The negative consequences of success are well documented among the ancient Greeks and Romans, illustrated in many tales, including those of Icarus who flew too high, Phaeton who dared to ride the chariot of the sun god, Arachne who wove more skillfully than Minerva, Prometheus who dared steal fire from the Gods, Polycrates, Midas, Croesus, and, of course, Oedipus. Divine jealousy *(phthonos)* becomes moralized as righteous indignation *(nemesis)* against the successful mortals via the cultural assumptions concerning success:

> Between the primitive offence of too much success and its punishment by jealous Deity, a moral link is inserted: success is said to produce *koros*—the complacency of the man who has done too well—which in turn generates *hubris,* arrogance in work or deed or even thought. (Dodds, 1951, p. 31)

The mere existence of a happy society was felt to be an offense, requiring divine intervention to reassert the heavenly superiority. Such a view has been common in the histories of earlier times, illustrated, for example, in this delightful passage from the sixteenth-century English historian Samuel Daniel:

> 'fierce Nemesis, mother of fate and change, Sword-bearer of th'eternal Providence' turned to the West, and was filled with resentment at the happiness she found there. . . . To put an end to their peace, she instructs Pandora to release all the swelling sciences, in order to make men learn everything except what is right; she is also to foster religious disputes and sin and make attractive two fatal instruments, printing and gunpowder. (Cited in Kelly, 1970, p. 186)

Sumner (1940) cites many cross-cultural and historical instances of aversion to success. For example, St. Augustine distinguished two cardinal sins: concupiscence and conceit *(superbia).* The idea of perpipeteia in the wheel of fortune links beliefs from many cultures in the negative consequences of success.

The Wheel of Fortune

A fear of success often stems from the common superstition that the higher one rises, the lower one will fall. This is a belief in the wheel of fortune, ever spinning through time, treating those who aspire to its rim to the heights of success and the depths of failure. The formula has been stated in many traditions. The philosopher Lao-tzu codified it in the ancient Chinese *Tao-te-Ching:* "Failure is the foundation of success; success the lurking-place of failure" (Section 58). The early Spanish playwright Pierre Corneille said the same in *Cinna* (1639, act 2): "Ambition, having reached the summit, longs to descend."[6] The classical Greek playwright Sophocles expressed the same in a pronouncement of the Chorus in *Antigone:*

> For time approaching, and time hereafter,
> And time forgotten, one rule stands:
> That greatness never
> Shall touch the life of man without destruction.[7]

So also with the Hebrew tradition, as exemplified by a passage from Isaiah (10:12–16): "I will punish . . . the glory of his high looks. For he saith, By the strength of my hand I have done it, and by my wisdom. . . . Therefore shall the Lord, the Lord of hosts, send among his fat ones leanness." In a mixture of Spanish Catholicism and Aztec religious belief, the sixteenth-century monk, Bernardine de Sahagún also wrote the formula in Mexico City: "For he who rejoiceth, who possesseth riches, who seeketh and coveteth our Lord's sweetness, his gentleness—riches and prosperity—thus endeth in great misery" (p. 66).

In his acceptance speech for the Nobel Prize in literature, Saul Bellow ominously quoted the Bible: "Woe unto you, when all men shall speak well of you!" (Luke 6:26). There were other predictions in that sermon by Jesus that the wheel would turn upside down: "Woe unto you that are full! for you shall hunger. Woe unto you that laugh now! for ye shall mourn and weep" (Luke 6:25).

Basic to this formulation is the construction of the vertical axis between heaven and earth.

> The tragic hero is typically on top of the wheel of fortune, halfway between human society on the ground and the something greater in the sky. Prometheus, Adam, and Christ hang between heaven and earth, between a world of paradisal freedom and a world of bondage. Tragic heroes are so much the highest point in their human landscape that they seem the inevitable conductors of the power about them, great trees more likely to be struck by lightning than a clump of grass. (Frye, 1957, p. 207)

[6]Perhaps this is why Goethe said "nothing is harder to bear than a succession of fair days" (quoted in Freud, 1930, p. 23).

[7]Lines 603ff. in the translation by Dodds (1951, p. 50).

But the energy which empowers also destroys. For a human ascending too high challenges the exclusive province of gods, arouses their jealousy *(phthonos),* and attracts their retribution. "The more your power, greater your fear should be."[8] Any human excess is brought back into the proper balance of the world of order: "What was great before, he [Zeus] brings to nothingness." Thus, as Might, the high police official who assists at Prometheus' torture, says: "There is nothing without discomfort except the overlordship of the Gods. For only Zeus is free."[9]

The higher the attainment, the baser the seed of failure within the success, as implied by Lao-tzu's statement. The Aztecs dramatized the equal and opposite nature of the zenith and nadir by treating their sacrificial victims like gods for a full year before the ceremony. This was also done in other cultures which had an annual sacred king (Eliade, 1960). Ralph Waldo Emerson (1841) also formulated this principle in his essay "Compensation."

Carl Jung gave this idea a place in modern psychology. He presented a striking case of success neurosis (though he did not label it so) in a self-made American business man, and interpreted it as a breakdown in the dynamic equilibrium of characterological opposites necessary to personality growth (1943, pp. 50–52). Jung related this case to the psychological law formulated by the old sage Heraclitus: *enantiodromia,* a running contrariwise, everything turning over time into its opposite. The more extreme, monarchic, or one-sided the success, the greater the imbalance, and the more likely an erosion or plunge towards a nadir lorded over by all that has been repressed and put aside in order to achieve the success. In a general sense, life leads to death, the exuberance and blind energies of youth are traded for the infirmities and insightful reflections of old age—it is when the course of our lives is past its zenith that the nagging questions about one's attainments and goals crumble the rationale for action in life's first half. "Changes of profession, divorces, religious convulsions, apostasies of every description are the symptoms of this swing over to the opposite" (Jung, 1943, p. 75).

The cyclical aspect of the widespread belief in the wheel is best expressed in the Greek myth of Sisyphus, doomed forever to push a

[8]Seneca in Seneca's *Octavia,* line 451.
[9]Two quotes from Aeschylus's *Prometheus,* lines 151 and 49f.

stone up a mountain until, when he reached "the very tip of the height, . . . the stone wobbled, trembled, and lapsed back upon him, and he rolled again down the whole long incline" (Miles, 1958). This process occurred over and over and over again as inexorable as the reappearance of each spoke of the turning wheel.

A poem by the architect Francis C. Klein using the Sisyphus theme notes the inexorable nature of the enantiodromia spoken of by Jung:[10]

> What would he have done having reached his height?
> Stake the great rock down with ropes and rods
> Driven through talus stones in Titanic might,
> Defying brutal judgements by the gods?
> Or only stand in sweat and watch hell's plains
> Roll away from his hands like a marble dream;
> The flatlands risen in burial mounds, and distant rains
> Bleaching a valley of dirty bones in a stream?
> No, he'd follow it bounding down the hillside,
> Splitting cracked olive stumps charred by the sun,
> Past the point where his straining arms had tried
> To break its fall, he stumbled and it won,
> Past the pit where beaten black he had cried,
> What could he do with himself if the thing were done?

Sisyphus shuns the success he struggles for but, if attained, would leave his life meaningless. It is the process, the changing, which gives meaning and majesty, albeit tragic, to Sisyphus's energy. To be statebound, even in success, would be real hell, as in Sartre's *No Exit*. In *El Dorado*, Robert Louis Stevenson expresses the same: "To travel hopefully is a better thing than to arrive, and the *true* success is to labour."

Tennessee Williams (1945, p. xiv) uses strikingly similar terms in a short piece entitled, "The Catastrophe of Success," concerning his sudden plunge into fame and fortune with the tremendous critical acclaim of *The Glass Menagerie* on Broadway:

> The sort of life which I had had previous to this popular success was one that required endurance, a life of clawing and scratching along a sheer surface and holding on tight with raw fingers to every inch of rock higher than the one caught hold of before, but

[10]My gratitude to Francis C. Klein for his permission to include this heretofore unpublished poem.

> it was a good life because it was the sort of life for which the human organism is created. I was not aware of how much vital energy had gone into this struggle until the struggle was removed. I was out on a level plateau with my arm still thrashing and my lungs still grabbing at air that no longer resisted. This was security at last. I sat down and looked about me and was suddenly very depressed.

Two seldom remembered facts from the Sisyphus story are related to the dynamics of success outlined in the psychoanalytic theories. Like Polycrates, Sisyphus was a king, ruler over Corinth. This *hubris* of social position was compounded by his observation of the rape and abduction by Zeus of the maiden Aegina. Oedipal themes are hinted at since God the Father punished Sisyphus for this witness in such a way that he would never fully succeed in the erection of his stone upon the mountain.

An example is given by Levy-Bruhl (1935) of a New Guinea tribe where excessive success is believed to *cause* failure directly. Too much success in hunting or in crops makes the tribesmen uneasy, and they attempt to worsen their performance. They fear a supernatural "mystic virtue" which will be fatal to those around the successful one. A dog always lucky in hunting is *maesa* (ill-starred, a bringer of evil); its master "will soon die, or his rice-crop will fail, or, more often still, there will be an epidemic among his cattle or pigs" (p. 46). Thus, while humans can voluntarily alter their performance to remain "twixt success and failure," the dog is usually put to death.

In her book comparing the death of a family of aristocrats in China with the Kennedy family, Pearl Buck (1970) suggests the dynamics behind the wheel of fortune:

> In the heart and mind of the common man, a basic fear arouses a natural hatred of the unusual, the talented, the brilliant, the innovator. This hatred is mingled at the same time with an unwilling "love," an envious admiration. . . . They [the aristocrats and the Kennedys] were too rich, too powerful, too successful, the men too handsome, their wives too beautiful, and so by the hatred of peasants and common folk they were destroyed. (pp. 4, 137)

Likewise, a bumper sticker in Mexico declares, "Down with everybody who is going up!" The fact that it is a bumper sticker with some popularity shows agreement with Buck's analysis.

Compare this with a comment in Wilde's (1890) *The Picture of Dorian Gray,* a morality play about excessive success:

> There is a fatality about all physical and intellectual distinction, the sort of fatality that seems to dog through history the faltering steps of kings. It is better not to be different from one's fellows. . . . we shall all suffer for what the gods have given us, suffer terribly. (p. 6)

Society is very much engaged in the moral training of the individual to avoid a narcissistic success, that is, an attainment which would withdraw that person's energy and accumulated resources from the social group (Slater, 1963). The voice of the revolutionary Shigalyov, from Dostoevski's *The Possessed,* announcing that since men of talent tend to rise, Cicero's tongue must be torn out, Copernicus's eyes gouged out, and Shakespeare stoned, is also not unfamiliar. Where there is a hatred of success for its elitism, its apparent inequality, its deviancy, or its insult to the abilities of others, there follows a fear of success. The social psychological interpretation will be elaborated in Chapter 3.

Advice to those fearing the inevitable negative consequences of the turning of the wheel is given in several places. The *Tao-te-Ching* abounds with it; for example, "If you are rich and of exalted station, you become proud, and thus abandon yourself to unavoidable ruin. When everything goes well, it is wise to put yourself in the background." This is, of course, what King Amasis advised the tyrant Polycrates to do. Expressed by the modern singer Cat Stevens, in his song "Drywood":

> Don't wish to win, and don't mind to lose
> That was just a cycle like a squirrel in a wheel

Christ's advice was

> Love ye your enemies, and do good, and lend, hoping for nothing again; and your reward shall be great, and ye shall be the children of the Highest. . . . For with the same measure that ye mete withal it shall be measured to you again. (Luke 6:35,38)

Fill the coffers of Fortune while you are able, against the day you find yourself at the bottom of the rotation.

For the individual not prepared to withdraw from worldly affairs, the Duc de la Rochefoucauld (1613–1680) likewise suggested

"There is great ability in knowing how to conceal one's ability" (Maxim 245). The same sentiment is in Francis Bacon's (1561–1626) counsel to the wise man to "do sacrifice to envy" (1612, p. 36) by averting attention from his talents and accomplishments. Niccolò Machiavelli (1537) likewise counseled the prince to let his nobles do the blamable dirty work, and even take the credit for favorable though risky endeavors. This is the same misattribution of one's deeds found among Ryan's "poor competitors"; only here this apparent devaluation of oneself is under control and in service of self-protection. If pride comes before a fall, as it must in the turning of the wheel, avoid pride and perhaps also anything you might be proud about, and you thereby avoid the fall.

In an article on "The Empirical Nature of Worry," A. Challmon (1974) saw this very belief at the root of self-imposed suffering of all sorts. He reasoned that we all have a conditioned association between suffering and relief; thus self-instigated and self-perpetuated worry is a mental activity which seeks to control fate through suffering. Belittling oneself, hiding or explaining away successes, persistent concentration on negative possibilities—these are as amulets to ward off the danger imminent to the successful and to start the wheel back on its upward course.

There is no clearer statement of the ultimate avoidance of the turning wheel of fate than A. E. Housman's poem, "To an Athlete Dying Young" (1896).[11] It is worth quoting in full, since every line marks the values implicit in this extreme romanticism.

The time you won your town the race
We chaired you through the market-place;
Man and boy stood cheering by,
And home we brought you shoulder-high.

To-day, the road all runners come,
Shoulder-high we bring you home,
And set you at your threshold down,
Townsman of a stiller town.

[11]From "A Shropshire Lad"—Authorized Edition—from *The Collected Poems of A. E. Housman*. Copyright 1939, 1940, © 1965 Holt, Rinehart and Winston. Copyright © 1967, 1968 by Robert E. Symons. Reprinted by permission of Holt, Rinehart and Winston, Publishers.

Smart lad, to slip betimes away
From fields where glory does not stay
And early though the laurel grows
It withers quicker than the rose.

Eyes the shady night has shut
Cannot see the record cut,
And silence sounds no worse than cheers
After earth has stopped the ears:

Now you will not swell the rout
Of lads that wore their honours out,
Runners whom renown outran
And the name died before the man.

So set, before its echoes fade,
The fleet foot on the sill of shade,
And hold to the low lintel up
The still-defended challenge-cup.

And round that early-laurelled head
Will flock to gaze the strengthless dead,
And find unwithered on its curls
The garland briefer than a girl's.

So death is preferable to the only aftermath of success. This poem has been standard fare at one point or another in English class between first grade and twelfth. What is appealing here to youth? Is it a vision of preempting adulthood, bypassing old age? A deeper question persists in my mind: how did the "smart lad" die? Is the avoidance of "the rout of lads that wore their honours out" worth actively seeking after a timely death? There have been suicides enough among the illustrious, but to hint that such is a possibility for the young shows the wretchedness of the mind caught in the wheel. George Orwell (1940, p. 228) analyzed his own boyhood infatuation with Housman's poetry as an adolescent preoccupation with "the simple, intelligible disasters that give you the feeling of being up against the 'bedrock facts' of life . . . murder, suicide, unhappy love, early death." A more modern author for the adolescent—Herman Hesse—has written many books with these themes, including one rightly entitled *Beneath the Wheel.*[12]

[12]At other times and in other cultures, the availability of a choice has been absent: "No man, Cyrnus, is responsible for his own ruin or his own success: of both these things the gods are the givers" (Theognis quoted in Dodds, 1951, p. 30).

In a similar manner, Samuel Butler (1890) hinted that death was preferable to a slower demise: "If I die prematurely, at any rate I shall be saved from being bored by my own success." Trollope formulated the same predicament in *Orley Farm* (1862): "Success is the necessary misfortune of life, but it is only to the very unfortunate that it comes early." Common sense persistently affirms that "one must take the bitter with the sweet" as expressed repeatedly in these excerpts.

What is the solution to this entrapment on the wheel? An old Hungarian proverb gives an answer: "Where ambition ends happiness begins." As the *Tao-te-Ching* says, the release from failure is found in the rejection of success, thus dispensing with the wheel altogether. These suggestions will be considered more fully in the last chapter.

CHAPTER 2

Achievement Motivation Theory and a New Theory of Fear of Success

---

APPROACH AND AVOIDANCE IN MOTIVATION THEORY

Neal Miller (1944, 1959) was influential in extending basic stimulus–response (S–R) concepts to general psychological principles, especially in describing the overt behavior of animals with respect to an object which represented both a goal and a threat. The classic illustration of Miller's model of conflicting gradients of approach and avoidance tendencies showed the approach tendency getting weaker and the avoidance tendency stronger as the object was closer to the organism. Thus the two tendencies crossed at some point away from the stimulus object. This explained how a goal might be approached and, on the verge of attainment, be rejected; again, if the sought-after goal could be labeled success, then the model described success avoidance. This work was instrumental in rejecting the popular Skinnerian view that inhibition was really only the modulation of approach in exact accord with the Law of Effect (see Schlosberg, 1937; and Herrnstein, 1970).

Scott (1956) extended Miller's theory to explain situational influences of what human subjects wrote stories about in the Thematic Apperception Test (TAT; see Murray, 1943):

> The net tendency to report the presence of event X in a stimulus situation is the resultant of two opposite tendencies, approach and avoidance. . . . The avoidance tendency with respect to X is a function of (a) the amount of fear associated with X, and (b) the degree of structuring of the cues with respect to X. (p. 344)

Scott varied the degree of threat in picture stimuli depicting various sorts of war scenes and, in a separate study, the degree of competition necessary to obtain admission to a college course. In both cases, "avoiders" could be identified by their reluctance to tell stories about anything which related to the threatening picture cue or situation, or, when they did tell relevant stories, by shorter stories lacking both in adaptive responses to the situation and in successful outcomes.

The popular motivational theory of David McClelland and John Atkinson (cf. Atkinson, 1964), most fully developed in terms of achievement motivation (McClelland, Atkinson, Clark, and Lowell, 1953; Atkinson, 1958; Atkinson and Feather, 1966; Atkinson and Raynor, 1974), relies most strongly on Miller's conception, both in terms of actual behavior in experimental situations and themes written to modified forms of the TAT. According to Atkinson's tradition of research and theory (see Weiner, 1972, for an excellent current review), motivation or a tendency to act toward a certain goal is based on a multiplicative relationship between Motive (latent, stable predisposition to action learned early in life), Expectation (cognitive judgement of the probability P of succeeding at the task), and Incentive (inherent attractiveness of the goal). Incentive (I), the "discrepancy between what is and what should be" (Heckhausen, 1967, p. 72), is assumed to vary inversely in relation to Expectation (P): $I = 1 - P$. Furthermore, Incentives combine with Motives to give the Value of the goal ($I \times M = V$); hence the name "Expectancy × Value" theory of motivation. With all the variables known (E, I, and M), one could determine the tendency to act in a certain way (T_A).

In this tradition of motivational theory, the motive to achieve (*n*Ach) has been assessed by a score taken from imagery in a TAT-type projective test. Stories written to several suggestive pictures were first checked to see if any of the characters in the story had an achievement goal, that is, did they want to perform better? If this achievement imagery (AI) is present, then ten additional categories of achievement imagery are scored: (1) stated need for achievement (N): an explicit statement about a desire to meet an achievement goal; (2) activity (Act): action taken toward attainment of the achievement goal; (3) anticipating success (Sa): thinking in the story about reaching the goal; (4) anticipating failure (Fa): thinking in the story about failing to reach the goal, or doubting that it will be reached; (5) personal block (Bp): some characteristic of the person in the story will be a block to his achievement; (6) world block (Bw): something in the environment will be a block to the achievement; (7) help (H): the person receives aid or encouragement from someone else; (8) positive feelings (F+): the person is pleased when the goal is reached; (9) negative feelings (F−): the person is discouraged when an achievement goal is not reached; and (10) theme (Th): the central plot of the imaginative story contains achievement thoughts and activities. More details on this system, as well as practice stories can be found in Smith and Feld (1958; also McClelland and Steele, 1972).

Fear of Failure

Achievement behavior was conceived as ultimately a function of a tendency to approach success minus a tendency to avoid failure. Although there were clearly supportive empirical reasons for this particular construction (Atkinson and Litwin, 1960), the formulation was based on the assumption that success was a hoped-for goal characterized by a favorable evaluation as a consequence of action, while failure was a feared threat characterized by an unfavorable evaluation (Atkinson, 1964, p. 241).[1]

The individual with a highly developed "fear of failure" (FOF or FF) or motive to avoid failure (M_{-F}, or M_{AF}) anxiously avoided any situation at which he or she might be evaluated and possibly fail.

[1]This construction was also highly influenced by the earlier work of Lewin *et al.* (1944) which concluded that level of aspiration and actual performance were the result of three factors: seeking of success ($f_{p,Suc}$), avoiding of failure ($f_{p,-Fai}$), and the cognitive factor of a judgment of the probability or likelihood of these events (J. W. Atkinson, personal communication, 1972).

> Motivation to avoid failure should always be conceived as inhibitory in character. This avoidance tendency always opposes, resists or dampens the influence of motivation to achieve success and extrinsic positive motivational tendencies to undertake some task. (Atkinson and Feather, 1966, p. 19, editor's note)

Thus "fear of failure" explained performance decrements or performance not up to the potential of the subject. A measure of tendency to avoid failure ($M_{-F} \times I_{-F} \times P_F$) was subtracted from a measure of tendency to approach success ($M_S \times I_S \times P_S$) to give a measure of Resultant Achievement Motivation. Though the whole McClelland–Atkinson tradition of motivation theory is very much identified with assessment of motives by TAT-type methods (Atkinson and McClelland, 1948; McClelland *et al.*, 1953; Atkinson, 1958), M_{-F} is curiously most often measured by questionnaire assessing some form of anxiety [either the Debilitating Anxiety Scale of the Alpert and Haber measure of anxiety, 1960, or the Test Anxiety Questionnaire (TAQ) developed by Mandler and Sarason, 1952].

Thematic Measures of Fear of Failure

Several attempts at assessing fear of failure using thematic scoring systems were made, but are not part of the mainstream of achievement motivation research. McClelland *et al.* (1953, p. 216) noted early that a preponderance of certain of the negative categories in the scoring system for need for achievement (*n*Ach)—e.g., personal or world obstacles, negative affect or anticipations—might be more a reflection of annoyance, hostility, or "fear of failure." Moulton (1958; also Raphelson and Moulton, 1958) and Clark, Teevan, and Ricciuti (1956) tried using subdivisions of the achievement scoring system as measures of fear of failure, with very little success. R. Anderson (1962, p. 294) extended Moulton's system to include several more categories, still a derivation of the larger measure of approach motivation: "failure imagery" was scored when there was any indication in the story of poor performance in customary achievement situations, doubt of ability to reach an achievement goal, anticipation of failure, discouragement or negative affect, desire to leave the situation, or daydreaming about something other than successful achievement. A different method for extracting a "fear of failure" score from the original *n* Ach scoring system was the categorization of the *outcome* of the story (deCharms and Dave, 1965; see also Arnold, 1962), a negative, failure, or questionable ending to an achievement-related story being an indication of "fear of failure." Heckhausen (1963; also 1967, 1968) scored for direct expressions of failure imagery, need to avoid failure, instrumental activity to avoid failure, etc. Birney, Burdick, and Teevan (1969), in an ambitious and lengthy program of research, developed a Hostile Press scoring system for "fear of failure" in TAT-type materials. Hostile Press was defined generally as

> assault on the well-being of the central figure by reprimand, affiliative-loss, natural forces, or personal failure. (p. 93)

The lack of popularity of a thematic approach to measuring "fear of failure" can be attributed to (a) confusion about the nature of avoidance motivation, illustrated by the sheer number of scoring systems that do exist to measure it and the generally unsuccessful findings of the studies cited above, (b) the confounding of negative, avoidance categories in the positive, approach scoring system for achievement (see Smith and Feld, 1958, for greater detail), and (c) the highly criticized low reliability of all these thematic measures (Klinger, 1966; Weinstein, 1969; Fiske, 1971; Entwisle, 1972), naturally increased when two or more such measures are combined to provide a total score.

The Possibility of "Fear of Success"

In the original statement concerning achievement motivation theory, McClelland *et al.* (1953) state that

> The child must begin to perceive performance in terms of standards of excellence . . . and to experience pleasant or unpleasant feelings about meeting or failing to meet these standards. (p. 79)

The above quote interestingly describes two outcomes and two valences to be associated with these outcomes—four possibilities in all. Thus instead of simply hope of success and "fear of failure," the motivational model would involve approach and avoidance tendencies which are independent (see N. Anderson, 1962; Lilly, 1958), in relation to two somewhat related outcomes, namely success and failure. This is clearly more in keeping with Miller's early formulation of the approach–avoidance conflict: a single object is experienced simultaneously both as a goal and a threat. A "motive to avoid success" would then be a logical extension of the original model. The fourth as yet unmentioned possibility, need to fail, has also been conceptualized and measured by Sarnoff (1967) and Maxwell and Gonzales (1972).

HORNER'S CONCEPTION OF "FEAR OF SUCCESS"

Matina Horner's recent work on "fear of success" is perhaps more widely known than any of the studies cited above. Her original study had two major parts of interest—the first concentrated on gender differences in the expression of themes in stories written to verbal story-writing cues, and the second related the presence of these expressed themes to behavior in an achievement task.[2]

In the first part, as part of a larger study, 88 male and 90 female college undergraduates were asked to write four-minute stories in response to several verbal cues, of which the following was the sixth: "At the end of first term finals, Anne finds herself at the top of her medical school class." Female subjects wrote about Anne at the top of the class and male subjects wrote about John. From an examination of all the different stories written to this cue, Horner described three major kinds of themes that might indicate the presence of a "fear of success": (a) social rejection or fear of losing friends as a result of the success indicated by the cue—"everyone hates and envies her," Anne has no boyfriends, her classmates physically harm her; (b) internal fears and negative affects because of the success—Anne feels

[2]The data for Horner's study were collected in the spring of 1964 and analyzed for her doctoral dissertation (1968). This study is summarized most thoroughly in two publications (1970a and 1974); it is summarized and further supplemented in a 1972 publication with the analysis of a number of smaller and more recent studies carried out by her students (1972a). There have been a number of other publications reporting the same initial study, each with unique secondary points in the analysis (Horner, 1968b, 1970b, 1970c, 1971, 1972b; Horner and Walsh, 1972). The popularization of this study has been accomplished primarily by articles in *Psychology Today* (Horner, 1969), the first issue of *Ms* (Gornick, 1972), and the *New York Times Magazine* (Gornick, 1973); this is important to note because many researchers who have attempted replications or variations of her study were familiar only with these last publications. Further details of her study are given in Part II.

guilty, unhappy, unfeminine, abnormal, etc.; and (c) bizarre or exaggerated hostile responses, or denial of the cue altogether—Anne is at the top but her boyfriend is *higher,* Anne is a code name for a group of medical students.

Two excerpts illustrate the sort of stories that were written:

> Anne feels guilty. . . . She will finally have a nervous breakdown and quit medical school and marry a successful young doctor.

> It was *luck* that Anne came out on top because she didn't want to go to medical school anyway.

Based on criteria suggested by Scott (1958, see above), Horner devised an eight-category system of thematic, TAT-type materials for "fear of success imagery," a measure of the "motive to avoid success." These are presented and discussed in Chapter 4. Fifty-six of the female undergraduates (62.2%)[3] revealed this "fear of success"imagery, while only 8 (9.1%) of the males did so. The male stories were characterized as extremely traditional in their achievement orientation, as "Horatio Alger" stories; the female stories revealed an anxious awareness that

> femininity and individual achievements which reflect intellectual competence or leadership potential are desirable but mutally exclusive goals. (Horner, 1972, p. 157)

To find out how these themes related to achievement behavior, Horner pretested all her subjects in a large room with males on one side of the room, and females on the other. They worked on the Lowell Scrambled Words task, unraveling as many mixed-up letters (such as EOVL and LPAPE) as possible within a certain time limit. In a second session, one-third of the subjects worked alone on a similar task (called the "noncompetitive" condition); one-third worked with a member of the same gender; and one-third worked with a member of the other gender ("mixed-sex competition" condition). The crucial measure of achievement in the second setting was the GENERATION anagram task, where subjects were asked to make as many words as possible in ten minutes from the letters of the word "generation." This score was compared with performance on the scrambled words task from the first session.

[3]In publications subsequent to her thesis (Horner, 1968), the data were reanalyzed and three more females were added to the fear of success group, bringing the total to 59 (65.6%).

Since the pretest had apparently been anxiety arousing, it was relabeled "large group mixed-sex competitive," and working alone in the second session became the baseline or control setting. Thus the two-thirds of the subjects who had competed against single partners were not used in her analysis. For the first third, most of the men (two-thirds) performed better in the competitive condition, while only half of the women did so.

Analyzed in terms of those females who had earlier shown "fear of success" imagery, 76% (13 of 17) performed better working alone than in the large group competitive situation. Of the females who had not written "fear of success" stories, 92% (12 of 13) performed better in the large group than alone, as did the men as a group (though in much higher proportion than the men). Horner concluded that women who showed "fear of success" imagery were also more likely to show "decrements" in performance when in competition with men.

Horner's conception of "fear of success" was founded on Atkinson's mathematical model of motivation. Indeed, she used the data showing a relation between "fear of success" imagery and changes in performance behavior as proof enough that this was a *motive* to avoid success (M_{-S}, or M_{AS}), that is a motive to avoid the negative consequences expected as a result of success. She further claimed that this offered a long-awaited explanation (as a heretofore unmeasured crucial variable) for the inconsistent and unpredictable behavior of women in two decades of achievement motivation research.

A number of comments can be made at this point about how Horner's conception of "fear of success" (hereafter termed FOS) fits in with previous conceptions of "fear of success." First of all, there is no special emphasis on early socialization experiences thought responsible for the development of this personality characteristic (but see Berens, 1972, and Veroff, 1969, on a developmental paradigm for FOS). Most striking is her idea that a "fear of success" is an important variable in the lives of women and not of men; this is the reverse of the position of previous studies which claimed either no differences in frequency or intensity for men and women, or assumed "fear of success" to be more a problem for men to the exclusion of women. The mechanism hypothesized to be at the root of a motive to avoid success was quite similar: repressed aggression which in certain situations of conflict causes anxiety which debilitates performance. The major difference between previous psychoanalytical theories and Horner's was her belief that FOS was not an exception (i.e., the learned reaction to an inordinately intimidating parent or sibling), but the rule. The repression of aggression was a part of the early gender-role socialization of all women. The result was a motive to avoid success in "intellectual competence or leadership potential" (Horner, 1972, p. 157).

The theoretical connections are summarized in the following manner: success requires achievement behavior, achievement behavior requires competition behavior, competition behavior is a "sublimated" form of aggressive behavior, but aggressive behavior is negatively sanctioned in this society as unfeminine. Therefore success is likewise negatively sanctioned as unfeminine. This conflict leads to anxiety and avoidance behavior in situations involving present or future success.

It should be noted that, while Freud's followers chose the term "fear of success" to describe cases of neurotic conflict in the face of occupational attainment, Horner was constrained to use this same term by the language of Atkinson's theoretical system: hope vs. fear, and success vs. failure. The explanation of this sytem in previous sections is intended to show that "fear of success" has a special meaning in Atkinson's system not in complete accord with the common uses of this term. The common sense meaning of the term has, however, been added on by interpreters of Horner's work, unfortunately leaving the clinical case studies and theory behind. However, by developing a concept of motive to avoid success within Atkinson's very practical and experiment-oriented theory of motivation, Horner made the phenomenon of success avoidance accessible to systematic social psychological research. Many other studies have been done in the past few years using the same or similar methods for assessing the presence of a "fear of success," reviewed in Part II.

Women and Achievement

Horner's work attempts to span the theoretical orientation to mathematical models for achievement behavior (above) and the tradition of writing and research pointing out the inconsistency between femininity—as traditionally defined in this society—and achievement—whether intellectual or manual, in academic or vocational settings. As Mead (1949) said much earlier:

> Each step forward in work as a successful American regardless of sex means a step back as a woman.[4] (p. 303)

Horner's conceptualization of FOS in women has been integrated into this mainstream of sociological thinking (cf. "The Uses of 'Fear of Success,'" Tresemer, 1976a, Appendix A).

Since there exist many other capable reviews of the incompatibility between femininity and achievement from the social psychological and clinical views (e.g., Douvan and Adelson, 1966; Fodor, 1974; Kagan, 1964; Stein and Bailey, 1973; Tresemer, 1974b), this complicated and bulky literature will not be reviewed here. A small number of oft-cited studies in the McClelland–Atkinson tradition of achievement motivation—particularly French and Lesser (1964, p. 128), who concluded "women who value intellectual attainment feel they must reject the woman's role"—is also not reviewed here because reviews are numerous and the details of these experiments far too complex for a brief summary.

SUCCESS

The metaphorical value of Horner's thematic cue ("At the end of first term finals, Anne finds herself at the top of her medical school class") at a time when medical school enjoys such popularity—especially for women—gave her study an important symbolic significance that might have been lacking had she used a questionnaire measure of anxiety or a score from the complex TAT. The cue brings up questions: why so much negative imagery among women and not men? What is success, anyway?

Deviance

In Horner's cue, Anne is more than just successful, she is "out of place" in two senses, both of which could evoke strong negative

[4]Compare also with the similar statements by deBeauvoir (1953, p. 662), Rossi (1965, p. 89), Maccoby (1963), and Korda (1973, Chapter 5, "The stigma of success").

success-avoidant imagery. First, Anne is excelling above *all* her peers, regardless of their gender (i.e., top of the class), a style of dominance *stereotypically* associated with men rather than women; and, second, Anne is doing competently at a task that has been defined in this culture as the behavioral territory or domain of the male (i.e., medical school). Publicly, Anne would appear to others as quite successful; privately, for the two reasons stated above, she might be experiencing a kind of personal failure. I would not expect this to be such a problem in the following situation: "At the end of first term finals, Anne finds she is *doing well* in her *nursing school* class." I would therefore expect negative success-avoidant imagery to be less in response to this second success cue. Perhaps, then, "success avoidance" is more a successful avoidance of situations where failure lurks.

The question immediately comes to mind: what about men? Perhaps, in line with Horner's theory, males experienced the John/medical school cue as nonconflictful and this was the reason they produced so much less negative success-avoidant imagery in Horner's study. Perhaps they would also experience (and express) more conflict to a verbal cue such as: "During his first term in nursing school, John finds he is getting along well with his classmates," a style and a domain that are gender-role-inappropriate.[5]

Success—Public and Private

Recall the quote by McClelland *et al.* (1953) in the original statement of achievement motivation theory:

> The child must begin to perceive performance in terms of standards of excellence . . . and to experience pleasant or unpleasant feelings about meeting or failing to meet these standards. (p. 79)

And later, the clarification:

> by achievement goal is meant success in competition with some standard of excellence. (p. 110)

At first externally imposed (by parents and other authorities), these standards of excellence soon become the internal measures of one's success in achievement. By defining failure as any action which results in an unfavorable evaluation, Atkinson (1964, p. 241) ignored

[5]Some of these cue manipulations have been tried—cf. Tresemer (1976a).

distinctions between (a) instances when there was concensus between individuals and society concerning which outcomes were to be treated favorably (success) and which unfavorably (failure) and (b) instances where this consensus did not exist. Thus, situations where, by public standards of excellence, the individual had succeeded, but by his or her own standards he or she had failed (and the reverse situation), could be interpreted as success or failure depending on the frame of reference. While to this point, "success" has been used simply as attainment of a desired goal,[6] we must now specify exactly what significance the goal has for the individual.

Public Success. A review of the literature, both psychological and otherwise, reveals a similar distinction between private personal success and public success. The latter is often derided as misdirecting and unworthy. It is "'Success' in its vulgar sense—the gaining of money and position" (Holmes, 1885, p. 260). Emerson in his "Success" (1870) speaks for many others when he separates public from private success:

> I fear the popular notion of success stands in direct opposition in all points to the real and wholesome success. One adores public opinion, the other private opinion; one fame, the other desert; one feats, the other humility; one lucre, the other love; one monopoly, the other hospitality of mind. (p. 290)

Indeed, Freud made a similar differentiation in his original article to explain the apparent contradiction of "those wrecked by success" (1915, pp. 325–326; see also Haimowitz and Haimowitz, 1958, p. 746).

Aristophanes (424 B.C.) showed the way to public success: "To plunder, to lie, to show your behind are three essentials for climbing high" (*The Knights,* 1, 428). Likewise, Samuel Clemens wrote "All you need in this life is ignorance and confidence, then success is sure" (1887, cited in Mencken, 1942). In *The Epic of Hades,* Lewis Morris declared: "How far high failure overleaps the bounds of low success."

Not only is "the fools' gold commonly called success" (Updegraff, 1941, p. 291) a dangerous siren for the undirected—Phaedrus

[6]"The prosperous achievement of something attempted; the attainment of an object according to one's desire" (from Onions's *OED,* 1972, p. 2066).

warned "success leads many astray to their ruin"[7]—but it corrupts its captors—Seneca told the Roman Senate that "success consecrates the foulest crimes" and Mosca declared "Success hath made me wanton" (Jonson's *Volpone,* act 3, scene 1). The trickery is complete when the aspirant is disappointed in his or her expectations: "Success rarely brings satisfaction" (Gracián, 1647), or, as Lord Byron wrote in *Childe Harold's Pilgrimage* (Canto II, lines 307–310, 1812):

> 'Tis an old lesson; Time approves it true,
> And those who know it best, deplore it most,
> When all is won that all desire to woo,
> The paltry prize is hardly worth the cost.

The taint or curse of success is expressed in several places:

> Success, which touches nothing that it does not vulgarize, should be its own reward. . . . the odium of success is hard enough to bear, without the added ignominy of popular applause. (Graham, 1902, p. 7)

Modern scientific research bears this opinion out: "success-striving" has been linked with a higher incidence of schizophrenia, psychoneurosis, and psychosomatic ailments (Ellis, 1952; Hollingshead *et al.,* 1954). Friedman and Rosenman (1974) link "Type A" behavior[8] with chronic heart ailments and heart attacks.

A famous statement about success as a contaminant or sickness comes from the illustrious psychologist William James, in a letter written in 1906 to H. G. Wells:

> The moral flabbiness born of the exclusive worship of the bitch-goddess SUCCESS. That—with the squalid cash interpretation on the word success—is our national disease.

"Our National Disease." James referred to the worship of success as our national disease. Achieving success has had a unique meaning in American history. Success was the promise of the new land; he who tried, and tried hard, would make it, maybe make it big. Success was also the burden—either to be the success one had to be

[7]From his *Fables,* book 3, fable 5; compare with the 1752 edition of *Poor Richard's Almanac:* "Success has ruin'd many a man."

[8]"Type A Behavior Pattern is any action-emotion complex that can be observed in any person who is *aggressively* involved in a *chronic, incessant* struggle to achieve more and more in less and less time, and if required to do so, against the opposing efforts of other things or other persons" (Friedman and Rosenman, 1974, p. 84).

or to be clearly on the way, or to be absolutely nothing. Many writers recorded this sentiment, some helping to fire it up more hotly in the American blood than others. Cawelti (1965) and Huber (1971) summarize hundreds of books guiding American youth to instant success, novels and advice pamphlets which continue to pour forth into our cultural mainstream.

Horatio Alger is perhaps the most famous of these "success writers," writing dozens of novels in the middle nineteenth century. According to Kenneth Lynn (1955, p. 7), the plot of every novel Alger ever wrote was the following:

> Alone, unaided, the ragged boy is plunged into the maelstrom of city life, but by his own pluck and luck he capitalizes on one of the myriad opportunities available to him and rises to the top of the economic heap.

The encouragement found in these tales for generations of young men is still passed on to future generations by the Horatio Alger Awards Committee of prospering businessmen in the form of plaques and money to young people who have shown these traits of character.

For other turn-of-the-century writers—Theodore Dreiser, Jack London, David Phillips, Frank Norris, and Robert Herrick—failure was a horror consistently linked with the worst degradations and death. But lurking beneath the praise for success in a culture oriented toward success, these writers revealed the horrors of winning. What was desirable when viewed from afar was upon closer inspection frivolous and dull; the success won by force and fraud was empty. "The pace that killed had to be kept up, but the enthrallment and the exhilaration attendant upon the rise were now replaced by monotony, boredom, exhaustion—and death" (Lynn, 1955, p. 242). Suicide was a haunting threat. The final insults to the rags-to-riches heroes were their children, the "second generation" of success—these were often characterized as snobbish and lazy, the source of a whole new kind of tension within the family. (Alger's neatly moral solution was to turn the wheel of fortune again, making the children poor, and thus returning them to the first generation's original level.)

Lynn's (1955) biographical analysis of the famous "success writers" from this time is telling—they were not successful to themselves or to their public, some attempted suicide, some degenerated at an early age. In the case of Horatio Alger, the famous stories seemed like orderly fantasies in utter contrast to his own life.

Never has this heritage of success-at-any-cost been so painful to the national spirit as in modern times where so many of the persons of greatest power in politics and business—"the best and the brightest"—are revealed for their lack of scruples, a scandal for the American success ethic.

Novelists have not been alone in hinting that the American dream of success is horribly misled. In addition to the professionals already cited, the reader can find a similar analysis in the following titles: "The Nightmare of Success," Ruzicka, 1973; "The Victims of Success," Wolman, 1973; "The Failure of Success," Milner, 1959, and Marrow, 1972; "The American Gospel of Success," Rischin, 1965 (cf. also Cawelti, 1965, and Huber, 1971).

In a Columbus day issue of *The New Republic,* Erich Segal (1976) makes the interesting suggestion that the American dream of success is actually not American, but a lingering European fantasy *about America* inspired by the tradition of Jason's capture of the Golden Fleece. Europe wrote abundantly of its hopes and visions of Paradise and El Dorado, of unlimited possibility, in the new land. But, as Melville complained, "Columbus ended earth's romance," which was thoroughly defeated in the disappointments of the "49ers" quest for California gold. The Americans were the ones left the task of recording the great disenchantment. In Faulkner, Santayana, Fitzgerald, Hemingway, Steinbeck, Bellow, and Salinger, Segal finds the spoiled success that spoils. Archibald MacLeish (1967) gives another such transformation—from the Nobel Prize-winning nuclear physicist into a modern tragic Herakles, who "after the Labors had been accomplished and the dog dragged from the gate of death, unknowing, killed his sons."

So "our national disease" takes on a chilling ambiguity—disease as discomfort, infection, or depravity. Melville (1851, pp. 111–112) indicated this in his warning: "Be sure of this, O young ambition, all mortal greatness is but disease." Segal credits Melville with substituting the White Whale for the Golden Fleece, and expressing our journey in the Pequod as a hopeless anti-Argo. Thus we find again the fear of success, indeed despair over it, in our cultural roots.[9]

This malaise over success need not be limited to our nation alone. Did not Lady Macbeth utter the same disappointed sentiments upon the attainment of her desires?

> Nought's had, all's spent,
> Where our desire is got without content:
> 'Tis safer to be that which we destroy
> Than by destruction dwell in doubtful joy.

"The Bitch-Goddess Success." James's apparent sexism is instructive. Success is commonly characterized by males as a female figure. There is the image of a demonic seductress or siren whose power over them erodes their leisure and happiness as their thirst increases for more; the extreme would be what is now labeled the "workaholic." Or there is the image of the coy mistress (cf. Huber, 1971), the romance kept separate and secret from one's human wife and family.

This is a typical form of the male's projection of the anima, C. G. Jung's term for the feminine aspect of the male personality, onto outside figures and events. Jung sees the bitch goddess as the most primitive figure for men's projections, widespread in pornography, popular books, films, and television. Tennessee Williams (1945, pp. xviii–xix) confessed a desire to "embrace the Bitch Goddess . . . with both arms and find in her smothering caresses exactly what the homesick little boy in you always wanted, absolute protection and utter effortlessness." Higher stages of maturity involve images such as the Madonna, Mona Lisa, and sister/partner. There are greater differences between individuals at these higher stages, and career and career success do not so likely become the unsatisfying surrogates for baser impulses.

The only piece of social psychological research designed to understand different kinds of success images among undergraduate males (Knapp and Green, 1964) found a statistical factor for "chival-

[9]Three titles show the currency of these themes: "Will success spoil B. F. Skinner?" (Hall, 1972); "Will success spoil [students voted most likely to succeed in their high school class]?" (McCabe, 1976); "Can Cesar Chavez cope with success?" (Solkoff, 1976).

ric, radiant success" (a shining sword, a triumphant song) negatively related to factors for "illusory success" (a castle of sand, a house of cards) and for "capricious success" (a roulette wheel, a vicious addiction). While explicitly female images were not used in their questionnaire, their research suggests the existence of different affective themes concerning success which might be used in research with persons in actual careers.

"Fly from It." After such a series of cogent arguments against success, "who with a spark of humour in his soul can bear success without some irritation in his mind?" (Graham, 1902, p. 7). It should certainly help to leaven the sense of moral outrage found in the current literature (Part II) that some people avoid success or even have a "fear of success." W. S. Maugham's (1938) advice is "You must not pursue a success, but fly from it." Frank Moore Colby (1926) affirms this position: "I have found some of the best reasons I ever had for remaining at the bottom simply by looking at the men at the top." Pearl Buck (1970, p. 167) concludes in her book on the Kennedy family that "no man or woman in his right senses could wish for great success." Even without demeaning success, there is a Japanese proverb: "The wise man should retire when fame is reached and great deeds done" (Siu, 1968, p. 15). As with all religions, the *Bhagavad-Gita* of the Hindus counsels against success-striving again and again.

These less scientific but consequently more agile citations are not alone in their condemnation of public success. Many professional psychological theorists also applaud the rejection of public success, thus encouraging what has been assumed elsewhere to be negative, maladaptive behavior. According to Marcuse (1955, p. 46), modern man is entrapped by the "performance principle," the internalized belief in work for work's sake. This regimentation leads to alienation and renunciation of the "freedom of the libidinal subject–object which the human organism primarily is and desires." Becker (1975) goes further, linking the urge to do better, to outshine others, with the creation of evil. Not only is this true of the wealthy capitalist seeking to accumulate "filthy lucre," but also for those who wish to increase "man's achievements," in medicine, for example, thereby gaining a little prestige and immortality for themselves. The counsel of these authors is to avoid the alienating marketplace and its "success."[10]

Subjective Success

It is clear from many writers that public success has nothing to do with private success. As Albert Einstein said (in a personal memoir to William Miller, an editor of *Life*, on May 2, 1955): "Try not to become a man of success but rather try to become a man of value." Nietzsche (1886) wrote "The higher the type of man, the greater the improbability that he will succeed."[11]

There is a single social psychological study of the difference between public and private success and failure. Kassarjian (1963) developed questionnaire scales for "psychological" success and failure to measure personal feeling and for "sociological" success and failure to measure how an individual thought he or she was regarded in the world. In an institutionalized sample and in a noninstitutionalized sample, the correlations between scores on these two scales was fairly low ($r \approx .30$), though for the samples combined the correlation was .51, still not very high. Thus, public success did not always go with subjective success. Furthermore, measures of self-esteem and the number of illness symptoms were not related to sociological success–failure but were closely related to psychological success–failure. This is what one would expect, but it needed demonstration for those researchers who persist in assuming that a popular public success such as being top in your medical school class is everybody's idea of success.

In the influential work by Lewin, Dembo, Festinger, and Sears (1944), total emphasis is put on the subjective definition of success: "What for one person means success means failure for another person" (p. 374; also Adler, 1935, p. 6). McClelland *et al.* (1953, p. 154), as well as F. Katz (1964) and Knapp and Green (1964), make similar distinctions about the many forms of success. Thus we cannot assume that any particular goal determined by the experimenter

[10]See also Fromm (1955, 1947), Horney (1939), May (1950, p. 162f), Henry (1971, pp. 336, 347, 363), and Buber (1937, p. 46) for parallel thoughts in very different contexts.

[11]Emerson's passage quoted earlier makes this differentiation quite clear. Also John Masefield: "Success is the brand on the brow of the man who has aimed too low."

(e.g., medical school) would have the same incentive for every person. We cannot even assume that a stereotypically male goal, e.g., occupational advancement, would be the chosen one in every case. For example, Bardwick and Douvan (1971, p. 54) write that for the female adolescent, "the establishment of successful interpersonal relationships becomes the self-defining, most rewarding, achievement task."[12]

But, given the developmental roots of achievement motives and the necessity that they be continuously validated by external feedback, I am constrained to the difficult position of accepting both internal and external influences on the experience of attainment of a desired goal (success).[13] Several theorists have tried to distinguish between sources of success feedback—e.g., autonomous achievement vs. social comparison achievement (Veroff, 1969), intrinsic achievement vs. extrinsic achievement (Smith, 1968). But in my view these can only cover the extreme cases. Overall, feelings of success and behavior towards and away from success are determined by multiple inputs, both internal and external.

McClelland and Watson (1973) give up the term "success" entirely in their study of motives, preferring to refer to particular kinds of incentives. They also remind us that public competition involves two kinds of incentives—achievement (doing well, completing the job) and power ("standing out," gaining prestige without work if possible, influencing the behavior of others). High achievement-oriented individuals are "thrown off" by public competition (pp. 123–124; see also Atkinson and Reitman, 1956). This is yet another ambiguity which we must accept when talking about fear of success—is shying away from being number one in a field where one is a member of a minority more indicative of a fear of power–success or a fear of achievement–success? Though power might be the more meaningful construct when talking about relationships between the genders (Holter, 1970; Silverstein, 1972; Lenski, 1966), achievement has certainly been one of the most popular constructs used to explain differences between the genders.

[12]The radical implications of these truths for experimental design are touched upon in the last chapter.

[13]Cf. Schilder's (1951) integrative definition: "Success is the realization of an anticipated ideal of oneself in relation to the outside world."

Fear of Failure and Fear of Success

The concept of "fear of failure" has been repeatedly used to explain success avoidance phenomena, and the similarity to previous conceptions of "fear of success" becomes clear in the thorough discussion of test anxiety (one of the most frequently used operational measures of FOF) by Sarason *et al.* (1960):

> We can assume that in the case of the test anxious child parental handling resulted in inordinately strong hostility and that attempts to defend against its expression were unsuccessful to the degree that it did not avoid the upsetting experience of guilt. . . . Another of the unconscious factors increased in strength in the test anxious reaction concerns the unconscious phantasies about the consequences of directing strong hostility toward parents. Essentially these are unconscious phantasies of retaliation on the part of the parents. (p. 14)

An investigation of the items used in the TAQ confirms this observation. For example, for item 13, "Before taking a group intelligence test to what extent do you perspire?," to what extent can an answer toward the pole "Perspire a lot" be said to be inherently an indication of "fear of failure" rather than "fear of success?"

The conceptual confusion between "fear of success" and "fear of failure" has been cited by others. Haimowitz and Haimowitz (1958, p. 751) and Marrow (1973) suggested that an apparent "fear of success" is rooted ultimately in a "fear of failure," while Schuster (1955, p. 416; and Rosenbaum and McAuliffe, 1972) stated that a real "fear of success" is often rationalized by patients as a "fear of failure."[14] For both concepts, however, fears are based on the expectation of and desire to avoid negative consequences of particular outcomes or events, and the observed behavior often involves avoidance of an apparently successful endstate.[15] The suicide attempt or sudden illness on the eve of a promotion are good examples of the overlap between an avoidance of success and an approach to failure.

[14]Empirically, Pappo (1972) found a moderately high correlation ($r = .54$) between "fear of failure" as measured by the Alpert–Haber (1960) measure of debilitating anxiety and her measure of "fear of (academic) success."

[15]Despite the obvious overlap between "fear of success" and "fear of failure" ideas, I have not included a full review of the large and difficult body of research on "fear of failure" (cf. Birney *et al.*, 1969).

We are in substantial agreement with Mills's (1940) critique of these terminologies of motives as really vocabularies of acceptable desires in particular social situations which have an often unspecified significance for a particular historical period.

In the last analysis, after arguments over definitions and techniques of measurement have subsided, this attitude–behavior complex of fear and avoidance will remain the focus of the researchers' concern and desire to help.

SUMMARY FOR CHAPTERS 1 AND 2

These first chapters lay the theoretical groundwork in the broadest terms for an understanding of a "fear of success." Psychoanalytic interpretations of fear and avoidance of success were compared with sociological, anthropological, and mythological understandings of similar phenomena. Horner's recent theory of a "motive to avoid success" was reviewed in terms of the tradition of motivational theory from which it was derived. Her formulation also joins the tradition of research documenting the incompatibility of femininity and traditional views of success. But the meanings of "success," and therefore of success avoidance, vary in different discussions. A basic distinction is made between popular and personal goals and sources of satisfaction. Depending on the kind of success goals sought and achieved and the way the search is conducted, this incompatibility between gender role and success may or may not occur.

CHAPTER 3

Social Psychological Perspectives on Fear of Success

From negative imagery written in a four-minute story coupled with a lower performance level in a competitive situation, Horner inferred the existence of an emotional state—a "fear" rooted deep in the personality, originating in gender-role socialization in childhood. Though the derivation of the psychoanalytic concept of "fear of success" is somewhat different, the clinical approach is in general agreement with the personality approach concerning the psychodynamics and early origin of "fear of success." This approach views behavior as evidence for unseen stable traits of the individual. The implication, of course, is that change in such an established behavior pattern is nearly impossible.

The modern social psychological approach to these phenomena is quite different. Behavior is seen as the appropriate response to a certain kind of situation, as more consciously manipulated and more malleable. In an area with as much relevance for social policy as "fear of success in women," this makes a big difference—the greater possibility of changing adult behavior in a publicized oppressed group opens the door for proposals to do just that. Social psychologists call the personality approach to the avoidance of success "blaming the victim" (e.g., Ryan, 1971; Condry and Dyer, in press) of an oppressive social system.

This chapter integrates various social psychological theories vis-à-vis the special case of a "fear of success." The statement of the social psychological position is fairly comprehensive since many researchers on "fear of success" have taken the currently popular social psychological view that "fear of success" is the relatively consciously controlled curtailment of gender-role-inappropriate behavior. At the end of the chapter, the merits of the personality and social psychological approaches are discussed in terms of their methodological stances toward "fear of success" phenomena. One approach cannot be unilaterally favored over the other; they must be integrated to deal effectively with a concept such as "fear of success."

A THEORY OF BOUNDARY MAINTENANCE

> The Erinys, the minions of Justice, would punish even the sun if it should "transgress his measures" by exceeding the task assigned to him. (Heraclitus, Frag. 94 Diels.)

In order to make systematic sense out of the theories, experimental results, and occasional criticisms and suggestions reported in Chapters 1 and 2 we need to present a theory of boundary maintenance. Actually, the central position and many of the corollaries of this so-called "theory" have been expressed in other bodies of theory and research—namely, (a) reference group theory (Merton, 1968; Merton and Rossi, 1950; Hyman, 1960; Eisenstadt, 1954); (b) social comparison theory and social evaluation theory (Festinger, 1954a,b; Thibaut and Kelly, 1959; Latane, 1966; Pettigrew, 1967); (c) the sociology of deviance and conformity, and labeling theory (Becker, 1963; K. Erikson, 1962, 1966; Goffman, 1957, 1963; Collins, 1973; Freedman and Doob, 1968; Scheff, 1966; Schervish, 1973); (d) field theory (Deutsch, 1969); (e) self-consistency theory (Lecky, 1945) and other social psychological balance theories (Hartmann, 1939; Heider, 1958; Festinger, 1957); (f) exchange theory and equity theory (Homans, 1950, 1961; Blau, 1964; Adams, 1965; Sampson, 1969; Walster *et al.*, 1973); and (g) the grandfather of all of these, role theory and symbolic interaction theory (see reviews by Sarbin and Allen, 1969, and Banton, 1968, and the recent compendium by Jackson, 1972). In these different areas of theory and research, many of the same ideas are expressed in different languages, and an attempt is made here to combine these superficially different but fundamentally similar approaches. Since this integration touches on all areas of social psychology, we can only touch on the central ideas, and must leave some areas out altogether.[1]

Role

The core concept of this theory is *role,* which we shall define classically as "a set of expectations that has an objective concrete reality and that impinges on individuals because they hold a given social position" (Veroff and Feld, 1970, p. 3); a *position* (or status) is the locus of a person in a network of social relationships. Persons are defined and define themselves in terms of shared understandings of how positions (or statuses) are allocated, and what rights (privileges, rewards) and obligations (duties, costs) go with them. The most important part of the definition of role is that the shared expectations are of *observable behavior* since what is not public cannot well be monitored by social norms. Consequently, the more obvious or public the positional differences, then the greater the difference in social expectations—the roles associated with differences in age, gender, and/or race are more distant from each other than other, less obvious criteria for divisions between people.

A person occupies several roles in several role systems simultaneously, one of which is usually dominant at any one time and is thus temporarily the determinant of appropriate behavior in that situation (Bates, 1956). Sometimes role conflict arises, and individuals must resort to one of various methods to overcome possible contradictions in the behavior required in these instances. The role literature is full of other terms for describing difficulties in role behavior: e.g., "role ambiguity" (Veroff and Feld, 1970), "role

[1]E.g., I have not included the huge literature from experimental psychology on shock-motivated avoidance behavior since the analogies between organisms (rats vs. humans) and situations (electric shock boxes vs. competition on paper-and-pencil tests) are not sufficiently clear.

strain" (Goode, 1960a), or "role overload" (Kahn *et al.*, 1964), all terms for stresses in "role enactment" which individuals seek to reduce through a sequence of "role bargains" (Goode, 1960a). How this strain arises and how it is dealt with will be analyzed later on.

Role systems exist within discrete areas of human collectivity and it is within each of these areas (e.g., males, doctors, male doctors, etc.) that different positions are defined, and different behaviors somewhat arbitrarily associated with each to affirm the difference. It was Cohen (1964) who used the term "social boundary-maintaining systems" for these role systems and for the separate roles within each system.

Commitment to Conformity

The labeling systems for social positions, the behaviors that accompany these positions, and rules for knowing which roles are appropriate (dominant) in which situations are learned early in life by means of various processes. Conforming to learned, and therefore usually traditional or at least conventional, role demands has such attractive power for individuals because it is linked (a) with fundamental affiliative rewards:

> The members of the group receive social approval in exchange for conformity and the contribution to the group their conformity to social expectation makes. (Blau, 1964, p. 259)[2]

(b) to the main values and norms of society (Eisenstadt, 1954); (c) to the achievement of a sense of self with "inner continuity and sameness" (Erik Erikson's definition of "identity"); and (d) ultimately to the person's sense of reality. Berger and Luckmann's (1966) treatment of this last feature illustrates the dynamic significance of roles for a person's sense of "place" in the world; for example,

> It can readily be seen that the construction of role typologies is a necessary correlate of the institutionalization of conduct. Institutions are embodied in individual experience by means of roles.

[2]See also Simmel's emphasis on the "sociability drive" (1949) and "web of affiliation" (1955) necessary for personality integration.

> The roles, objectified linguistically, are an essential ingredient of the objectively available world of any society. By playing roles, the individual participates in a social world. By internalizing these roles, the same world becomes subjectively real to him. (p. 69)

These factors in conjunction show how the legality of the system is linked with loyalty (sense of responsibility) to the system (Cohen, 1964).

Perhaps more powerful than the attractive features of conformity to social roles are the threats for deviance from expectation which are avoided by conformity. The expectations of behavior for a particular role usually define a range of possible behavior with more or less rigid barriers; behavior which is not in that range has exceeded the inexact and somewhat arbitrary limits of tolerability, or boundaries. Role strains of various sorts arise for exactly the reason that one or several boundaries have been trespassed, and the individual faces the sometimes rigorously applied negative sanctions normally deployed by others for nonconformity (deviance) which threatens the homeostatic stability of the social matrix (Getzels and Guba, 1954).

Legal systems as well as informal enforcement systems cull out and label certain quotas of persons as deviant (or taboo or polluted) in order to identify the normative boundaries of society (K. Erikson, 1966; Currie, 1968; Douglas, 1966). H. S. Becker (1963, p. 9) stated this most baldly: "deviant behavior is behavior that people so label." But K. Erikson (1966) was more thorough:

> The chief ways that individuals in a group learn about the norms of that group may be from boundaries made salient by those who violate them. The cost of boundary violation may be illustrated through the isolation, chastisement or ill fortune of the deviant. (p. 11)

The attentional bias toward possible negative outcomes has been documented by Kogan and Wallach (1964) in the case of risk-taking, by Thibaut and Kelly (1959) in the case of small group behavior, and by Kanouse and Hanson (1972) for evaluations of objects, situations, and persons; generally, individuals are "more motivated to avoid potential costs than to seek potential gains"

(Kanouse and Hanson, 1972, p. 61). The result is high attentiveness to possible trespass of boundaries.[3]

In a brilliant paper on the libidinal basis of the social matrix, Slater (1963) outlined the sometimes drastic measures legitimized by a society for insuring that the basic cohesion is maintained. In the life cycle, deviance is controlled at first in the form of actual punishment, then through a combination of threats (as described above, in the form of public demonstration of deviance) and self-regulation. From habitualization or internalization of learned programs[4] as well as from external control or threat of control, the individual's social conduct is controlled within limits tolerable to society.

Social Comparison

To this point, role behavior has been described for the most part as mediated by abstract knowledge of what behaviors are expected. While this is partly so, far more important are repeated contacts with others whom one thinks of as members of one's social position (reference group). While the first is referred to as a normative function, the second is known as the comparative function of groups Kelly, 1952). In dichotomous role systems (notably gender, though there is a tendency to dichotomize ascriptive labels in any situation), potent referents for behavior are also members of the other group (negative reference group): their norms are rejected as alien to one's own in favor of counternorms.

Several early theorists emphasized the importance of comparison with similar others, and the allocation of a judgmental faculty to an internal standard of behavior and attitude based on one's own conception of how one ought to be; the basis for this role prescription was how one perceived similar and/or important others to be.

[3]"Socially and morally, he [Man] tries to be an armored crustacean alert only for attack or defense: the price of selfishness is eternal vigilance" (Frye, 1947, pp. 348–349).

[4]The helpful term "program" is used by Mills (1940, p. 356f.), Berger and Luckman (1966, p. 58ff.), and Lilly (1970) to denote a set of elements and functions (or operations) that interlink them—i.e., an entire system of rules for behavior in a particular situation. The interactive concepts of "roles" and, more concretely, "programs" are constructs more in accord with Mills's (1940) suggestion of a terminology for situated actions than the more general vocabulary of "motives."

Thus G. H. Mead's (1934) "generalized other" and Cooley's (1922) "looking-glass self" both involved the comparison of one's self (defined in each moment by particular behaviors and/or attitudes) with an internal social referent. The later, similar formulations of Leon Festinger (1954a, 1954b) were quite systematic, and have led to a host of investigations, including the theory and research associated with cognitive dissonance (Festinger, 1957, 1964; Brehm and Cohen, 1962).

Festinger postulated a fundamental "need to know" about oneself. Since in many cases a behavior or attitude had no possibility of external objective measurement and could only be compared to the relative performance or opinions of others, he reasoned that this led to a desire to seek out similar others, with whom one felt a basic identification, in order to compare oneself with them. But in order to remain similar enough to be able to "know where one stood," there was a pressure to conform to the opinions and behaviors of this group as perceived by the person. The resultant is stated in Festinger's (1954b) crucial Derivation D_1:

> When a discrepancy exists with respect to opinions and abilities there will be tendencies to change one's own position so as to move closer to others in the group. (p. 126)

Support for this hypothesis can be found in any of the reviews of this literature (e.g., Pettigrew, 1967; Radloff, 1968). The mediating variables stated above, however, were shown to be still very important. Chapman and Volkman (1939) found that the more unfamiliar the task, i.e., the less experience with the task and thus the less set one's personal standards for performance at the task, the more performance can be modified by reported norms for a reference group. Further, the more salient the membership in such a reference group, the more behavior is altered (Charters and Newcomb, 1952; Dittes and Kelley, 1956; Bass, 1961).

Similar explanatory constructs have been McClelland's (1971) "motive to consistency," and Mischel's (1970) "motivation to avoid uncertainty." However, in a critique of Festinger's early statement of his theory (1954a), Nissen (1954) felt that the basic "need to know" was not enough to explain conformity, and suggested other operative factors—namely, "gregariousness, a drive to be part of and identify with the group" (p. 223), similar to Simmel's (1949) "sociability drive." Later research, while accepting the basic ideas presented, have emphasized the part played by self-perception and the perception of the "generalized other" (e.g., Asch, 1956; Latane, 1966; Bem, 1972).

These statements are often understood in terms of a congruity principle (Veroff and Feld, 1970; Sampson, 1969). Behavior or opinions which transgress the boundaries of one's group are role-incongruent or role-inappropriate because the socially prescribed role (e.g., adult male) and the enactment (e.g., wearing frilly clothes) contradict each other. In these cases of conflict, the individual strives to return to a state of role-congruence. The cognitive mechanics of this process are described by Tedeschi *et al.* (1971) as impression management: role-inappropriate behaviors elicit face-saving behaviors to maintain self-consistency of one's image to oneself and to others.

The research spawned by these theoretical statements has confirmed that a drive for self-evaluation leads to group-joining and conformity. The link with affective experience follows. Schachter (1959) found that the tendency to affiliate with others undergoing a similar experience and to judge one's own reactions from others increased when subjects were made anxious. Rasmussen and Zander (1954) took this one more step; they hypothesized that "conformity to group standards is tantamount to achievement of the person's ideal and should result in feelings of success" (p. 241), which they experimentally confirmed. Consequently, nonconformity or role-inappropriateness of behavior could be expected to lead to a sense of failure (demonstrated with autonomic indicators of anxiety by Lawson and Stagner, 1957, and Back *et al.*, 1963). Likewise, Duval and Wicklund (1972) argue that a state of "objective self-awareness," resulting from awareness of a discrepancy between oneself and an internalized standard for behavior, leads to negative affect and is avoided. Research on "fear of success" documents this phenomenon in the special case where apparent (public) success is also a personal (private) failure, due to a conflict between prescribed and enacted role.

An example comes from the reaction of a fifth grader to her mother, who in turn had been told by the girl's teacher that her daughter's superior performance warranted skipping a grade or, better, attending a private special school. The young girl responded,

> "Mother, if I'm smarter, I don't want anybody to know it. I'm going to stay with my own grade. I'm going to go to the same school that I go to. I'm going to live here the rest of my life and I'm going to be with these people, and I don't want them to think that I am one whit different or better than they." (Options in Education, 1976, Part 4, p. 5)

Justice and Transgression

Other theoretical approaches again demonstrate success avoidance in the face of transgression of boundaries. Homans's (1961) two forms of fundamental societal norms of distributive justice—equity and equality—both lead to similar, though not identical, responses to inappropriate success (cf. an early discussion by Ichheiser, 1943). From the approach of equity theory, a number of experiments (Jacques, 1961; Adams and Rosenbaum, 1962; Adams, 1963; and Leventhal *et al.*, 1969) have shown that those who receive *more* than they deserve feel distress (usually in the form of guilt[5]), and act to reduce rewards to an equitable level. There is evidence that within more cohesive groups (e.g., among preadolescent male classmates), the equality solution to the sharing of rewards is preferred (Morgan and Sawyer, 1967; Sampson, 1969), also leading to the homogenization of behavior. Parallel to equality and equity norms are larger social forces that restrain individual potential: extreme equalitarianism in the urge for the classless society and hereditary stratification within existing classes (Gardner, 1961; Burt, 1975).

There is another sort of transgression in the violation of the norm of reciprocity by excessive success. There are no gifts for "the person who has everything"—the successful cannot be given to, and

[5]Through a combination of hard work and brilliance, Norman Podhoretz (1967) leaped from the Brooklyn lower class to the upper middle class, but the achievement was tainted by guilt: "There was a kind of treason in it: treason toward my family, treason toward my friends" (p. 4).

so are outside the network of exchange so fundamental to social interaction.

On all levels, the person who has exceeded in his behavior the boundaries of the system (termed a "harm-doer" by Walster *et al.*, 1973) can reduce this stress through self-deprivation, self-punishment (Walster *et al.*, 1973, p. 156), self-deprecation, ingratiation (Blau, 1964, p. 48), self-criticism (Aronfreed, 1964), self-accusation (Fromm, 1942), or "tactical conformity" (Jones and Gerard, 1967, p. 588). These concepts differ only slightly from the somewhat outdated but vivid terms expiation, indemnification, and atonement.

Irwin Katz's (1964) concept of "social threat" for Negro children is an excellent example of a boundary-maintenance conception of success avoidance. Compare his description to Horner's (1968) construct of M_{-S}:

> Another way in which social threat may impair (academic) performance is by causing Negro children to abandon efforts to excel in order not to arouse further resentment and hostility in white competitors. . . . When academic success is expected to instigate white reprisals, then any stimulus which arouses the motive to achieve should also generate anxiety, and defensive avoidance of such stimuli should be learned. (p. 226)

According to Katz, the key is the attribution of "coercive power" (French and Raven, 1960) to a powerful social environment.[6] The conflict between apparent (public) success and personal failure at the foundation of success-avoidant behavior takes place in a social field, and is interpreted cognitively; according to Katz the response is a defense against anticipated anxiety.[7]

Inappropriate excellence leads to social threat in Katz's conception, and is also a threat to the moral basis of the social order, as described simply in R. D. Laing's analysis of repression of female intelligence (1970, p. 23):

[6]Note the further similarity to the idea of hostile press, the basis for Birney *et al.'s* (1969) measure of "fear of *failure!*"

[7]See also Vaillant (1971) on a view of anticipation, carefulness, and general avoidance as "mature defenses." Deutsch *et al.* (1962) similarly speak of "dissonance reduction," including the cases of rejection of unexpected success, as a "mechanism of defense" similar to "rationalization."

> It is bad to be clever, because this shows
> how stupid they were
> to tell her how stupid she was.

In every case, reactions to transgression of social boundaries are both social and personal.

Disconfirmed Expectations: Unexpected Success

From another research tradition, disconfirmed expectancies are found to be generally unpleasant (Tolman, 1959):

> Events which coincide with self-relevant performance expectancies are consonant, pleasant, sought out; events which are discrepant from these expectancies are dissonant, unpleasant, avoided, or minimized. (Aronson and Carlsmith, 1962, p. 178)

Naturally, an unexpected failure is unpleasant. Not only is the event of unexpected success also experienced as unpleasant (Carlsmith and Aronson, 1961), but it leads to changing already correct answers on a test or "faking bad" in order to reduce dissonance (Aronson and Carlsmith, 1962; Carlsmith and Aronson, 1963).

Since the demonstration of Aronson and Carlsmith (1962) of subjects who, after unexpected success, avoided further success and/or "sought to fail," numerous attempts have been made to replicate this rejection-of-success phenomenon (Ward and Sandvold, 1963; Silverman, 1964; Cottrell, 1965; Brock *et al.*, 1965; Silverman and Marcantonio, 1965; Lowin and Epstein, 1965; Mettee, 1971; Maracek and Mettee, 1972; Taylor and Huesmann, 1973; Weaver and Brickman, 1974). In some cases, the self-enhancing properties of an unexpected success proved stronger than the need to reject it as inconsistent with one's conception of one's past behavior. In others, the success was sabotaged when it was unexpected. Silverman (1964; also Deutsch and Solomon, 1959) found self-esteem to be a central individual difference variable mediating this specific phenomenon. Maracek and Mettee (1972) combined a number of the proposed mediating factors and concluded that

> persons for whom success is inconsistent (i.e., chronic low self-esteem subjects) will reject or minimize success only if they are certain of their low self-assessment and the success is self-determined. (p. 104)

Thus, in addition to the personality variable of low self-esteem (measured by the self-acceptance and social presence scales of the California Personality Inventory), the factors of (a) the degree of reliability experienced concerning the experimental information about one's previous level of performance and (b) the degree of responsibility felt for the discrepant event were found to be crucial to obtaining this effect. Mettee, Williams, and Reed (1974) summarized this research on rejection of unexpected success in terms of resistance to self-image enhancement among those with a negative self-image (an alternative language presented at the beginning of this chapter). This is the hamartia or tragic life script of the "born loser" who zealously rejects anything positive as a threat to his or her fundamental identity (Steiner, 1974).[8]

Along the same lines, Seligman (1973) explains depression following career success as the result of a situation where "reinforcements are no longer contingent on present responding"—the person gets reinforced for "who he *is* rather than because of what he is *doing*" (p. 45), an objectionable state where expectancies would be unrelated to rewards.

In the literature on the self-fulfilling prophecy (see Rosenthal, 1973a, 1973b), the expectations of others are clearly shown to have potentially inhibiting effects on performance. Teachers resist accepting too much success from students whose ability they have pegged. Children who have done "too well" are regarded as less well-adjusted, less interesting, and less affectionate (Rosenthal and Jacobson, 1968); their unexpectedly high performance earns them labels such as "maladjusted" and "troublemaking" (Shore, 1969; also Leacock, 1969); and, in response, the ratio of praise to criticism by the teacher is significantly decreased for these students (Rubovits and Maehr, 1972). There are clearly hazards to disconfirming the expectancy of a powerful other.

High Achievers

Several sources suggest that these effects may be greater for high achievers than for low achievers, perhaps for the very simple reason

[8]The central ideas of a small corpus of literature on "ego threat" (see review in Holmes, 1974), not included in this review, are similar to those expressed here.

that performance level is more easily inhibited than bolstered. Festinger (1954b) postulated a "unidirectional drive upward" for abilities in addition to the pressures to conform. Therefore, possible conflict between behavioral tendencies is greater for high performers or those who "stand out." According to Festinger's theory, they are more vigilant to their own differences from others, and more subject to the anxieties and external social pressures for deviance. Radloff (1966) found expressions of this conflict in "superior deviates" in the form of a wide range of evaluations of their own performances, much less accurate than the evaluations by performers who had been told they were average. Dreyer (1954) tested how this conflict might lead to success avoidance and found that:

> the person doing considerably better than the group average and not given the opportunity to change the other group members' abilities or performance should be the first person to stop the activity. (p. 177)

Indeed, Lewis (1943) and Zorbaugh *et al.* (1951) cite evidence that gifted children often perform far below capacity, show greater behavioral maladjustments in the form of withdrawal, and doubt their superiority despite massive evidence supporting it. O'Connor *et al.* (1966) cited social comparison theory to explain why high ability students performed better in homogeneous ability groups than in heterogeneous peer groupings. Likewise, Lecky (1945) attributed persistent avoidance of successful performance in classroom situations to a self-conception which will not allow the transcendence of too high a level of performance.

Philip Slater (1963) also outlined how low performers are far more easily integrated into the social group than those who "stand out" by their excellence. Levin (1951) has even explained decapitation and scalping in this light. Societies do not tolerate too much individuation; in the eyes of culture, "it is a crime to own a head" (p. 269). When a person stands "head and shoulders" above his or her fellows, the revenge for this transgression is to take away the head, individuality at its most intensive point. Perhaps we can understand the greater susceptibility of high-ability students to the debilitating effects of blame (Costello, 1964, p. 198). Beheading is the ultimate social castration since in society it is the head which sticks out, differentiates one from the others, and expresses one's personal power. Naturally, Norman O. Brown (1966) has already said this—the head is the penis, for both genders.

Also recall the earlier quoted sections of Benedict (1934) concerning the Zuni Indians, and of Haimowitz and Haimowitz (1960) concerning widespread primitive prejudices against the conspicuously successful. Haythorn (1953, p. 284) found that even among NROTC sophomores, "effective group functioning was facilitated by cooperativeness . . . , 'striving for individual prominence' reduces group cohesiveness and friendliness." Blau (1964) summarizes a great deal of naturalistic observation of groups of workers in the following:

> work groups often discourage competitive endeavors to attain superior rewards as revealed by the restriction of output and social disapproval of rate busting. (p. 258)

See also Roethlisberger and Dickson (1939), Roy (1952, 1953), and Homans (1961) on the specific forms of quota restriction, goldbricking, etc.

Interesting in this context are the obvious exceptions, the high achievers who stand apart from the crowd and appear unscathed. Examples are Muhammed Ali, Israel's General Dayan, Father Divine, corporate presidents, Krushschev, and indeed most political and military leaders in time of crisis. It is a difficult role; in order to step out of the sea of faces without incurring the wrath of the social boundary-maintaining mechanism, they must flaunt the particular riches gained through their powers, and cause people to believe that there is a special magic in them which might rub off on others too. It is a fulltime confidence job to convince society that one's independence and unique capabilities are good for it. Only then does the "Satanic pride" of the nonconformist not arouse "social anxiety" and lead to threats and finally retribution. In every case, they pay ritual obeisance to their followers or to "the people," dedicating at least a part of their lives to volunteer organizations, to support of worthy causes, to giving back. We must not forget that renunciation of success is sometimes used for another sort of gain: status as a hero of altruism.

The individual narcissistic withdrawal has the appearance of actually increasing the cohesion of the rest of the social matrix and is supported by the society. Freud (1922; and also Machiavelli before him) identified this urge of the group as the need to set up a father figure above themselves, a person on whom they could project their loves and also their parricidal impulses. When the magic or the special powers are thought to be lost or outdated, the leader is "done away with" by coup, vote, or neglect. Thus, the exceptions prove the rule.

Perhaps another set of reasons for the susceptibility of high performers is the difficulties and costs of maintaining such a level of performance. Lanzetta and Hannah (1969) found that when student teachers thought a learner had a "high potential," rather than low, they rewarded him with the larger sum of money when he was right, and shocked him more severely when he was wrong. Such are the wages of success.[9]

Against a background of mediocre performances, a success stands out; but against a background of successes, the mediocre performances seem like failures.[10] Perhaps the general negativity bias in self-evaluations (Kanouse and Hanson, 1971) is a defensive reaction against the latter perceptual set. The result is a derogation of one's level of successfulness.

It is also believed that, through the cycles of time, good fortune (success) will necessarily lead to an equal and opposite misfortune (see, for example, Lilly, 1970). Certainly this was the case for Polycrates, the tyrant of Samos; Flugel (1945) linked the psychoanalytical views of the precursors of success avoidance (reviewed in Chapter 1) with the enforcement of limits in present-day social boundary-maintaining systems through this tale. According to Flugel, taboos on infantile sexuality are internalized as guilt over getting what one wants. The result can be attentiveness to trespass of boundaries in others:

[9]Concerning the harrassment by the tax authorities of Ingmar Bergman, Vincent Canby explained: "He was considered to have gotten too big for his britches. Bergman, the internationally acclaimed filmmaker, had somehow spoiled Swedish symmetry by being a large lump in a flat landscape, by being recognized, critically and financially, for his genius, and genius is something they don't dispense in government-run clinics. It was as if the Swedish national organism automatically was trying to reject him. The aberration had to be excised" (Canby, 1976).

[10]In demonstration tours after winning international acclaim for several perfect scores in gymnastics at the 1976 Olympics, the young Rumanian Nadia Comaneci was greeted with groans and boos for anything less than perfect performances.

> it is felt that such pioneers (kings, magnates, or famous scientists) are guilty of Hubris, and that if they had their way they would involve all mankind in the penalties incurred by those who presume 'above their station.' (Flugel, 1945, p. 152)

Thus the successful arouse suspicion and distrust in others.

Likewise, Horner predicted that "fear of success" would be higher among high performers than low since an outcome of success would be relevant to the former and not to the latter. Indeed, she found that "Honors" students showed somewhat more FOS imagery than "Non-honors" students (Horner, 1968, p. 110). Extending the parallel to thema that have been labeled "fear of failure," Birney *et al.* (1969, pp. 108–111) report seven studies showing a statistically significant association of "fear of failure" (measured by hostile press thema in TAT-like stories) with high grades and being in honors programs. Success is quite simply more an issue for those for whom a public success is possible.

The Envious Evil Eye

The widespread belief in the evil eye serves as an anecdotal focal point for several of the social psychological notions about the dynamics of success avoidance. Folk beliefs hold that through fascination a gifted operator of the evil eye can affect the mental state or damage the physical state of his or her victim by speaking, touching, or merely looking. Where the idea is firmly entrenched, there is a great fear of the intentional or accidental malevolence of the possessor. For example, in Naples, fear of the evil eye regularly creates panic in the streets (Bryon, 1964). On the appearance of a reputed *jettatore* (one who throws out evil from the eyes), a hushed word or signal is passed up the street. Even in a crowded area, there is at once a stampede into shops, alcoves, or anywhere out of sight and so out of danger, notwithstanding the fact that everyone has about him or her some charm or antidote.

While cripples, old women, and the thrice unlucky are primary suspects as possessors, "All those among the ancients who in any way surpassed conspicuously the common standard, as, for instance, in athletic or physical strength or size, were dreaded as possessors" (Elworthy, 1928, p. 610). An example of a famous person thought to have the evil eye is Pope Pius IX (1792–1878). As he was being driven through the streets of Rome in 1846, his glance happened to fall upon a nurse who was standing in an open window with a child in her arms. A few minutes later, the child fell to the pavement and was killed. The Pope immediately earned the reputation for the evil eye. Indeed, when he blessed the column erected to the Virgin in the Piazza de Spagna, a worker fell from the scaffold to his death. When he said mass at the Basilica di Santa Agnese, the floor collapsed. The stories continue, as they do about any exceptional person in this culture (cf. *National Enquirer* and other such periodicals).

Not only are the envied suspected but also the envious, the successful, and "they that desire to excel in too many matters" (Bacon, 1612). The covetous irritation of unattainable desire makes vulnerable those on either side of success—as victims of the evil eye, or as victims of being labeled a possessor—as shown by numerous examples given in Elworthy (1895, 1928), Maclagan (1902), Gifford (1956), Haimowitz and Haimowitz (1958), and Bryon (1964). Indeed success can separate the closest of relationships with envy. As Aeschylus wrote in *Agamemnon* (line 832), "Few men have the natural strength to honor a friend's success without envy. . . . I well know that mirror of friendship, shadow of a shade."

In an advocacy of boundary-maintenance, Francis Bacon (1612) marked those who would incur envy and applauded this primitive power as a good protection against excessive success:

> those are most subject to envy which carry the greatness of their fortunes in an insolent and proud manner being never well but while they are showing how great they are, either by outward pomp, or by triumphing over all opposition in competition. (p. 36)
>
> public envy is as an ostracism, that eclipseth men when they grow too great; and therefore is it a bridle also to great ones to keep them within bounds. (pp. 37–38)

In contrast to the Greek explanations for success avoidance—"what the gods demand is contrition" (Kott, 1970, p. 155)—Bacon's is a truly social-psychological theory since the normative order is seen entirely in terms of human social dynamics.

Bacon's practical recommendation was that the wise men "do sacrifice to envy" (1612, p. 36), suggesting specifically that

> the wiser sort of great persons bring in ever upon the stage somebody upon whom to derive the envy that would come upon themselves. (p. 37)

This is a brilliant application of modern attribution theory. The public is confused into blaming and punishing the stooges (political advisors, subsidiary corporations) of a central figure whose success has exceeded bounds.

There is a related widespread superstition concerning the danger arising from praise or admiration. For example,

> you have seen my cousin J.'s third boy. He was the finest and nicest looking of all children. When six months old he was a very pretty child. One day a woman came into the house; the baby was on his mother's arm, and the visitor began to praise the child, and praised it very much. She was hardly away when a man came, and he began to praise the child as the woman had done. After he went away, like a shot the baby took ill. (Maclagan, 1902, p. 76)

An appeal and an attribution to a higher power can be found among many when they receive compliments, ranging from "Mashallah!" to "Lord be wi' us!" to "Kein Ayin-Hara!" "Don't praise me" goes hand in hand with "Don't blame me" and "Don't envy me." Among the Romans, the well-mannered speaker of praise accompanied his speech with *praefiscini dixerim* ("Fend evil I should say").

Naturally, to avoid the dangers of covetous praise meant to avoid any grounds for praise: "Children, horses, and asses were disfigured amongst the Moslems to protect them from the risk [that] they would suffer if beautiful" (Haimowitz and Haimowitz, 1958, p. 743).

The danger of self-praise and over-boasting is familiar. It seems that, just as one proclaims a success in not breaking anything for years, one drops the old glass that belonged to grandmother. After Tennessee Williams' (1945) success with *The Glass Menagerie,* "things began to break accidentally," reminding him that we can't get too far beyond the physical clumsiness of our human condition. This event can be perhaps explained as an increased awareness of whether or not one is breaking things. The salience of the thought makes one more aware of exceptions. Likewise, perhaps we are more aware of the tragedies to and near the successful not because they are more frequent among this class but because any doings of the successful are more newsworthy. However, in the glass-breaking example, perhaps the claim to a sort of success draws to itself its opposite, a mysterious dynamic equilibrium spoken of in all cultures. One is compelled to break something by a host of social and psychological programs, detailed in these chapters.

The case of the success of Tennessee Williams bears further comment. With the production of *The Glass Menagerie* on Broadway he was "snatched out of virtual oblivion and thrust into sudden prominence" (Williams, 1945, p. xiii). In his new expensive Manhattan suite, "things began to break accidentally," cigarettes would fall onto the furniture, the windows would be left open in a downpour and the room flooded—events that had never happened before to him. He became severely depressed. "Sincerity and kindliness seemed to have gone out of my friends' voices. I suspected them of hypocrisy. I stopped calling them, stopped seeing them." He then took an excuse to go to the hospital for an optional eye operation; his eyes were covered with a gauze mask and he could not see for several weeks. He could, however, now bear his friends to be with him and look upon him. He felt again that they were his friends. Upon leaving the hospital, with the mask off, he immediately left for Mexico where he knew no one, "where you can quickly forget the false dignities and conceits imposed by success" (Williams, 1945, p. xvi). The escape to Mexico enabled him to write again. There he wrote *The Streetcar Named Desire,* and some may find in that play further evidence of his atonement.

I find it fascinating that Rollo May (1961) reinterpreted the Oedipus myth not only in terms of castration anxiety but in these same terms of too much greatness, ostracism (Oedipus exiled himself from Thebes), and the blinding of the evil eye (Oedipus gouged his eyes out). The reaction of Tennessee Williams to success was remarkably similar, and suggests another twist. Not only are the eyes of the transgressor blinded but this blinding shields the person from the envious eyes of others: he does not see that he is seen.

Dissection of Behavior

As this chapter (and Chapter 1) makes repeatedly clear, the reason that there is apparently so little research on "fear of success" and "success avoidance" is that these phenomena are so common in the social boundary-maintaining systems of everyday life that they have been assumed in larger models. Indeed, Homans (1950, pp. 294–312) sees "restriction of output" as a subsidiary special case of the most general processes maintaining social equilibrium. Lecky (1945) saw a distinction between approach and avoidance or positive and negative behavior as false, based on the assumption that the organism is divided against itself. Far more important was the general unity or self-consistency of the organism which was constantly being maintained. In their summary of work on the psychology of inhibition, Diamond *et al.* (1963, p. 376) also reject conflict models in favor of a model of the organism as "a pattern of mutually inhibitory response dispositions inherent in the integrated organism." Similarly, Backman and Secord (1968) emphasize how individuals "fashion" themselves to better fit a role category to which they belong; the emphasis is not on making use of all one's potential but on shaping all one's behavioral possibilities to achieve self-consistency and the interpersonal benefits of a consistent role portrayal. And, as mentioned above, Tedeschi *et al.* (1971) integrate research on cognitive dissonance phenomena under the concept of impression management and maintenance of a consistent self-image. Speaking just about success avoidance or "fear of success" is thus one-sided. We can, however, benefit from concentrating on the specific phenomenon of success avoidance in a clearly defined situation by finding out how competing demands of different roles can serve to diminish personal development and perhaps also how these limits can be altered. We can do this if we do not for a moment forget that any part of the boundary-maintenance system cannot be perceived without the whole.

Alternatives in Achievement Motivation Theory

The tentativeness I am suggesting about labeling a negative thema or an observed performance decrement as "motive to avoid success" or "fear of success" comes from the number of "plausible rival hypotheses" (Campbell and Stanley, 1963)—or alternative languages—for explaining the success-avoidance phenomena. Both Chapters 1 and 2 are full of examples of alternative languages. Most challenging perhaps are alternative interpretations of the "fear of success" effect within Atkinson's own mathematical model.

To begin with, a performance decrement after success or in the face of success can be explained merely in terms of motivation to achieve: $M_S \times I_S \times E_S$. Using the metaphor of "top of the medical school class," once Anne has found herself in that position, the expectancy of what we assume is the success (E_S) would then be very high. The incentive value of the success would consequently, by Atkinson's definition, be very low, since $I_S = 1 - E_S$.[11] Thus, the theory would anticipate that in subsequent work the motivation to achieve would drop to a low level. Indeed, Hoppe (1930) found early on that after repeated or profound failure or success, people quit—in the latter case, there is no chance for further improvement and thus incentive is lacking.

In addition, the proposed gender difference in performance could be explained as follows: females have lower expectancies of success (E_S) than males, especially in competition. Or females attribute success at a task to their own efforts less than males do (Crandall, 1969; Tresemer, 1974b; Deaux and Enswiller, 1974; Feldman-Summers and Kiesler, 1974). Each of these interpretations invokes the ideas of differential socialization and "role" outlined above, without actually using these terms; they also do not hypostatize a new "motive."

Other "plausible rival hypotheses" involve the operation of other motives. A popular interpretation is that need for affiliation (*n* Aff) is a moderating influence of achievement (Walker and Heyns, 1962). Sorrentino (1974) showed that "overmotivation"—need to achieve along with need for affiliation—led to performance decrements in a Together situation compared with an Alone situation, a parallel to Horner's experiment. Thus, too many positive or approach programs or tendencies can be debilitating, pulling the person in too many directions at once. Negative ideation as found in the TAT-type stories is then explained as anxiety in response to the more basic process of conflict between primary motives.

Of course, the conflicting requirements of achievement and affiliation touch several of our previous discussions; to make this point, I include an illustrative reminder from Rose Thorpe's "Whom Others Envy" (1890):

[11]This example might acquaint the reader with how this assumption is at once true and absurd.

A millionaire:—he bartered love for this,—
Love binds the wings of him who would arise.
He rose unfettered. Now with famished eyes
He gazes on another's Paradise,
While Memory taunts him with a shy, sweet kiss,
A frightened, fluttering thing, the first, the last.
No childish voices echo through his past:
He wears his laurels, but he paid their price.

As discussed earlier, fear of failure, the fear of power component of power motivation, and general debilitating anxiety can also be used as explanations for success-avoidance phenomena.

Finally, some (Veroff, 1969; House, 1973) have realized that what is popularly called "achievement" can be effort in relation to one's own past performance ("autonomous achievement orientation"), to the performance of others ("social comparison achievement orientation"), to social approval ("external achievement orientation"), or to beating others (also "external achievement orientation").

Any of these alternative languages can explain success-avoidance phenomena, and it is sometimes difficult to imagine an experiment which would discriminate one explanation from another. None of these explanations requires the concept of "a latent, stable personality disposition acquired early in life . . . a disposition to become anxious about achieving success" (Horner, 1972, p. 159).

The social-psychological frameworks presented earlier in this chapter are much easier to understand, and provide a clear framework from which to test ideas. Perhaps the difficulties of the Atkinson motivational framework (1964; Atkinson and Feather, 1966) in handling this social psychological level of theorizing are (a) its "quasi-cognitive" nature (Weiner, 1972)—the drive theory of experimental psychology in which this theoretical tradition has its roots would never have this problem in the definition of success (see Schlosberg, 1937, on "success" in the conditioning of rats)—and (b) the inability to systematically assess the impact of social situations.

In regard to the latter, Rotter's (1955) model of the determinants of human behavior, though structurally similar to Atkinson's (1964) Expectancy × Value theory, defines expectancy not in terms of subjective probability of being able to successfully complete a task but rather in terms of the probability held by the individual that a particular *reinforcement* will occur as a function of a specific behavior in a specific situation. Thus the social situation and what it allows must be taken into account. Rotter's model, while perhaps closer to the complexities of real situations, loses, however, the research-generating simplicity of Atkinson's theory. Yet both frameworks treat the individual isomorphically, with little apparent awareness of the essentially social nature of identity and ongoing identity-related processes (cf. Cohen, 1964).

The most recent formulation by Atkinson (Atkinson and Birch, 1970) is clearly more open to a conception of behavior that is determined by multiple "instigating forces" (a language which they prefer to "motives"), leading to actions and redirective "negactions." A particular behavior at any time is determined by the dominance of one "family of functionally related tendencies" rather than another. Appealing as these new theoretical developments are, the language of boundaries developed in this section is preferable for its familiarity, and seems no more handicapped in explaining avoidance phenomena.

THE CASE OF GENDER-ROLE BOUNDARIES

> Last week, the regional vice president called Liz into his office, praised her, and offered her a promotion to assistant office manager in charge of hiring and training all clerical employees. The position included a private office and a salary that exceeded her father's. Liz was in a terrible quandry. She just couldn't see herself as a manager giving orders to girls like she had been herself a few years before. And she did not want to be thought of as a career woman.
>
> This morning Elizabeth Sternberg quit her job and went home. (Webber, 1975, p. 140)

What about boundary maintenance in the special case of gender roles?[12] From the research cited in the section on women and achievement in the previous chapter, it would seem that females are

[12]Classification by "sex" refers to the dichotomous distinction between male and female based on physiological characteristics; classification by "gender" refers to the psychological and cultural definitions of the dimensions "masculine" and "feminine," and only tends to dichotomy. When speaking of learned roles, the proper term is "gender role" (Stoller, 1968; Oakley, 1972; Tresemer, 1975a, 1975b; also Holter, 1968, and Bernard, 1971).

far more handicapped than males in the range of tolerated social behavior. Indeed, there is a great deal of additional writing not reported here which implicitly or explicitly makes that claim. On the contrary, there exists now a growing set of references showing how gender-role boundaries are actually narrower and more restrictive for the male, especially in adolescence (Seward, 1946; Faris, 1952; Hacker, 1957; Hartley, 1959; Douvan, 1960; Hartup *et al.*, 1963; Brenton, 1966; Jourard, 1964; Ruitenbeek, 1967; Holter, 1968; Levy, 1972; Rosenberg and Hyde, 1973; Goldstine, 1973). Deviation for the male is more harshly penalized (e.g., in the form of shock-based behavior modification treatments for effeminate behavior; see Green and Money, 1969) than female deviation from prescribed gender roles.[13] To clear up this argument, I constructed a scorecard of studies predicting which sex would conform more in a situation of transgression of gender-role boundaries (before Maccoby and Jacklin, 1974, was available). It ran to dozens of studies with no strong indications of which gender avoids gender-role-incongruent behavior more. Even when it comes to the loosely defined "achievement situation" or "performance situation," it seems that there is a slight contradiction overall between being female and doing well, but this effect is often reversed when the tasks are verbal ones, at which females are expected to be more proficient. The major reasons for this multiplicity of findings are the tremendous range of psychological situations tested, and the fantastic complexity of the personality–situation interaction. In a number of studies, it seems clear that there is an antagonism between the genders, each using the other as a negative reference group, leading to different attitudes and behaviors. But the universal nature of this difference remains elusive while variation among individuals lends far more variability to the results than variation between groups. Maccoby (1972), Maccoby and Jacklin (1974), and Rosenberg and Hyde (1973) have strongly criticized the assumption that gender differences exist in all situations.[14] Given the contradictory evidence from the literature, I agree.

[13]Millman (1971) has claimed that the nearly exclusive application of social role interpretations of social science data to women and not to men is constraining to both genders.

[14]Despite the existence of empirically derived adjectival lists of gender-linked behaviors (e.g., the program of research reported in Broverman *et al.*, 1972), there exists little overall agreement on the universal, situation-free content of gender roles (Parsons, 1942; Goode, 1960b; Angrist, 1969).

The form which the theory of boundary maintenance takes in the case of responses to gender roles is as follows: widespread images of appropriate gender roles, associated with the general (normative) reference groups of men and women, give normative direction to the formation of gender-role identity; the process of enforcement of these norms takes place via social comparison with the immediate group of similar others (or peer group). For the most part, gender roles are learned (Maccoby and Jacklin, 1974). According to Kohlberg (1966, 1969), to control his environment and reduce uncertainty about the self, the child seizes upon obvious physical differences between the sexes and elaborates upon them. Being a "male" or "female" as defined by the social context is, even in the absence of external reinforcement, intrinsically gratifying to the individual in terms of feelings and senses about the self and identity as they emerge.

In support of the point made earlier about the greater strength of prohibitions in maintaining appropriate role behavior, Margaret Mead (1949) commented:

> Where an occupation or an art is defined as feminine, the males who are attracted to it are either already in some way injured or may be injured if they try to practice it. . . . When an occupation is defined as masculine, the women who first enter it will be similarly handicapped. (p. 353)

In other words, given the negative consequences for transcending role boundaries which Mead talks about, individuals strive to avoid gender-role-incongruent behavior and to act in a way congruent with their appropriate gender role. To establish stability and consistency in a personal sense of identity, to receive the expected praise for proper behavior, and to avoid censure from without, people tend to strive to conform to, and tend to fear to deviate from, the opinions and behavior dictated by these prescribed roles. Perhaps, because the threat of "injury" appears much more specific and clear-cut than the possible advantages of praise for conformity or confirmation of an individual's sense of self, concerns about negative sanctions seem more common than concerns about acting exactly in the "right" way. The consequences of not conforming are severe:

> It is always possible for society to deny to one sex that which both sexes are able to do; no human gift is strong enough to

> flower fully in a person who is threatened with loss of sex membership. (M. Mead, 1949, p. 352)

According to Sheehy (1976), internalized proscriptions are powerful enough; for a woman, a masculine success poses the threat that "just as she is about to seize control of her own destiny, that inner custodian, thwarted by her disobedience, might run amuck" (pp. 114–115).

Documentation of these points comes from diverse sources. In terms of behavioral styles, Letailleur *et al.* (1958) and again Cheek (1964) (as well as McClelland and Watt, 1968; Reed, 1957; and Chesler, 1972, p. 56) report a reversal of gender roles observed among hospitalized schizophrenics; Cheek (1964, p. 399) explains that the "overactive, dominating female and underactive, passive male are cultural anomalies" and in their nonconformity to cultural stereotypes are more susceptible to hospitalization. Burhenne (1972) found that college subjects rated a hypothetical person as having less likability, ability, and mental health if that person had used gender-role-inappropriate adjectives to describe himself (or herself). It has been found that women concerned about their lack of femininity (Wilsnack, 1973) and men concerned about their lack of masculinity (McClelland *et al.*, 1972) turn to drink to let them act and feel as if they have crossed the boundary into gender-role-congruence. In addition, Kimball (1953) found that under- and overachieving males showed a feminine identification, perhaps their accommodation to their perception that they had transcended the boundaries of their gender reference group. Among males, feelings of inferiority, even in the presence of social success, are associated with effeminacy (Hartman, 1949; Aronfreed, 1960; Kassarjian, 1963). Fenichel (1945, p. 336f.) linked homosexuality and feminine identification in men with the avoidance of success. In a study of second, sixth, and twelfth graders, Stein and Smithels (1969) observed that it was more important to learn what was inappropriate to one's group, not what was appropriate. Dornbusch (1966) summarizes this point:

> variation in the inappropriate area of behavior has been found to be a better predictor of other behavior than variation in the approved area of behavior. (p. 213)

Another level of analysis involves not styles but tasks. Analyses of the results of gender typing of fields of graduate study (Davis,

1968) and professional occupations (Rossi, 1965; Epstein, 1970a,b) show the degree of segregation between the sexes. Though women are often kept out of professional occupations completely, one well-documented case of a gender-role-inappropriate occupation for males is nursing (Segal, 1962; Etzkowitz, 1971)—they have to accommodate to being often mistaken for doctors and don't do well as nurses. Goldberg (1968) found that college women valued the professional work of men more highly than the identical work of women when the professions were law, city planning, etc.; Pheterson (1969, cited in Pheterson *et al.*, 1971) found that professional articles that concerned traditional feminine occupations (e.g., marriage, child discipline) received significantly higher evaluations for female than for male authors.

Experiments by Bem and Bem (1971) have shown that a single intervention (change in the gender typing of advertisements for telephone operators and linemen) can drastically alter the perception of boundaries for proper behavior, and consequently the attractiveness for once inappropriate behavior. This research highlights the pervasiveness of the vigilant avoidance of the transgression of existing boundaries. Perceptions of appropriateness are also central to performance on school tasks (see above; also Levy, 1972). Milton (1958, 1959) found that females improve their mathematics performance if the problems are rewritten so that they involve cooking and gardening. In this case, gender differences in problem solving are reduced (though there remains a comforting *apparent* difference in the content of the problem).

The concept of boundaries highlights the constraint of individuals within the system to persistently attend to their standing within the system. In Goode's (1960a, p. 495) words, "no one can ever escape the role market." In terms of personality, the basis of external separation between groups is repression of that internal part of oneself which is attributed (projected) to the other group (Freud, 1911; Brown, 1966), in this case the "repression of one's congenital contrasexuality" (Neumann, 1970, p. 112). The dynamic nature of the tension between the repression and the desire to transgress (Henry, 1971, p. 347) makes the entrapment referred to above understandable. In the case of gender, separation is necessary to the definition of self:

> A clear elaboration of sexual types is always essential for the polarization of the sexes in sexual life and in their respective identity formation. (E. Erikson, 1965, p. 236)[15]

This is exacerbated by the tendency to perceive gender as rigidly dichotomous. Levi-Strauss (1966) and Piaget (1970) peg this binary thinking as the most primitive, which can be seen in the exaggerated absoluteness of gender label in situations, for example, where the term "the opposite sex" is used (cf. also McCall and Simmons, 1966).

Thus, gender referents are fundamental to personal identity, especially during adolescence. Gender-role incongruence will therefore be avoided. Finally, we can predict that success that is gender-role incongruent will elicit avoidant or reparative responses.

Previous Related Research

Some previous research has been done relating the experimental manipulation of the gender-role appropriateness of a task and avoidance of success on that task. The program of research by A. H. Stein and others has been couched in the Crandall *et al.* (1960) model of motivation emphasizing the specificity of achievement behavior to particular types of achievement and success outcomes, thus more responsive to the situation than Atkinson's (1964) conception of latent, stable predispositions to action. Stein (1971) found that children's gender-role standards for six achievement areas (mechanical and spatial, athletic, math, reading, art and music, and social skills) were related to their attainment values (importance which an individual attaches to competence in that area), expectancies of success, and standards of performance (minimum score that would be satisfying) among sixth and ninth graders. Stein (1967) tried to extend these associations to "masculine" and "feminine" classes of tasks, and beyond indexes of motivation to actual behavior (persistence at a task). She asked eighty boys and girls between the ages of eight and twelve to work on a task that "measured potential skill at building and fixing things" (which she labeled "masculine"), then on a task that "measured potential skill at taking good care of a baby" (which

[15]A complementary and perhaps stronger statement is made by Lief (1967, p. 863): "In both sexes conflicts and confusion over gender identity and role may be potent sources of recurrent anxiety attacks."

she labeled "feminine"). The results were complex. Boys were more persistent on a masculine task only when tested by a male experimenter. Girls showed no differences in persistence. Contrary to prediction, both boys and girls stated higher expectancies of success on the feminine task. It was naturally unclear whether these findings applied generally to masculine and feminine tasks or were specific to the tasks used in the study.

A recent study by Stein *et al.* (1971) was intended to clarify and extend the previous findings in a sophisticated design. Ninety-six sixth-grade boys and girls were given three tests introduced as measures of masculine, feminine, and masculine-and-feminine ("neutral") skills. For example, for the feminine skills, the experimenter pointed to a box marked "Girls," and introduced the contents by saying: "This test helps to show how good you would be at girls' subjects in school, like home economics. People who are good at this test are good at things like cooking and sewing and other things you learn in home economics." The explicitness of the introduction was intended to offset uncertain assumptions about the gender-role linkage of school subjects, and associated the various tests with reference groups more than with particular tasks. The boys behaved exactly in accord with the hypotheses: attainment values, expectancies of success, and achievement behavior (persistence) were greatest on the gender-role-appropriate test, intermediate on the "neutral" test, and least on the gender-role-inappropriate test. For girls, while time scores did not differ between conditions, attainment values and expectancies of success were significantly lower on the masculine (gender-role-inappropriate) test than on the others. This result for females suggests that the gender-role incongruency was the motivating factor, a gender-role-congruent task being no more motivating than a neutral one. A premeasure of masculine or feminine role preferences (checking on individual differences effects) only partially predicted the girls' attainment values and time scores but was unrelated to any of the measures for the boys. Thus gender labels of a task (situation) were sufficient to influence children's motivation for an activity, supporting Kohlberg's (1966) cognitive approach to gender-role learning and behavior.

Similar to the study of Stein (1971), Dwyer (1972) found that gender-role standards about reading and arithmetic explained a significant amount of variance in reading and arithmetic achievement scores; the effect was somewhat stronger for males than for females. Montemayor (1972) found that, for both boys and girls, performance on a new game was highest when the game was labeled gender appropriate, intermediate when no gender label was given for the game, and lowest when the game was labeled gender inappropriate. Appropriate and neutral games were rated as similarly attractive, both higher than the inappropriate game. Hartup *et al.* (1963) found that objects labeled as gender inappropriate were avoided by both sexes, more by eight-year olds than by three-year olds.

Lambert *et al.* (1967) told one set of male and female subjects that men normally withstand more pain than women, another that women normally withstand more pain than men, and a third set nothing at all about gender differences in the tolerance of pain. Then they measured thresholds of intolerable pain using a sphygmomanometer applied to the forearm with sharp rubber projections sewn on the inner side. For both experimental conditions, men increased their thresholds over a pretest level; for the first condition, women conformed by taking less pain, though they did not increase their thresholds in the second condition above the control group level. The particular dependent variable used in this case clearly had a certain meaning for the traditional definition of masculinity and femininity that no experimental manipulation could alter. When the salience of religious membership group (Jewish vs. Protestant) was increased using the same procedure (Lambert *et al.*, 1960), the dependent variable had a completely different contextual meaning, and confounded the results in an altogether different way.

For each of the last five studies using gender labels, individual gender-role preference or identification (some using Brown's, 1956, IT scale, some Gough's, 1952, 1957, M–F scale) was unrelated to actual behavior.

Though confirming of the boundary-maintenance model, this research, with the exception of the Lambert *et al.* (1967) study, does not have the feature of experimental design that the subjects are used as their own controls over time (as is found in Horner's, 1968, research). It is therefore more difficult to relate these findings to individual modulations in approach or avoidance. In addition, there are no measures of latent ideation (as with TATs or TAT-like instruments) which might serve as further indications of what processes might be involved in this apparent success avoidance. Lastly, there is the problem in some of these studies that the experimenter has made the assumption that a particular task (e.g., "cooking" or "sewing" or "fixing things" or "taking pain") has a particular gender association for the subjects, and that the degree of femininity for the "feminine" task is the same as the degree of "masculinity" for the "masculine" task. This is a common practice in research on gender differences and gender roles but suffers from the obvious problem that the experimenter cannot know if these assumptions are true with that particular population in that particular situation. Indeed, few studies have found that the clear, binary demarcations assumed by the experimenters have led to such clearly different results. But despite the noncomparability with the research on "fear of success," this research does suggest that success that is gender-role inappropriate is avoided to some extent.

THE SOURCES OF SUCCESS AVOIDANCE

To sum up the wide range of forms that success avoidance can take and the various theories put forward to account for it reviewed above, the point should be made that all the sorts of apparent avoidance of attainment of a desired goal—from inhibition of symbolically sexual achievement based on parental prohibitions experienced in childhood to "restriction of output" among workers in a machine shop to superstitions about the overly successful based on transgression of expectations—are related to each other, even if not as systematically as might be desired. In each case, a limit of intolerability set up by a personal or social normative system has been exceeded and there exists an expectation of negative consequences for performance above a certain level.

Though the sources of success avoidance may come from diverse directions, the avoidance of success can be logically attributed to three major modalities found in the material of this chapter:

1. A desire to avoid the stress on self-perception entailed by an outcome (or series of outcomes) that is "out of character," that

disconfirms expectancies about oneself. It is important for one to know how well one does in most situations; one derives important aspects of one's self-conception from this information. Consequently, it is uncomfortable to achieve outcomes very different from one's expected performance level and as a result be labeled differently (e.g., more successful, more of a failure) than one perceives oneself (Bem, 1972). In the case of the abnormally successful performance, not only will the sheer inconsistency between this new outcome and one's self-conception be experienced as uncomfortable and lead to success-avoidant behavior (Aronson and Carlsmith, 1962), but the noxious aspect of an expected down-turn in future performances will also lead to success-avoidant behavior in anticipation of that possibility (Mettee, 1971; cf. the research from equity theory cited above).

2. A fear of the extremity of the demands inherent in the role of being a "successful person." Continued success requires continued high levels of effort. This is true in the long run where the factor of luck or fate loses its power, and even where natural ability is relatively high and difficulty of the task relatively low (see Weiner *et al.*, 1972, and Weiner, 1972, for the discussion of the exhaustiveness of these four perceived causes of behavior). Often associated with the highly focused persistence of instrumental activity necessary to maintain this role are such negative consequences as physical ailments (heart attacks, ulcers, gout), chronic tension, anxiety symptoms, defensiveness, nervous breakdowns, and so on (French and Caplan, 1972).[16] Also associated are the numerous limitations on other valued parts of one's personality—camping, spending time with friends, hobbies, or relaxing must give way to working at one's occupational task. An additional side-effect is that, while more capable and successful people receive greater rewards for their superior performance, they also receive greater punishment when they do fail (Lanzetta and Hannah, 1969). Perhaps the greatest causes for despair in success are the isolation and lack of the positive value of community which result from excessive individualism (May, 1950). Such Pyrrhic victories, the results of the "success syndrome" (Beecher and

[16]This is so despite the longer lives of the thousand *highest* executives in the United States ("Longevity of Corporate Executives," 1974).

Beecher, 1966; Marrow, 1973), might rightly be rejected along with the behaviors leading toward success by persons who realize such are the possible outcomes.

3. A fear of the social ostracism resulting from success. Persons who perform very well relative to others in the social groups to which they belong are sometimes envied by the others, sometimes rejected as no longer a member of the group, and are often under pressures to do like the others do. These punishments for doing *too* well (and thus threatening the established behavioral tolerances of the social group) discourage exceptional performances in situations where results can be measured and are public.[17]

The first and third sources above have in common the idea that one's place in a social group is of importance to individuals, and that this can be evaluated in particular social situations; they are summaries of the above material on boundary maintenance. While the first has been amply demonstrated, my attention has in this chapter been put on the third: how one's relationship to social boundaries determines one's level of performance.

The second source above involves yet another view of "success" and deserves mention. Let us go back for a moment to Horner's experiment. Perhaps the women responding with such negative imagery to Anne at the top of her medical school class were aware of the hazards of such a professional position. Indeed, they may have been aware that, even though suicides among male physicians and medical students account for more deaths than any other accidental cause, rate of suicides among female physicians and medical students far surpasses even that for males, a dramatic reverse of the situation in the population in general (Ross, 1973). The effects such knowledge might have is a matter of conjecture.

More probably, these females were aware of the inappropriateness of medical school to the feminine gender role. Relevant in this

[17]Interestingly (and this fact was discovered after these had been written) these sources correspond to the three feared consequences of *non*attainment or three forms of "fear of failure" described by Birney *et al.* (1969) in the conclusion of their program of research (pp. 201–225): devaluation of the self-estimate, nonego punishments (i.e., undesired side effects of the outcome), and social devaluation. These modalities take a somewhat revised form when the negative outcome is success, but the similarities are indeed striking.

regard are the statistics for the actual number of women in the first year of medical school in the academic year 1963–1964 (the year in which Horner collected her data): of 8772 entering students, 684 or 7.8% were women (Dubé, 1973, p. 187). Although it is doubtful that Horner's subjects would have known these exact statistics, Tresemer and Pleck (1974; see also Touhey, 1974) cite evidence that even younger subjects sexualize professional occupations in a way very closely related to the actual percentages of males and females in those occupations. Indeed, the wording of the famous medical school cue—" . . . Anne *finds* herself . . ."—puts special emphasis on the Meadian I–Me distinction (Mead, 1934). The self that is the object of observation is the social self, the enactor of roles; reflection on the appropriateness of these roles is encouraged by the cue (cf. Gergen, 1971; also Duval and Wicklund, 1972). The social-psychological view would posit that avoidance of transgression of social boundaries (third source above), mediated by processes of social comparison (central to the first source above), account for the expression of "fear of success" and the avoidance of success.

PART II

RECENT RESEARCH ON FEAR OF SUCCESS

In the spring of 1964, 178 students from the introductory psychology course at the University of Michigan fulfilled a course requirement that they participate in a psychological experiment by spending two hour-long sessions filling out questionnaires and taking written tests. Some worked alone with a tape recorder giving them instructions, some worked in pairs, and all in the first session worked together in a large auditorium. These students also wrote creative stories to several one-liner settings, such as "Tom is looking into his microscope." After writing five such stories for four minutes each, the students were given the story cue: "At the end of first term finals, Anne finds herself at the top of her medical school class." Males wrote about John at the top of his class; females about Anne.

The study was designed by Matina Souretis Horner, a graduate student working toward the Ph.D. under the supervision of Professor John Atkinson, known for his Expectancy × Value theory of human motivation (Atkinson, 1964). Completed in 1968, Horner's doctoral dissertation (Horner, 1968) dealt mostly with further work on the relationships between the motive to do well or need for achievement, need for affiliation, performance (at verbal tasks such as unscrambling mixed-up words like LPAPE), and level of aspiration for doing well at such a task. However, stories written to the "medical school" cue had shown strong differences in negative imagery between the male and female students, 62.2% of the women having expressed conflict over the success in their stories, while only 9.1% of the men expressed such conflict. A portion of Horner's thesis proposed that women had a "fear of success" and demonstrated behavioral proof that this negative or "fear of success" imagery was related to avoidance of success (doing well at the verbal tasks) when competing against men.

Soon after Horner's dissertation was completed, a brief article about the "fear of success" portion of the research appeared in *Psychology Today* (Horner, 1969), the fledgling forum for popular psychology. This stimulated a flood of articles in places such as *The New York Times Magazine, Ms., Time, Newsweek,* as well as many newspapers, all serving to disseminate this new explanation for women's unequal occupational attainment in the American success hierarchy. It soon became an axiom of gender-role differences.

None of the theories of "fear of success" mentioned in Chapter 1 has stimulated much in the way of social-psychological research. In marked contrast is Horner's more recent theory of "fear of success" (FOS). This theory has achieved a powerful status in the psychological marketplace—in grant proposals, in introductory texts, and in the professional journals. In addition, Horner's theory has been one of the few psychological theories to be embraced and disseminated by the popular press. Indeed, FOS tests, like achievement tests (M. Levine, 1976), have become an absolute criterion in themselves—"FOS-present" has become a far-ranging judgment about a person and his or her past and future.

The use made of Horner's study via citations of Horner's work as support for critical points in key papers by psychologists and sociologists has been most interesting. In an appendix to the annotated bibliography of studies on "fear of success" (Tresemer, 1976a) is summarized the import of many such citations. They range from substantiation of an alleged female "will to fail" to the higher suicide rate among women psychologists to females' negative attitudes toward the career role for women to the debilitating gender-role socialization of American women. We shall see in the following chapters the extent to which such statements can rely on the research on "fear of success."[1]

Why has there been such a boom in research on "fear of success" when several other previous conceptions received only scant attention? The reasons are complicated. Horner linked the dramatic displays of anxiety about success from the creative story-writing exercise with modern methods of social-psychological research. For many, this link meant that the relatively new science of social psychology, often so dry and overflowing with tongue-twisting neologisms, was enriched by raw data, really raw data. Quotes of young women's unconscious fears about being at the top in medical school stimulated the parallel fantasies of the readers in a way that would have been impossible with more "objective" methods such as seven-point Likert-type scales asking questions like, "Are you afraid of being top in your class?" The interest, indeed fascination, in a "fear" of success could only have developed in a culture oriented toward success. The touchingly personal revelations of the young women's stories could then be linked to commentary on large social groups, namely achieving women or even all women. Undergraduates in some introductory courses were encouraged to be scientific about their more passionate involvement with the Women's Liberation Movement by having their friends or specified samples simply write stories. This seemed so much more interesting than filling out questionnaires.

There have been numerous programs of research by competent and careful professionals either using Horner's technique of measuring "fear of success" or using her research as a guideline for a complementary research design. These programs of research are cited and thoroughly annotated in Tresemer (1976a).[2] Chapters 5 and 6 summarize and discuss the most important of these studies. These

[1]An example too recent to be included in the annotated bibliography is from Gail Sheehy's popular book *Passages* (1976); she cites Horner as proof that "the more competent the woman, the greater her conflict about achieving" (p. 114). This claim is directly addressed in Chapter 6.

[2]Available in photocopy or microfiche from the Journal Supplement Abstract Service, American Psychological Association, 1200 17th St., N.W., Washington, D.C. 20036. Many of the original manuscripts can be found in the Fear of Success Collection, Sophia Smith Library, Smith College, Northampton, Mass. The annotated bibliography on which these analyses were based is exhaustive to January 1, 1976.

chapters have been organized in terms of the most important recurrent questions in this field:

(a) Do females show more "fear of success" imagery than do males?

(b) Do males respond to a cue depicting an achieving female with more "fear of success" imagery than do females?

(c) Have the proportions of "fear of success" imagery elicted by men and women in response to verbal cues changed over the last decade?

(d) What are the correlates of "fear of success"?

(e) What is the relationship between "fear of success" imagery and performance in different kinds of situations (e.g., female achievement behavior in competition with men)? The answers to these questions are summarized at the end of Chapter 6 in "The Performance of FOS."

Chapter 4 is an introduction to the research tradition on which Horner's research and most contemporary work on "fear of success" is founded. This includes attention (a) to the theoretical background of the experimental approach to achievement-related phenomena, and (b) to the technical details of the experimental lab as utilized in this research tradition. A full understanding of these matters requires spending time with several rambling tomes of collected writings in this tradition (e.g., McClelland *et al.*, 1953; Atkinson, 1958; and recently Atkinson and Raynor, 1974); these will guide the reader toward many other sources of current and of historical interest for this research tradition. This research approach certainly deserves to be called a "paradigm" in psychology in the sense that it defines what should be studied, what questions should be asked, how they should be asked, how to collect pertinent data, and how to interpret them. The tradition has certain ways of understanding social and psychological realities—for example, in the definition and measurement of an individual's need for achievement and achievement behavior—which are hinted at in this chapter.

Chapter 4 is also intended as a primer for the use of thematic methods, as background for a great deal of the research summarized herein, although an acquaintance with the literature on the use of the Thematic Apperception Test (cf. Rapaport, Gill, and Schafer, 1970, and Murstein, 1963) would be very useful in this regard.

CHAPTER 4

Scoring Success-Avoidance Thema in Responses to Verbal Story Cues

FORMAT

The use of story writing for assessing motivation began with the adaptation of procedures used in Henry Murray's Thematic Apperception Test (TAT; 1943; 1951) in a study of the arousing properties of hunger by J. W. Atkinson and D. C. McClelland (1948). A description of this adapted technique is found in Atkinson (1964, p. 223).

> A series of pictures which suggested food-seeking or eating in varying degree were selected from some of Murray's original set of TAT pictures and from ordinary magazines. Following a general instruction that the task was to construct interesting and imaginative stories, each picture was shown for 20 seconds and then withdrawn. The subjects were then given four minutes to write a story about the picture. The general questions that are normally given verbally in clinical use of thematic apperception were printed at equal intervals on otherwise blank story forms to guide subjects through the plot of a story. The guiding questions were:
>
> 1. What is happening? Who are the persons?
> 2. What has led up to this situation, that is, what has happened in the past?

> 3. What is being thought? What is wanted, by whom?
> 4. What will happen? What will be done?
>
> As soon as the four minutes allotted for writing a story was up, another picture was shown. This procedure continued for 16 to 32 minutes, depending upon the number of pictures employed. It produced a substantial "thought sample," or sample of imaginative behavior, induced by certain picture cues under controlled motivating conditions.

The use of verbal cues as in research on "fear of success" alters the demand characteristics of the stimulus; there is much less information than in the pictures from the TAT. Additionally, one of the central characteristics of the TAT has been its ambiguity, thought to create variance in responses and thus reveal more of the respondent's personality. This characteristic is also highly stressed by McClelland *et al.* (1953) in their discussion of cues to be used for assessing achievement motivation. However, this is not true of Horner's "medical school" cue, and the relative specificity of this cue can perhaps be likened more to studies in social psychological research on reactions to word stimuli than to the traditional clinical uses of the Thematic Apperception Test. Attempts have been made in subsequent research to reinstitute the traditional ambiguity of stimuli.

VALIDATION OF THE SCORING SYSTEM

The normal validating procedure for demonstrating the existence of a motive and the way of assessing it thematically was used first in the Atkinson and McClelland (1948) study of hunger and remains the model for this type of research. Subjects are put into a situation thought for theoretical reasons to arouse a particular latent, stable predisposition to action (Atkinson's definition of motive); they then write stories at that time. Thus, the stories are representations of the "redintegration by a cue of a change in an affective state" (McClelland *et al.*, 1953, p. 28).

The latent thema of the stories are understood as projections of latent need states and are scored as indications of these needs. To facilitate this projection outward, Atkinson and McClelland (1948, p. 655) emphasized that the most effective eliciting stimuli "should be vague and contain characters with whom the person can identify," a recommendation based on a large earlier study by Symonds (1939). In nearly every investigation since then, this has meant using cues depicting at least one same-gender figure.

The thema in the stories of the aroused group are compared with stories of a control (nonaroused) group and a scoring system is thus empirically derived from the differences.

Finally, a new group of nonaroused subjects writes stories which are scored with the new criteria. The stories are used to predict individual differences in behavior in an experimental situation. The importance of the second step is clear as a validation of the scoring categories in terms of actual behavior.

Horner's original study (1968) was based only on the second step and, as such, remains an important demonstration study; use of her original scoring criteria do not constitute a measure of a *motive* to avoid success, though it seems clear from her original study and subsequent work that these thema do have something to do with success avoidant behavior. Work on the first step in this traditional validation procedure is currently underway (cf. Horner *et al.*, 1973, and summary in Tresemer, 1976a).

The above description of the validation technique for a motivational scoring system is very conservative. While this has been the preferred technique for guaranteeing content, construct, and predictive validity in several scoring systems (see Atkinson, 1958; Winter, 1973), other techniques have been used. From an empirical point of view, any paper-and-pencil behavior that relates to a performance behavior sufficiently constitutes a measure, though the face and content validity of that paper-and-pencil behavior is necessary to know what it is measuring.

HORNER'S FEAR OF SUCCESS

Horner's criteria for scoring "fear of success" in her sample of responses to the "medical school" cue were presented as follows (1968, p. 105):

> A very simple present–absent scoring system was adopted for fear of success imagery. The stories were scored for Fear of Success if there was negative imagery expressed which reflected concern about the success. For instance,

a. negative consequences because of the success
b. anticipation of negative consequences because of the success
c. negative affect because of the success
d. instrumental activity away from present or future success, including leaving the field for more traditional female work such as nursing, school teaching, or social work
e. any direct expression of conflict about success

Also scored was evidence of

f. denial of the situation described by the cue
g. bizarre, inappropriate, unrealistic or nonadaptive responses to the situation described by the cue.

The above criteria were derived in part from Scott's (1958) application of Miller's (1944) approach–avoidance paradigm to thematic reactions to threatening stimuli.[1] In one later publication (Horner, 1970a, p. 59), another category was added: "denial of effort in attaining the success (also cheating or any other attempt to deny responsibility or reject credit for the success)."

These criteria were supplemented by more detailed descriptions of the three major groups of responses which Horner found for her female subjects. The descriptions and especially the examples used to illustrate them, have become for many subsequent researchers additional (or the only) categories for scoring Horner's "fear of success." They are as follows:

1. Fear of social rejection: "fear of losing one's friendships, the loss of one's datable or marriageable quality, actual isolation or loneliness as a result of the success and the desire to keep the success a secret and pretend that intelligence is not a part of her." This includes wondering or worrying about others' reactions.

2. Doubts about one's normality as a woman, and guilt and despair about the success.

3. Denial of the cue or denying effort or responsibility for attaining the successful outcome; and bizarre stories. Two examples of denial were given by Horner (1968, p. 106) as follows:

[1]There are also similarities to the negative categories of the need-achievement or *n* Ach system (especially I-, Ga-, Bp, Bw, and G-; see Smith and Feld, 1958) and to scoring systems developed for assessing "fear of failure" (Moulton, 1958; Birney *et al.*, 1969). See also the similarities to Beck's scoring system for depression in dreams (Beck and Hurvich, 1959).

> Anne is really happy she's on top, though Tom is higher than she—though that's as it should be . . . Anne doesn't mind Tom winning.

> It was luck that Anne came out on top of her med class because she didn't want to go to med school anyway.

An example of a bizarre story was given by Horner as follows:

> She starts proclaiming her surprise and joy. Her fellow classmates are so disgusted with her behavior that they jump on her in a body and beat her. She is maimed for life.

CLARIFICATIONS

In my experience with scoring Horner's "fear of success" (the score hereafter abbreviated as FOS), I required a clarification of the terse available scoring criteria. I rescored 85 of the stories in her original study, carefully checking against her decisions after each of the twenty stories. I shall summarize this additional material here.

These examples are from responses to the following cues used in a study of high school juniors (Tresemer, 1974b):

> "Project" cue: "John (Joan) has just successfully completed his (her) own project, which he (she) has been working on for several months."

> "Gotten what wanted"cue: "After much work, David (Judy) has finally gotten what he (she) wanted."

> "Smile" cue: "Paul (Judy) is sitting in a chair with a smile on his (her) face."

> "Pleased" cue: "Joe (Anne) seems particularly pleased."

Compared with the specificity of the "medical school" cue, these cues signify a return to the stimulus ambiguity characteristic of the TAT. Yet, there is a task or affective "success" which must be integrated into the respondent's story in some way.

Success can be linked with a negative affect resulting from it, or with a subsequent downfall:

> ("Pleased" cue) Anne is particularly pleased today. In her hand she tightly grasps a letter from her brother who is fighting in the war. Her face changes from one of pleasure to a horrified questioning look. She drops the letter on the floor. The first line is showing through "We regret to inform you . . ."

("Gotten what wanted" cue) It took David two years to earn enough money for his new motorcycle. He always wanted a new bike and now he finally had one . . . David would most likely try to show off and in doing so he would kill himself.

("Smile" cue) Last night, Judy had a dream that she was Cinderella. She dreamed that a big pumpkin was turned into a coach but that her fairy godmother did not change her rags into a gown. So, in the dream, Judy was continually embarrassed and felt poor in her rags on the way to the ball. When she arrived, the Prince did not fall in love with her, but mistook her for a gallery maid.

Fear of a future disaster or failure can also be scored as an expected negative consequence.

Rejections by other people are also a common sort of negative consequence for success, as are mentions of anticipated affiliative loss.

("Project" cue) John has completed his project that people in his town have been waiting forward to seeing. His project is a work of art so he says which will be placed in the common. The unveiling takes place this afternoon. Many people are coming to see the unveiling. Right now there is a white sheet draped over a 23 foot statue that no one has seen, now it has been unveiled and yeck, disappointment overwhelms the town . . .

("Project" cue) . . . Joan goes upstairs and tries the dress (she has made) on. Then Joan goes over to her mother and asks if the dress looks alright. Joan's mother is a bitch so she says no and Joan goes to her room and destroys the dress.

Seeming accidents, attributed to fate (negative consequences not contingent to the person) or in some way linked to a fault of the person (contingent), are central to FOS.

("Project" cue) The project that John has been working on is a stereo cabinet in wood shop . . . John finishes his project and brings it home only to find out that it is a foot too long for the space where it was going to go.

("Project" cue) Joan has just finished her project, she has been working on for months. She was home doing the dishes one night, she heard a crash, she went in to see what it was, her cat had jumped on her desk, knocked her project over. She feels terrible . . .

("Project" cue) . . . John's project fell on the floor today and broke and John flipped out.

Doubts about the desired goal, implying conflict over the success should be scored only in the most obvious cases—that is, when it seems clear that such conflictful ideation was part of or might lead to success avoidance. This is illustrated in the following two examples.

> ("Gotten what wanted" cue) . . . She has been saving and going without other things that she has really wanted. Judy has finally saved enough money to buy a car, but now she wonders if it was worth it.

> ("Pleased" cue) . . . He had worked all year so that he could buy the car, and he finally did it. But now he is afraid of cracking it up, and he is starting to have second thoughts about his new car . . .

BIZARRE STORIES

Although bizarre or wildly inappropriate stories are scored in Horner's "fear of success" system, it seems that the fault in these stories was at a completely different level from the others. Instead of accepting the stimulus cue as presented and creating a story which might or might not terminate negatively, the bizarre stories seemed to reject the cue and the task altogether. Perhaps bizarre stories should be seen as a category of their own. A definition of bizarre stories is as follows: Any extremely violent, weird, or nonsensical stories. It should be noted that, while many of these stories are quite comic:

> ("Pleased" cue) Yes, Joe does seem to be pleased, and with good reason. Joe just got a job as the head banana peeler in a banana recycling plant. All his life Joe has worked to get a job as good as this. He never has been able to get a good job, partly because he has an IQ of four, but mainly because he has a neurotic compulsion to kick people. Here, though, he can kick anybody he wants, because they wear shin guards.

most often the same flair for exaggeration turns into sadistic violence:

> ("Gotten what wanted" cue) . . . So today when Judy came home from school she locked her mother in the basement. There are rats in the basement and Judy's mother can't get out. No one can hear her or see her either. Now Judy has finally gotten what she

> always wanted. She has control of the family now. She had voodooed her father's car and he had had a fatal accident . . .
>
> ("Project" cue) . . . By the way, John fed the lizard guts to his little sister and she died . . .

Sometimes the achievement-oriented pursuit of a desired goal is tainted by the nature of the ends or means, to create a bizarre situation:

> ("Smile" cue) He feels a great sense of triumph. He's sure no one will ever figure out that it was him. He disposed of the body so neatly and inconspicuously, but he's beginning to get a little nervous the crime was so perfect that something must go wrong like in a lot of those Poe stories.

It should be clear from at least some of these examples that bizarre stories exaggerate to an extreme some of the same story elements found in other categories of FOS. Although differentiation of this category proved unhelpful in one investigation for its small size (Tresemer, 1974b), further work is needed to assess the worth of including this category in the FOS score.

NEGATIVE ANTECEDENT

Subjects sometimes construct a story in response to success (e.g., a finished project) that does not have a negative *consequence*, but describes a negative *antecedent* to the success. The success is then often regarded as a miraculous unexpected change in fate, or sometimes the fruits of hard labors to rise out of the originally negative situation. It seems that this might be an alternative route for subjects to integrate the "success" of the verbal cue into a story, but still express their discomfort about accepting success in a way that differs from imagining ultimate negative outcomes.

It could be argued that the "expectancy of negative consequences" is as strong in such a story and that the different plot construction reflects only a difference in style from FOS. Indeed, Lionel Ovesey (1962, p. 84) identified two major groups of unconscious fantasies in those showing a "fear of success": fantasies of destruction and fantasies of magical repair. While Horner's conception includes stories terminating in or anticipating various forms of destruction, this category picks up stories showing previous destruction followed by either magical or hardly earned repair. This form of success avoidance through megalomania has also been described by Fromm (1942, p. 150) and Reich (1960).

Another system which contrasts these two categories was developed in a study by Robert May (1966) of gender differences in fantasies expressed to ambiguous picture stimuli. The parallel to FOS was the style of enhancement followed by deprivation (ED):

> a pattern of success followed by failure, gain followed by loss, high expectations followed by unsatisfying achievements. (p. 579)

The current category would be seen as the opposite (deprivation followed by enhancement or DE).

While Ovesey saw themes of this sort simply as alternative expressions of a "fear of success," and May saw them as more typical of the female personality, deCharms and Dave (1965) saw them as indications of a "hope of success." Their scoring system is based solely on the outcome of an achievement-related story: negative outcomes (scorable for FOS) scored as "fear of failure," and positive outcomes as "hope of success." Symonds (1949, p. 89) suggests, on the other hand, that conflictful stories that end happily indicate guilt tendencies in the adolescent author.

Negative Antecedent imagery clearly involves a completely different Gestalt from Fear of Success Imagery. In Negative Antecedent, to a mind imbued in the cultural belief in the wheel of fortune, a success may be borne only by one who has failed or had sufficient misfortune. As a Romanian fairy tale says, "only kings rule who have suffered many things" (Bettelheim, 1976). Essentially, "he has paid his dues." This is why Horatio Alger stories are acceptable—the eventual hero starts off a ragamuffin, weak, and maligned. Indeed, most romance novels, after a brief introductory thesis, emphasize the negative strophe or antithesis before the achievement of the happy synthesis is permissible.

The scoring criteria are as follows: a bad grade average, nagging parents, a broken leg, exhaustion from the excessive strain or work, feeling unhappy or feeling bad about not doing well on the last test, and so on are assumed to indicate a previous state of deprivation if they happen before the reference to the success in the story. Worries about possible failure on an upcoming test which is then studied for and passed successfully are also scored; such expectations of negative consequences can be scored as FOS only when they concern consequences following a previous success.

Also included are statements of deprivations from hardships endured in working toward the successful outcome; this does not mean references to hard work but to something extremely distasteful or involving loss. For example, talking about working nights at a supermarket or gas station in order to earn extra money to attain the desired goal of a new car is insufficient to be scored as a Negative Antecedent; if, however, this is linked with loss of friends or other sorts of suffering, it does qualify as a Negative Antecedent. The following example illustrates several sorts of loss:

> ("Pleased" cue) Joe Smith seems happy because he has just gotten his report card. All year long his parents have been haunting him about his grades but Joe was more interested in sports. But in his senior year Joe found out from his football coach, Mr. Albert, that he could not play football on a good college team unless his grades improved immensely. Joe sacrificed many things in order to do better in school. His girlfriend Sally Fudd stopped coming to see him at night. He stopped watching television schoolnights and quit drinking on weekends. It paid off.

Further examples of the distinction between hard work and hardship are in order. References to unelaborated difficulties are *not* scored:

> David has been trying to get a group together for two years and he has really been trying hard. Now his reward has come and he has found some kids to jam with.

References to anticipations of a goal are *not* scored:

> She has been waiting for this for a long time.

In the sentence, "She works all day from 7:00 to 5:00, breaking her back for her boss," the first phrase is *not* scored (long hours, hard work), but the second phrase *is* (depiction of extreme hardship).

Previous deficits in the person are also a frequent type of response:

> ("Project" cue) Joan has been after Artie for several months. He is charming and really cute. Joan on the other hand is fat and ugly. She went on a crash diet and used Noxema for two months.

At the beginning of the third month Joan gave up on Artie. Several days later who called her on the phone for a date! Yup! Artie did. Now Joan is pregnant and they are planning a June wedding.

("Smile" cue) . . . everyone, including her friend, thought she was barren, but it finally happened, Judy's pregnant . . .

These should be scored only if it is clear that the personal attribute is experienced as deprivatory. This can be assumed with references to such extreme states as ugliness, barrenness, mental retardation, and so on; but situations where this is unclear such as a gymnastic contest where Judy is against tough competition are not scored unless the problems are labeled as or associated with some sort of deprivation (e.g., Judy is only 5 ft, 3 in.).

Other scorable mentions (all to the "Project" cue) are as follows:

Joan has given up many, more fun, activities in order to complete this.

. . . months of agony . . .

. . . the good times he had forfeited during these four years.

John had tried before but he had failed . . .

. . . After he had experienced many crying sessions at the library, his frustration paid off in a well-done project.

Tresemer (1974b) found the presence of this kind of negative imagery to be unrelated to FOS; for 187 high school juniors the correlation was −.059 for the two themes scored from the same two stories, and a month later with a different set of stories the correlation was +.088. Since in that study, Negative Antecedent related to some variables to which FOS did not, it seems unfortunate that the newer scoring system for FOS (Horner *et al.*, 1973) does not differentiate this form of imagery from FOS.

GENERAL INHIBITION THEMA

Another distinguishable category for negative thematic imagery was used by Tresemer (1974b), where it was defined as follows:

General Inhibition Thema: These are symbolic "leaks" indicating that the situation is highly charged for the individual and that he or she may experience unacknowledged difficulties in approaching it. This can be interpreted as a powerful fear of one's own lack of control which would result in hurting self or others, leading to the symbolic statement: "I'd better not . . . or else." Score any explicit mentions in the story of:

> severe loss (orphan's home, divorce), illness, death, suicide, retardation, exhaustion; severe anxiety or depression, fainting, passing out, feeling cold or cold weather; punishments, torture, voodoo, blood, murder, guns, pain, robberies and thefts, rape, biting or being bitten, accidents, physical handicaps, amputations, crashes, fires, hospitals, plagues; jail, prison; unreal powerful forces (UFOs, monsters); explosive or implosive outlets for pent-up energy (alcohol, drugs, violence, sexual excess, sleeping a lot); or other characteristics of this sort.

Score whether related to an action or not.

Examples:

> "Paul is watching the house burn."
>
> "Jane is really stoned."
>
> "She murders him that night."
>
> "Suddenly she has a heart attack from the shock."
>
> "A group of young people are gathered on the beach on a cold, clear day."
>
> "That night he and his 'gang' go out and get bombed on beer, wine, whiskey, sex, and highness. In the midst of all this, John falls into a deep remorse, for he knows how little the grades mean, how little he knows—and he commits suicide."

As is clear from this definition, General Inhibition Thema is one way of measuring general negativity in a story, even if this negativity is unrelated to a disastrous (or even to a positive) outcome. It should be noted that a similar category was used with some success by Rotter (1940, p. 30; 1946, p. 88) and Lindzey and Newburg (1954, p. 592) to measure signs of anxiety in stories told in the TAT. These themes have also been used as indicators of depression, maladjustment, and psychopathic character disorder (see Lindzey *et al.*, 1959, pp. 14, 15, 26, 38, 41, 57). Tresemer (1974b) found a statistically significant predominance of General Inhibition Thema in stories written by males rather than females (e = .04, a "small" effect), a replication of observations made by Symonds (1949), Harrison (1965), and Gottschalk and Glaser (1969, p. 72). General Inhibition

Thema were also associated with FOS themes, correlating at +.332 ($p < .001$) in one set of stories and at +.369 ($p < .001$) in another set a month later.

RESPONSIVENESS OF NEGATIVE THEMA TO SITUATIONAL DIFFERENCES

Different theories about the properties of fantasy lead to different ideas about whether the incidence of negative themes will increase under arousal or not. Most of the arguments about the structure and function of fantasy have involved whether it reflects primary process—nondirected immediate discharge of tensional energy, behavior which feels nonvolitional and of which the organism is fundamentally unaware—or secondary process—where the organism sets out with considerable effort to obtain an effect and is quite aware of the direction of mental activity and feedback from the environment (Klinger, 1971). Many theorists see fantasy as far more determined by primary process, and seek out the latent (vs. manifest) aspects of expressions of fantasy as measures of dominant predispositions to behavior (Freud, 1900; Rapaport, 1951; McClelland *et al.*, 1953; McClelland, 1965). Klinger (1971) helpfully parallels this distinction to a Skinnerian differentiation between respondent and operant responses. In this sense, responses to story-writing stimuli are respondent (nonvolitional, reactive) in form. And, to the extent that these cues are "ambiguous" (i.e., nonspecific yet still engaging), the responses may be reliable indications of the dominant integrated behavioral predisposition of the organism (or the "regnant subself;" see Klinger, 1971).

The above applies to so-called neutral situations; but when affect (e.g., anxiety) is aroused in a particular context, it can operate either as a potentiating influence or an interrupting influence on expression (Klinger, 1971). The bulk of existing theory predicts the first. Though primarily based on conceptions of positive affects in response to positive incentives, the same reasoning has classically been extended to negative situations also. For example, Bramel (1962) found that defensive projection increased as the negativity of a self-referent cognition (arousing cognitive dissonance) increased. Birney *et al.* (1969, p. 93) found that a failure experience arranged with the false-norm technique increased themes of "assault on the well-being of the central figure by reprimand, affiliative-loss, natural forces, or personal failure." Lindzey and Kalnins (1958) observed increases in stories showing aggression following frustration. McClelland *et al.* (1953), using a similar arousal technique, noted a preponderance of negative affective state themes (G− in the achievement scoring system) and positive goal anticipation (Ga+), suggesting that the state of failure would eventually be replaced by more positive outcomes, simply relying on the law of averages.

Both of these latter studies, however, are not really comparable to a situation which might arouse the ambivalence about the goal which characterizes anxiety about success. Both of the settings for failure were among groups of male subjects in competition with rival groups of males; the success condition in the latter study unambivalently increased the preponderance of positive affect (G+), while lowering the incidence of personal obstacles (Bp), need (N), and negative affective state (G−). There was one indication of increased negativity after success: while after failure against competitors, positive goal anticipation (Ga+) had risen, after success it decreased, suggesting the expectation of less positive outcomes after a very positive one [taken as evidence by McClelland *et al.* (1953) of the "Polycrates complex"—see Chapter 1].

Other research has indicated that the *de*creased appearance of inhibitory themes is the proper indication of the degree of arousal of a situation (Lesser, 1958; Clark, 1952; Clark and Sensibar, 1955; Clark *et al.*, 1956).

McClelland's (1951, pp. 494–500) early formulation of factors affecting expression of positive and negative themes integrates these various possibilities in a different way. This model was used by Clark *et al.* (1956) to try to explain a decrease in negative themes in a situation where, based on theory and previous research, they expected such ideation would predominate. McClelland's model showed two interacting curvilinear response curves for positive ("Goal imagery") and negative ("Deprivation imagery") expressions depending on the degree of stimulation or arousal of the person. In the protected Wish-Fulfillment stage of low situational arousal and uninterrupted introspective reverie, the incidence of positive fantasy is at a high and negative at a low. At an intermediate stage of Push Toward Reality, anxiety upon meeting real problems in the real world drives negative themes to a high and positive themes to a low. Finally, in the Defense stage, hard realities become overwhelming and the negative themes decrease while positive themes increase again. This last change is especially pronounced past a certain threshold, where the capability of the ego to encompass the increased stimulation is at its limit, a factor which must vary from individual to individual and depend on a host of unique and expected developmental and situational factors.

This model nicely integrates the various theories about the nature of fantasy in different settings. For example, the Defense stage explains some findings such as the *decrease* of fear or anxiety responses when the negative or mixed incentive is closest and thus more intense—observed for soldiers stationed at 4000 yards from the site of the detonation of a nuclear device who were tested at intervals before the explosion (Walker and Atkinson, 1958), for parachutists approaching the time of a jump (Fenz and Epstein, 1962), and for emotionally disturbed and maladjusted children and adolescents as compared to normals (Symonds, 1949; Cox and Sargent, 1950). Likewise, McClelland *et al.* (1953, p. 103) observed decreases in imagery of all sorts in response to arousal that was too extreme.

Another prediction was that operant responses would only be possible in that large midrange of Push Toward Reality. But an experiment by Bobbit (1958) extended this to respondent behavior as well. She suggested to hypnotized subjects that they had run from the scene of an automobile accident and introduced various levels of moral condemnation for this act, then studied the differential level of recall for the act. Under both total repression and complete recall, "complex indicators" (that is, symbolic word associations) were inactive; partial repression was associated with moderate interfering anxiety, and here the thematic measure was most indicative of the subject's latent anxiety.

An attractive feature of McClelland's model is its single gradient for arousal, combining the classical Yerkes–Dodson (1908) curve of positive imagery with its symmetrical opposite for negative imagery.

In a study closely related to McClelland's model R. Anderson

(1962, p. 297) found that the incidence of negative themes used as a measure of "fear of failure" had a curvilinear relationship to arousal, and explained the decrease under high arousal as "a defensive reaction to an anxiety-provoking situation."

Since, however, it is difficult to know just where on that curvilinear continuum any situation might be for any individual, we don't know whether we should predict an increase or decrease in negative themes under arousal conditions. While a number of authors (cited above) have observed a decrease in expression of negative themes under arousal, others (Scott, 1956; Moulton, 1958; and see Birney *et al.*, 1969), using less extreme arousal situations, have found increases in arousal situations. Incidence of and changes in negative imagery can thus be seen as dependent on the arousing power of the situation.

A situation could be defined in terms of McClelland's model if *both* positive and negative themes were measured, but this has not to my knowledge been systematically researched. I tried this in one study (Tresemer, 1974b) by calculating the relative preponderance of Negative Antecedent over FOS.[2] That is, the emphasis on justification of a success depicted in the cue by reference to previous hardships (Negative Antecedent) can be seen as "Goal imagery," and the emphasis on retribution for a success in a story with a tragic ending (FOS) can be seen as "Deprivation imagery;" their relative strengths can then be interpreted as an index of anxiety in McClelland's model. Using this index as a dependent variable, I found a much lower preponderance of Negative Antecedent over FOS when performance feedback was related to (fictitious) gender-role norms than when performance feedback was not related to (fictitious) gender-role norms. Gender-role-incongruent success resulted in the lowest values for this index: doing well at a task on which the opposite gender normatively does better is not the time for justification (Negative Antecedent imagery) but rather for retribution (FOS imagery). This would suggest that the gender-related success (and especially gender-role-incongruent success) feedback was more anxiety provoking, more in the Push Toward Reality sector of McClelland's model, while

[2]This measure was adapted from the early work of McClelland *et al.* (1953, pp. 153–154) for comparing the incidences of two themes in the same projective materials.

other sorts of success feedback were less anxiety provoking, more in the Wish-Fulfillment sector of McClelland's model. These results demand further inquiry into the arousal of negative affect, and into the distinction between kinds of negative imagery.

PRODUCTION

Some studies using thematic measures have sought to measure the length of the protocol as an important variable affecting the number of themes found in the story, and with few exceptions have found it to be an important covariate. In addition, the most successful critique of the use of thematic productions in motivational research (Entwisle, 1972) has suggested that productivity is the single most important mediating variable between motive measures and the behavior that they are supposed to predict, as well as the variable that would account for the observed gender differences in achievement. Tresemer (1974b) found a low positive correlation between FOS and story length ($r = +.199$, $n = 221$, $p < .01$). Short and Sorrentino (1974) also found a positive relationship [$F(1,162) = 5.55$, $p < .05$].

In the study by Tresemer (1974b), the number of words in one story was compared with the number of lines in that story (an occasional index of story length). The correlation between the number of lines and the number of words was +.682 ($n = 187$), indicating that, time-consuming though it may be, actually counting the number of words in the story increases accuracy appreciably.

FURTHER THOUGHTS ON THE CUE AND PROJECTIVE METHODS

Rather than tapping a direct expression of motive strength, i.e., something latent and stable about the personality, perhaps the medical school cue is eliciting more a reaction to the superficial content of the verbal cue. With the ambiguous and complex pictures used over and over again in the Thematic Apperception Test (TAT), common themes or biases due to the obvious subject matter have been taken into account; these common themes and cliches have not been taken too seriously when they arise in a protocol. No such standardization of cue material has yet been made in this field. Thus the problem with the "Anne at the top of her medical school class" cue is the explicitly structured nature of its presentation: are the responses telling us something about (1) the person's feelings about success, or (2) the person's feelings about being the top of the class, or (3) the person's feelings about success at medical school, or (4) the person's feelings about success in a "traditionally male occupation," or (5) the person's guesses about or reactions to a hypothetical woman who would (perhaps unlike the person) have the background and desire to enter medical school and spend the time to come out on top? The first definition is the entity of theoretical interest in Atkinson's Expectancy × Value theory of motivation. Assumptions, however, are frequently made that definitions (2) through (5) are the same as the first. But if one changes the cue to a different form of success, the results change (cf. Tresemer, 1976a), invalidating these assumptions.

An additional problem with this cue (and with projective methods in general) is the possibility of conscious control of content. Scorers in other systems have been unable to distinguish faked stories from neutral ones (Holmes, 1974). In addition, popularity of Horner's work has led to preknowledge among research subjects (Tresemer, 1974a). For example, the following story was obtained in one study:

> Anne is being congratulated by the male and female members of her class. The males are somewhat chagrined, as is Anne. However, Anne has read *Psychology Today* and knows that studies such as this indicate that this is an expected reaction. Anne will try to continue to do well—because she wants a career—but not necessarily number one.

Naturally, this story was not used in the analysis. But how many of the other stories from that sample were similarly "contaminated" by exposure to Horner's *Psychology Today* article (1969)?

Reading hundreds of stories leads to an awareness different from a simple familiarity with scoring criteria for a particular sort of imagery. Through experience one fallibility of the scoring system for "fear of success" is revealed. Stories that have what we think of as an interesting plot—that is, a story that includes positive and negative elements in meaningful relationship with exciting turns of fate and so on—are put in the same category with those that have disturbing indications of possible psychopathology, of anxiety and conflict. They are both called "fear of success." The first kind of story might be called "creative," but current scoring systems have been unable to distinguish it from the anxiety ridden. It seems impossible to design specific scoring criteria which will make this distinction; the differentiation must be based on a subjective experience of the story as a whole—its tone, choice of words, plot, etc. Of course, specific characteristics of form and content in a single story should not be used as "pathognomonic indicators for a given clinical syndrome" (Eron, 1965, p. 470), but must be interpreted in the larger context of the story as a whole, the series of stories, and what is known about the person. This appraisal is like when we say that J.R.R. Tolkien or C. S. Lewis are joyously constructive with their tragic events while Edgar Allan Poe or Jerzy Kosinski are brooding, never recovering from perverse disasters.

There are too many stories that do *not* show FOS imagery which could also be called Polyannish or dull or not realistic about life. It is a relief after reading several of these stories to encounter a truly imaginative story which shows a fresh approach to the cue material; these latter stories are often scored for FOS because they include the right kind of negative imagery, even though the negativity is often overcome or resolved in some way. However, I wonder if they are reliable evidence for a "fear of success" when compared with the Polyannish stories.

Here are some examples to illustrate the point. Several anxiety-ridden stories suggesting a crippling fear of success are quoted earlier in this chapter. The following story to the "medical school" cue is typical of the Polyannish type:

> Anne is so happy because she really wants to be a doctor. She worked very hard to do well in school. And now she has finally made it. She will be a good doctor.

This story scores relatively well for achievement imagery and there is no "fear of success" imagery, but its immaturity is clear. A more interesting story had essentially the same introduction until the last sentence, where the author continued:

> However, Anne is not so sure she wants to be a doctor after all the work it takes to be #1. She decides to spend less time studying and more having fun. Of course, her grades will drop but that's OK with her.

Although this story would be scored for FOS, it displays a more developed realization of the choice before Anne, the possible costs of her success, and the fact that we can't have everything all at once.[3]

These "clinical judgments" based on very short stories take time and some experience with reading between the lines and are very hard to communicate. We must simply consider the possibility that the "fear of success" system is befuddled with stories that do not necessarily imply a "fear," and work to improve upon it.

These problems remain mootly present throughout the discussions in the next two chapters. Some are addressed and provisionally resolved in those chapters.

[3]I once informally interviewed two dozen medical students and doctors from different schools about just what the top student in their class was like. The reader can certainly guess (and be scored for FOS): nearly all of their responses contained some sort of FOS imagery.

CHAPTER 5

The Cumulative Record of Research on Fear of Success

Several questions have been addressed repeatedly in research in the area of "fear of success" (FOS). The most frequently studied has been the gender difference in FOS, especially since Horner concluded on the basis of her results that American women feared success and men did not. Other questions frequently addressed by researchers interested in "fear of success" involve changes in FOS levels over the last decade, gender differences in responses to a cue depicting an achieving female, the correlates of FOS, and the relationship of FOS to performance criteria in different kinds of situations (e.g., competition with men).

This last question may perhaps be the most important of all, for without a relationship to behavior just what might "fear of success" mean? However, I will concentrate on the first questions in this chapter, and deal with the more complex question of relationship to performance in the next chapter. The conclusions are summarized in the overview at the end of Chapter 6.

Throughout this chapter and the next, I use the term FOS not only as a convenient abbreviation for "fear of success" but to remind the reader that we are dealing with a hypothetical construct that may or may not have much to do with the reader's commonsense idea about an anxiety about doing well, i.e., a "fear" of "success." Thus, FOS denotes only the name of the measure for fear of success, more properly an indication of a person's judgment of certain kinds of negative imagery in another person's writings. I do not here make the assumption that the measure of "fear of success" actually measures a fear of success, but sidestep the issue for a later discussion.

EFFECT SIZE

The concept of effect size is so integral to the following analyses that I shall summarize its definition and meaning here.

The conventional practice in current research of setting limitation on the p level (the probability of Type I error) at .05 or less as the single criterion of the statistical significance of the study has received repeated criticisms from many authors (e.g., Bakan, 1966; Cohen, 1962, 1969; Greenwald, 1975; Rozeboom, 1960; Signorelli, 1974). The choices made with this model are (a) reject or (b) not reject the null hypothesis of no effect. "No rejection" is not seen as support for the null hypothesis, but rather as a reason to redesign the study or drop it altogether (cf. Greenwald, 1975).

Since the p level is dependent on the degree of truth of the hypothesized effect and also on the sample size (n), employing many more subjects in a study of the proposed effect can result in a statistically significant finding even if the effect is very small, or "really" insignificant.

The question, particularly for reviews of many studies in an area, is "how big is this effect?" Methods are available (cf. Cohen, 1969; also Tresemer, 1975b), for calculating the *effect size estimate* from many kinds of statistics that is not dependent on sample size. Since these estimates are based on considerations of the many issues concerning statistical power (i.e., Type II error) in a design, they will be presented only briefly here (see Cohen, 1969, for a thorough treatment).

For a comparison of two means, the effect size, d, is calculated as $(\bar{X}_A - \bar{X}_B)$/s.d. where s.d. is the usual pooled estimate of the population standard deviation and the $\bar{X}_i$ are the group means for groups A and B. Thus d measures the difference between two groups in terms of the variance found in those groups. If the difference between means is large but the variance is also large, then the size of the effect is attenuated. Cohen (1969) has proposed conventional values for d, calling $d = .50$, or a difference equal to half a standard deviation, a "medium" effect size. This is the magnitude of the difference in height between 14- and 18-year-old girls (about one inch where s.d. = 2). A "large" effect size ($d = .80$) is illustrated by the difference in IQ between holders of the Ph.D. degree and typical college freshmen, or between college graduates and persons with only a 50–50 chance of passing in an academic high school curriculum (cf. Cohen, 1969, p. 25). Other comparisons with real-life differences between groups can be made by the reader in areas in which he or she has a "feel" for the relationship of mean difference to dispersion.

The effect size index d is naturally related to other statistical indices: $d = 2t/(df)^{1/2}$ (for samples of equal size and equal variance). In terms of the proportion of variance explained (r^2) by membership in one of the two groups, $r^2 = d^2/[d^2 + (1/pq)]$, where p is the proportion of As in the combined A and B populations and $q = 1 - p$. The correlation index r and its square r^2 are good metric-free effect size indices without any transformations.

For an analysis of variance design, the effect size, f, is defined as σ_m/σ, where σ_m is the standard deviation of the k population means—$[\Sigma(m_i - m)^2/k]^{1/2}$—and σ is the population standard deviation, estimated by $(MS_e)^{1/2}$. In terms of the eta-squared measure of association, $f = [\eta^2/(1 - \eta^2)]^{1/2}$. η^2 has values similar to r^2. Thus, for the comparison of two means, $f = d/2$. For the computation of f from an interaction planned comparison in a matrix of r rows and c columns

$$\sigma_m = \{\Sigma x_{ij}^2/[(r - 1)(c - 1) + 1]\}^{1/2}$$

with $x_{ij}^2 = m_{ij} - m_{i.} - m_{.j} + m_{...}$

For the chi-square statistic the effect size e is equal to the sum over all cells of $(P_i - P_o)^2/P_o$, where P_o is the null or expected proportion and P_i is the observed proportion. Thus, $e = \chi^2/n$.

The above should give an idea of how the effect size indices are metric-free measures not dependent on sample size, though more complex designs require more complex computations for estimating the effect size. For more detailed statistical relationships, see Friedman (1968) and Cohen (1969).

By convention, Cohen (1969) argued for setting power at .8 and the p level at .05, a 4-to-1 bias against Type I error over Type II error. With these determinants in mind, Cohen's conventions for effect size in the social sciences are helpful guidelines and allow comparisons between different effect size indices. These values are given below.

	Effect Size		
Index	"Small"	"Medium"	"Large"
f	.10	.25	.40
η^2	.0099	.0588	.1379
d	.20	.50	.80
e	.05	.10	.20
r	.100	.243	.371
r^2	.010	.059	.138

Of course, the judgment of "large" or "small" depends for any effect on the *social* significance of that effect. Even for a "large" effect, the proportion of variance explained (r^2) is only 14%. And the percentage of the population with the lower average value that still exceeds the average of the population with the higher average value (O_2 from Tresemer, 1975b) is 21.2%. For a "small" effect, which Cohen defined as real but not clearly visible to the naked eye, the variance explained is 1.4%. Here, O_2 is 42.1% or nearly a complete overlap of the distributions of the two groups ($O_2 = 50\%$). How much of a debilitated performance on an anagrams task is necessary for the FOS group before educational and social policy should be changed? A concrete way to address this problem in terms of the "fear of success" area is suggested at the end of Chapter 6 ("External validity").

By combining the results of many studies, we can make a more reliable approximation of the effect sizes of interest. In reviews of research on a pyschological phenomenon, assertions are often supported or undermined by a listing of references which found a statistically significant effect in the predicted direction compared with a list of references which did not find the statistically significant effect in the predicted direction. I call this the "one study–one vote" method of review. It fails on two counts: (a) it does not take into account the different effect sizes of the various studies (with different n_i) but rather relies on p values; and (b) it does not provide a composite effect size based on all the studies combined. Methods are used here which provide a more accurate appraisal of the research done to date.

Fortunately, the "fear of success" area has been so controversial that many attempted replications of parts of Horner's research have been reported, even when statistically significant results were *not* obtained. The practice of publishing (or writing up) only those studies in which the findings reached statistical significance increases the occurrence of Type I error; in the area of FOS research, however, the probability of bias due to Type I errors has been minimized.

In this cumulative report, the results of a large number of studies of FOS have been combined in order to assess our current state of knowledge about this topic. The individual studies upon which this cumulative report is based have not been cited, except in unique circumstances. Reference to specific works can be found in Tresemer (1976a), a thorough data-oriented annotated bibliography of studies on FOS, a manuscript of nearly 190 pages with well over two hundred citations.[1]

WORKING ASSUMPTIONS

There are several assumptions necessary in order to proceed with some of these analyses. I will state these assumptions and later criticize their verity.

Working Assumption 1. All the samples being combined were independent and randomly drawn from the defined population. For example, if the population of interest was white college women, then it was assumed that every observation (subject) was independently drawn in a random fashion from that entire population.

[1]Available from the American Psychological Association, 1200 17th St. N.W., Washington, D.C. 20036. My apologies for not personally recognizing the many diligent and prolific workers in this area. Many of their manuscripts can be found in the Fear of Success Collection, Sophia Smith Library, Smith College, Northampton, Mass.

Working Assumption 2. The judgment of FOS was of uniform reliability. That is, every researcher would agree completely about the presence or absence of FOS. We must assume we are combining data about one thing, namely FOS. In the following analyses, only results based on Horner's 1968 scoring system for thematic materials, and with one exception on studies that used same-gender cues to measure FOS have been used.

Working Assumption 3. FOS was reliably measured by a wide range of verbal cues. That is, the great variety of cues used to elicit FOS imagery yield comparable results.

Working Assumption 4. All assessments of FOS were made under the same conditions. We cannot really assume that FOS score is not affected by the demand characteristics of the situation (as is assumed for many trait measures). To compare these studies one with another, we must assume that those situations are about the same for the individuals being assessed for FOS.

Criticism

The social scientist will recognize these assumptions as reasonable and customary in any review of past research. Nonetheless, the limitations of the above assumptions should be made clear. Depending on one's judgment about the robustness of these analyses in the face of a violation of assumptions, the strength of the conclusions may be attenuated.

Working Assumption 1. The annotated bibliography in Tresemer (1976a) makes it quite clear that this assumption is true in a restricted sense only. Researchers took what subjects were available, often local college students in psychology courses. This is the usual situation in many areas within the social and psychological sciences. However, as far as I know, there is no serious *systematic* error in this practice if the subsample is noted: that is, we cannot conclude much from this collection of data about "women" or "men," but we can say some things about "white college women" and so forth.

Working Assumption 2. I have previously noted (Tresemer, 1974a) discrepancies between the scoring criteria used by different researchers on FOS. Since there has been no scoring manual as for other thematic scoring systems (e.g., achievement, power, affiliation) until the more recent manual by Horner *et al.* (1973), researchers have been forced to rely on their own judgment about what constitutes FOS. The difficulties arising from the lack of a standardized scoring method for FOS are illustrated in the results of a systematic study by Moreland and Liss-Levinson (1975). They sent 20 stories written in response to the "Anne at the top of her medical school class" cue to 13 investigators who had published articles on this topic before October, 1974. Eight of the thirteen responded to their request to score the 20 protocols. For the five researchers who had used the original scoring system as outlined in Horner's thesis (1968), eight stories of the twenty were scored in the same way by the eight investigators. The average proportion of agreement between scores was, however, .75 (the median, .775). This rate of agreement between scorers is not up to par but is also not grossly less than the rule-of-thumb minimum of .80 for interscorer reliability in thematic scoring systems. Nonetheless, specific methods have been employed in the following analyses to diminish the dependence on this assumption.

One further problem with this assumption is the finding by Robbins and Robbins (1973) that female scorers found more FOS than did male scorers. The effect was small (data inadequate to estimate effect size) and has not been investigated since, so it is difficult to know how serious a problem this is.

Working Assumption 3. There has been a tremendous range of cue material used in all these studies, which must have had some effects on the FOS levels obtained. It is not clear whether FOS is as easily expressed to one cue as to another—some findings point in one direction, and some in another. Since most studies have measured FOS from imagery to only one cue, it is not known how seriously the occasional report of low split-half reliability (e.g., correlation of FOS score from one story with that from another) should be taken. Horner *et al.* (1973) have dispensed with this problem by proposing the use of a few *non*specific achievement-oriented and neutral verbal cues for assessing FOS, thus avoiding the trend toward tapping subjects' reactions to complex situations having little to do with the self. This assumption again attributes variation due to cue to nonsystematic or random error.

Working Assumption 4. From the information given in each study, it is impossible to determine what sort of social or psychological atmosphere existed when the subjects wrote stories to verbal cues, whether the situation was comparable or not. I believe this is generally due to the lingering absence of a taxonomy of situations (more complete than Relaxed vs. Neutral vs. Aroused, cf. Heckhausen, 1967) so needed in the social sciences. The atmosphere of the setting where stories are written is a key determinant of the observed rates of FOS, as can be seen in the studies where FOS is a dependent variable (e.g., Patty, 1976). I think this is the weakest working assumption. It is also the most exciting in terms of directions for future research needed to clarify the meaning of FOS. I think variation in setting will be able to account for the problems with low test–retest reliability, currently cited as a negative feature of the thematic measure of FOS.[2]

These are the working assumptions necessary to proceed with the following analyses. By stating them, I am focusing attention on those areas which need further clarification if the conclusions of this report are to be improved upon. While the little bits of evidence pertinent to an evaluation of these assumptions do not always confirm them as good assumptions, I would say that at this point they are not unsatisfactory assumptions for research on FOS.

GENDER DIFFERENCES IN INCIDENCE OF FOS

A matter of some debate has been the alleged prevalence of FOS among women as compared with men. To test this assertion, only those samples were used where both males and females from the same subpopulation were assessed for FOS. This comprised 56 samples in all from 42 different reports of research, representing data from 2939 males and 3151 females. An additional 53 samples were excluded because in 52 samples only females were tested for FOS, and in one only males were tested.

Most of these studies involved the simple measurement of FOS and the details of measurement are not important to note in the face of a large cumulative analysis. Three studies, however, stand out among the rest. In 1971, Lois Hoffman attempted to copy Horner's

[2]Low autocorrelations (test–retest) have been explained in the *n*Ach literature as unimportant in the face of high predictive validity (McClelland, 1965; Ray, 1974; also Rosenthal and Rosnow, 1975). The predictive validity of FOS is treated most directly in Chapter 6.

"large-group mixed-sex competitive" setting (Session 1 from Horner, 1968) in exact detail: data were collected at the same point in the academic year in the same academic course in the same room with the same seating arrangement with the same sort of experimenter wearing the same kinds of clothes with the same questionnaire books and instructions. The "Anne at the top of her medical school class" cue was sixth in a series of verbal story-writing cues, as in Horner's original study. For three of four subgroups, however, three other verbal cues were given in place of the "medical school" cue. The results showed a percentage writing FOS (62.0%) almost identical with Horner's original scoring (62.2%). Does this mean we can conclude that the setting is the chief determinant of the arousal of FOS? Perhaps, but the percentage of males writing FOS to the medical school cue was much larger: 76.2% compared with Horner's 9.1%. Only by testing FOS proportions in several carefully defined settings in the same study can we know to what extent a situation, and what aspects of that situation, influences the result. Hoffman's (1974) study must be considered as additional data points on a par with the fifty others used in this analysis.

The other two studies were the only ones to use adult men and women with real careers in the "real" world. Wood and Greenfield (1976) tested 18 male and 18 female executives from the Atlantic Richfield Company, writing to the following cue:

> When Janet (Jeff) graduated from college, she (he) went on to get a graduate degree in business. Early in the spring quarter, she (he) is the first in her (his) class to be offered a top management job.

Forty percent of the men and thirty percent of the women showed FOS imagery in their responses.[3] The investigation by Wood and Greenfield has been the first comprehensive study of males and females actually in the career settings where the negative aspects of FOS are supposed to take their ultimate toll.

Glancy (1970), with Horner's help, analyzed the responses of several hundred graduates of Harvard Law School to a mailed questionnaire including the following open-ended items: "If you were to receive an announcement that George Andrews has become a part-

[3]The results of this study were not available until after the compilation of the annotated bibliography and were not included in the analyses of this chapter.

ner in a large New York law firm, how would you describe him?" and "If Barbara Robbins, formerly president of the Harvard *Law Review*, had just been appointed Deputy Solicitor General, how would you describe her?" (Half of the respondents received a female name in the first setting and a male name in the second.) Nearly 10% of the responses from males showed FOS imagery, while FOS imagery for women from the 1950s classes was 38.5%, from the classes of 1960 through 1964 46.7%, and from the classes of 1965 through 1969 51.1%. Unfortunately, the nonresponse rate for males, as well as the number of returned questionnaires that were blank for these items, was extremely high. Males' nonreturn and nonresponse was also much higher than for the females, who often expressed great personal interest in the questionnaire study in terms of their recent involvement in Women's Liberation issues. Also unfortunately, it is not known if mailed questionnaires, subject to a multitude of variations in the situation in which they are filled out as well as a lack of time limit and thorough instructions for response, are directly comparable to data obtained in the psychological laboratory or in a controlled interview setting.

These two studies represent an important extension beyond the vague and uninformed fears about "medical school" and other careers among college underclassmen. Like the Hoffman study, they must be considered as additional data points in a larger cumulative analysis.

Restricting the analysis to 56 samples permitted the use of methods to combine degrees of association between FOS and gender, an approach which makes most kinds of violations of Working Assumptions 2 and 3 irrelevant. That is, if two researchers agreed on which stories in a sample *definitely* did or did not show FOS, but one researcher tended to score more of the uncertain stories as showing FOS than did the other researcher, this bias would not greatly affect the degree of association with gender found for each researcher. Naturally, I still made Working Assumptions 1 and 4.

Statistical Methods

The method for combining these data was from Fleiss (1973) and is summarized for those interested in the following: First the data were arranged in a 2 × 2 or FOS (present or absent) × gender (male or female) table, with cell values a, b, c, and d. The common odds ratio o (the ratio of the products of the diagonals in the 2×2 table, or ad/bc) was then calculated to four significant digits. Then the logit, or natural logarithm of the odds ratio, $\log_e o$ or L, was computed. This was transformed into a chi-square statistic using an estimate of the standard error of L as follows: $[\text{s.e.}(L)]^2 = (1/a + 1/b + 1/c + 1/d) = w^{-1}$. The overall chi-square ($\chi^2_{\text{total}} = \Sigma w_i L_i^2$) can be divided into a component for association (χ^2_{assoc}) with one degree of freedom, representing the overall common degree of association, and a component for homogeneity (χ^2_{homog}) with degrees of freedom equal to the number of samples minus one.[4] The latter must be small to indicate homogeneity or agreement between the studies before the chi-square for association can be taken seriously.

Cumulative Results

For all 56 samples, the χ^2_{assoc} was 11.998, a statistically significant difference ($p < .001$) for a tiny effect size ($e = .002$), indicating that females told a slightly greater proportion of FOS stories than males. But the χ^2_{homog} (53) was 161.884 ($p < .001$), clearly showing tremendous variability between studies.

In such cases, the chi-square must be further partitioned to reduce heterogeneity. I reduced the acceptable samples to those measuring FOS with the same-gender "medical school" cue alone, for white college students from the United States. I included only papers by professional psychologists, most published in professional journals, including one paper being submitted for publication and one doctoral dissertation. Though this excluded several master's theses and undergraduate papers, I thereby avoided a decision about their quality, and kept the restricted sample small. I did not use any data collected before March of 1971 or after the Spring of 1973. This left nine samples from nine studies by professionals who themselves had personal experience in projective motive measurement or were collaborating with someone who had such experience (this point is made as a further gesture to Working Assumption 2). The studies were by Feather and Raphelson (1974; American sample only), Heil-

[4] χ^2_{assoc} is $[\bar{L}/\text{s.e.}(\bar{L})]^2$, where $\bar{L}$, the estimate of the logarithm of the common odds ratio, is $\Sigma w_i L_i / \Sigma w_i$, and the standard error of $\bar{L}$, s.e.($\bar{L}$), is the reciprocal of the square root of Σw_i. Of course, $\chi^2_{\text{homog}} = \chi^2_{\text{total}} - \chi^2_{\text{assoc}}$.

brun, Kleemeier, and Piccola (1974), Hoffman (1974), Jackaway, Steinberg, and Teevan (1972), Krusell (1973), Levine and Crumrine (1975), and Robbins and Robbins (1973). Combining the gender difference data from these studies yielded a χ^2_{assoc} of 1.147 (*n.s.*, $e =$ .001), but a χ^2_{homog} (8) of 16.364 ($p < .05$), still a high degree of variability among studies.

Further work with partitioning the data by date of collection, age of subject, or rough estimates of the achievement-related atmosphere of the testing situations led to no better homogeneity among studies or to any greater difference between men and women.[5]

This finding is, in itself, puzzling. The social psychological approach to Horner's work has construed FOS as a perception of what is and is not culturally appropriate gender-role behavior. Thus FOS responses to the "medical school" cue would be expected to be greater for females writing about Anne than for males writing about John. Negative imagery in response to an appropriate setting should be absent, in response to an inappropriate setting rampant. The lack of gender difference in FOS responses in studies using the "medical school" cue appears to suggest that FOS means something other than a response to gender-role-inappropriate achievement.

Perhaps what is scored for males as FOS is different from what is scored for females as FOS. It has been found repeatedly that males more often than females wrote cynical, bizarre, pessimistic, hostile,

[5]As a further check, a method due to Dave Kenney (personal communication, May, 1975) was employed to better control for this heterogeneity among studies. This method treats the data more in an analysis of variance model, using gender as a fixed factor and study as a random factor. The task is to delete the variability due to study and find what is left for the gender factor. The result is a conservative chi-square for gender differences equal to:

$$\frac{\{\Sigma[\text{s.e.}(L)]^2 L/\Sigma[\text{s.e.}(L)]^2\}^2}{\Sigma[\text{s.e.}(L)]^4/\Sigma[\text{s.e.}(L)]^2}$$

where L is the natural logarithm of the odds ratio for each sample, and s.e.(L) is its standard error. In Fleiss's (1973) notation, this would be

$$\frac{(\Sigma w_i^{-1} L_i)^2}{(\Sigma w_i^{-1})\ \Sigma[(w_i^{-1})^2]}$$

Using this method for the nine studies subject to restrictions concerning cue, quality, etc., the chi-square estimate for the relationship of gender to FOS ($df = 1$) was .065 ($e = .000$). Using this statistic for 56 samples yielded a chi-square of .534 ($e = .000$). The indication was again no difference between genders.

and/or joking stories, containing violence, death, devaluation of success and achievement, and doubt about the worth of sacrifice for success. Females more often than males wrote stories depicting (fear of) social rejection, loss of femininity, and affiliative loss.

Due to the lack of standardization in the assessment of these particular thematic differences, a summary of findings to date has not even been attempted. Such a thematic difference raises the question that FOS as measured might have different psychodynamic significance for males and for females. However, we can not rely on this explanation for the lack of gender difference in FOS until systematic work is done with the sorts of images produced by both genders.

In conclusion, the hypothesis that there is a gender difference in FOS is not supported. Perhaps the high degree of variability found in these studies is entirely due to violations of our Working Assumptions; I also feel it indicates that individual variability in responses to traditional career success far exceeds gender-role differences. It may be, as I have suggested elsewhere (Tresemer, 1975a), that generalizations about gender differences are a convenient fiction for psychologist and subject in the service of gross categorizations. But, in material not quite so obvious such as the TAT or other story-writing tasks, these gender-role stereotypes fall away as individual uniqueness becomes more prominent. We may indeed be finding the general negativity about successful attainment so deeply rooted in our cultural psyche which, as we saw in Part I, does not differentiate between the genders.

RESPONSES TO CROSS-GENDER CUES

The tradition of motivation research in which Horner's study was based seldom questioned that a subject should respond to "characters with whom the person can identify" (Atkinson and McClelland, 1948, p. 655), assumed to be of the same gender as the subject.

Several current researchers have, however, been interested in having males write about Anne at the top of her medical school class, and females about John. In some cases, this interest has stemmed from a prejudice toward crossing all experimental factors to unravel possibly confounded effects. Occasionally, higher FOS scores for males writing about Anne have been interpreted not as a measure of the male's predisposition (or "motive") to avoid success, but rather as an indication of his hostile attitudes toward achieving women. Specifically, the comparisons have been made between levels of FOS imagery expressed by male and female subjects in response to a cue depicting an achieving female. When males have written more FOS than females about the achieving female it has been seen as evidence for male backlash against female competence, as *more* potent than females' own self-sabotage, in line with other current research (Entwisle and Greenberger, 1972; Feldman-Summers and Kiesler, 1974; Deaux and Enswiller, 1974; Touhey, 1974).

Several authors have given descriptions of the males' negative reactions to female achievement. For example, Doerr (1973) reported her experiment with the "medical school" cue in her high-school social-studies classes:

> In one class, the boys, given the story of John, foresaw a generally happy and prosperous life for him; the girls, given the story of Anne, told of her getting married or becoming a nurse. In another class, the assignment was switched: the boys were told to complete the story about Anne, and the girls to complete the story about John. Most of the girls saw a happy future for John; more interesting was Anne's fate at the hands of the boys. Two students, working independently of each other, wrote that Anne, happily leaving the classroom where the first term grades and class standings were posted and walking out into the street, was promptly run over by a truck and killed.

Lockheed (1975; Lockheed-Katz, 1974) also described the responses of the male authors to the exceptionally bright female medical student in a school where she is the only female as well as top of her class:

> Explanations for Anne's success in the all-male environment tended to cluster around her sexuality: she is sexually distracting to her male classmates or professors, she "buys" her success with her body, she is tricky, and she receives help from her classmates for sexual reasons. (p. 46)

These examples were presented as clear evidence of the males' disproportionately negative reactions to the deviantly bright female.

I evaluated these assertions using the combination methods from Fleiss (1973) for 21 samples of white subjects of all ages, totaling 893 men and 893 women. I compared FOS levels for males and females to a cue depicting an achieving female within each sample. The resulting χ^2_{homog} (20) was 24.950, statistically nonsignificant, indicating that the assumption of homogeneity was acceptable. The average logit (natural log of the odds ratio) was .168, yielding a measure of association that was not statistically significant [χ^2_{assoc} (1) = 1.680], and an effect size estimate that was very small (e = .032, males more FOS). Thus, males have not written appreciably more FOS imagery to a female cue figure but rather have written about the same amount. This in itself is a point worth noting: that males and females seem to respond similarly to an achieving female. Though this does not agree with the view that males more than females resist achievement by women, it does support the social psychological model set forth in Chapter 3: attitudes about social objects (a female who is first in her medical school) are similar in different groups.

CHANGES IN FOS OVER TIME

Assertions have been made that FOS has been decreasing for females and increasing for males over the years since Horner's study. To assess this, I grouped the samples by academic year in which the data were collected (academic year includes the following summer, e.g., September 1969 through August 1970). I only analyzed the data for white college men and women from the United States from those samples for which date of assessment was available. Working Assumption 1 is relied on heavily since the data from several samples in one year have been added together to give a single proportion for that year. Working Assumptions 2 and 3 are also in greater use in this analysis than in previous analyses.

The composite data and the statistics for a linear regression based on these data (cf. Fleiss, 1973, pp. 96–99) are given in Table 1.

For white college men from the United States, there was a statistically significant tendency for the proportion showing FOS to decrease with time ($\chi^2_{slope} = 4.38$, $p < .05$), with an average decrease of 2.4% per academic year. With four degrees of freedom (the num-

TABLE 1
Proportions of White College Men and Women from the United States Showing FOS by Academic Year

Academic year	Proportion showing FOS (number of samples)		
	College men (all cues)	College women (all cues)	"Medical school" cue[a]
1963–1964	8/88(1)	59/90(1)	59/90(1)
1964–1965	—	19/35(1)	—
1965–1966	—	—	—
1966–1967	—	129/195(3)	105/145(2)
1967–1968	—	—	—
1968–1969	—	17/20(2)	17/20(2)
1969–1970	28/57(1)	230/487(4)	84/104(2)
1970–1971	35/101(2)	134/235(12)	57/137(2)
1971–1972	304/594(9)	474/1460(16)	376/882(8)
1972–1973	153/403(8)	365/939(11)	124/294(4)
1973–1974	66/174(1)	161/381(3)	143/348(2)
1974–1975	49/114(2)	75/179(3)	34/80(1)
	Linear regression (for years below line)		
Grand average	635/1443(23)	1439/3681(47)	835/1865(21)
b (slope)	−.0236	−.0141	−.0481
χ^2 linearity[b]	22.78	80.57	104.24
χ^2 slope ($df = 1$)	4.38[c]	4.83[c]	25.82[d]

[a]This subgroup of samples is subject to more restrictions than stimulus cue; see text.
[b]Degrees of freedom for this chi-square discussed in text.
[c]$p < .05$
[d]$p < .001$

ber of years minus 1), the chi-square for linearity was statistically significant ($\chi^2_{\text{lin}} = 22.78$, $p < .001$), indicating that the decrease was not a linear one.[6] An argument could be made that there are really about 20 degrees of freedom for this data, a little less than the number of samples combined. In this case, the chi-square would not be statistically significant and the hypothesis of linearity in the data would hold. The data points and fitted regression line are shown in Figure 1.

For white college females from the United States, the chi-square for linearity was 80.57, statistically significant with 4 *or* 40 degrees of freedom. Nonetheless, the data points and fitted regression line are

[6]Perhaps Fleiss (1973) should have called this the chi-square for *non*linearity.

given in Figure 2, showing a general though scattered trend to lower proportions showing FOS over the years.

I again used a restricted sample of white college females from the United States responding to the same gender "medical school" cue as described in the section on gender differences in FOS. However, as in Figure 2, I did accept studies using only females. The chi-square for linearity for this set of studies was 104.24, statistically significant at 5 *or* 20 degrees of freedom, and the picture in Figure 3 reveals why. FOS imagery assumed a stable level from the academic year 1970–1971 on, while proportions before that time were higher and widely dispersed.

It is tempting to try to match these data points with the social and political phenomena of those years, but the process is difficult and results may possibly be misleading. However, one such matching experiment appears particularly relevant for the arguments about what FOS imagery means. FOS is viewed by some as a negative reaction to the inappropriateness of medical school for women, fully in line with research that has demonstrated that occupations are gender-linked according to the proportions of men and women in them and that occupations are avoided if gender-role inappropriate (e.g., Tresemer and Pleck, 1974). In three publications by Dubé

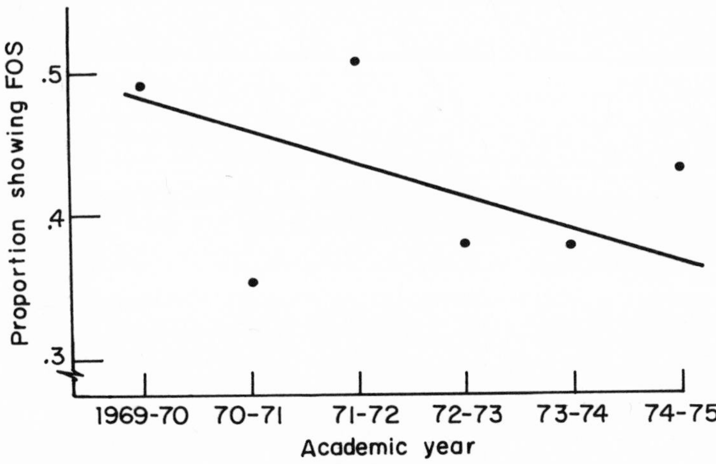

FIGURE 1. Proportion of white college males showing FOS by academic year when data were collected, including fitted regression line.

(1973, 1974, 1975) can be found the actual proportions of women entering the first year class of medical school in each academic year. This is an opportunity to compare trends of the number of women entering medical school with negative reactions to Anne at the top of her medical school class. Presumably, the more women in medical school, the less "out-of-place" Anne would be at the top, and the less FOS imagery found in response to this situation among knowledgeable college students. Figure 3 shows the points for one minus the proportion of women entering medical school. Actual enrollments and number graduating follow the same pattern but seemed less appropriate as indicators of current trends. In addition, "at the end of first term finals" is usually understood as during Anne's first year.

The clearcut trends seen in the proportion of women entering medical school have no parallel in the FOS data. One interesting coincidence emerges: just at the time the proportion of women dips below the stable .90 (or 10%) mark to start its steady increase in admissions to medical school, there is the sudden drop in FOS imagery to what appears to be a stable level around .42. This was the end of 1969 through 1970, significant years in anyone's memory. Perhaps the proportion of women entering medical school and the

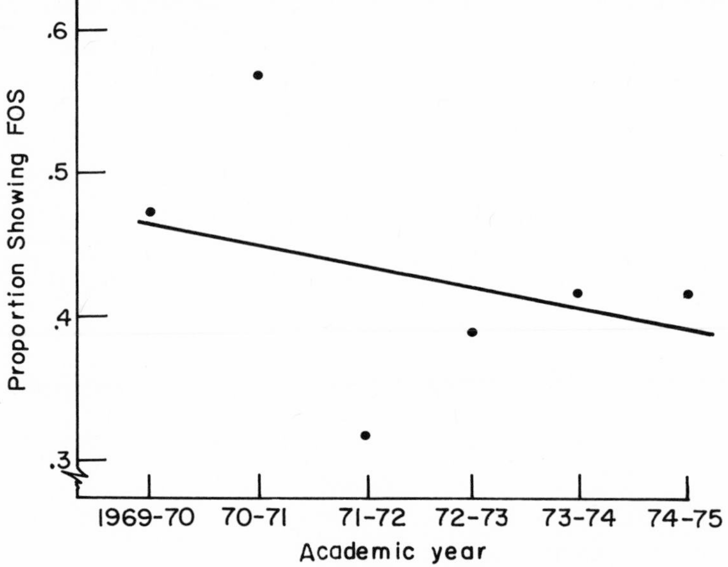

FIGURE 2. Proportion of white college females showing FOS by academic year when data were collected, including fitted regression line.

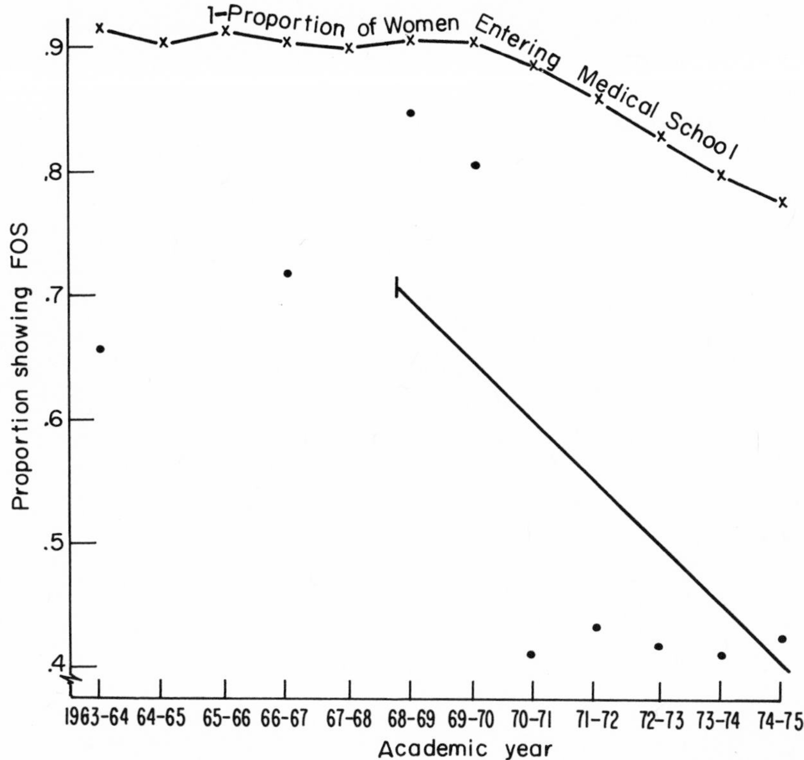

FIGURE 3. Proportion of white college females showing FOS to the "medical school" cue in a restricted set of studies by academic year when data were collected, including fitted regression line (solid line), and including curve for one minus proportion of women entering medical school.

proportion of college women writing FOS to the "medical school" cue were both subject to the same large-scale social changes.

CORRELATES OF FOS

In many of the studies cited in Tresemer (1976a), the correlates of FOS are often stated without any index of relationship (e.g., size of *r*) because that was all the information that was available, especially if the correlation was statistically insignificant. Indeed, determining the variables to which FOS was *un*related—an important task for any review of past findings concerning a particular relationship of interest—was most difficult. For this reason, summary statistics were not computed. Below are brief overviews of correlates in five areas that, because of the inherent interest in their relationship with FOS, were often reported even if statistically insignificant.

Ability

FOS has been hypothesized to be greater for high-ability women, since for them success is within reach. The measures of ability came in the form of reported SAT scores, SAT scores available from transcripts, grade point average (GPA), various IQ tests, school track, honors status, performance on verbal achievement tasks such as the Lowell Scrambled Words Task and anagrams, plans for college, and career goals. (Actually, all of these can be seen as measuring varying mixtures of ability and effort.) Taking the studies that measured these relationships as a whole, FOS has shown no relationship to ability.

Gender-Role Identification

FOS has been hypothetically related to a more traditional gender-role orientation in women, since success in a masculine-dominated field such as medicine would then be more conflictfully inappropriate. There have been various measures of gender-role identification employed, all with a view toward discriminating identification with stereotypically traditional roles vs. other. There are numerous scales, measures, and questionnaire items designed for this task. Also related are the traditionality of career choice, traditionality of college major, whether or not the mother was employed and how traditional her job was, political activism or lack of activism, and so on. Taking the studies that measured these relationships as a whole, FOS has shown no relationship to gender-role identification.

Anxiety

FOS might be expected to relate to other measures of anxiety. With various anxiety scales, including the Debilitating Anxiety scale of the Alpert–Haber Achievement Anxiety Test and the Test Anxiety

Questionnaire of Mandler and Sarason, there has been overall no relationship with FOS. In the very few instances where the thematic scoring system for Fear of Failure from Birney, Burdick, and Teevan (1969) has been used, there has been a positive relationship with FOS; this relationship needs further examination (cf. Jackaway and Teevan, 1976). In one study, Pappo's (1972) scale for "fear of (academic) success" has been found to correlate highly with the Alpert–Haber scale, but has also been found (in one study only) to be unrelated to FOS (Curtis *et al.*, in press).

External Control

Attribution of one's achievements and life outcomes to external factors (i.e., the difficulty of the task or luck) rather than to internal factors (i.e., ability or effort) has been claimed as an integral part of the FOS syndrome. FOS does seem to be related to Rotter's internal-control–external-control dimension. Those higher in FOS also score higher on the external control side [e.g., Midgley and Abrams, 1974, d (females) = .58, and Patty and Shelley, 1974, r (females) = .45, and for Pappo's measure of "fear of success," r (males) = .42, and r (females) = .12]. One would expect this correlation to extend to other tests of attribution for performance outcome. Indeed, Krusell (1973) found that FOS-present students of both genders attributed to themselves less responsibility for the success and more for the failure of a subordinate they had trained to perform on an achievement task than did FOS-absent students. However, Feather and Simon (1973) found that "fear of success subjects who succeeded saw task difficulty and luck factors [external factors] as less important causes of their outcome than fear of success subjects who failed, whereas the opposite applied for subjects who did not express fear of success in their stories."[7]

Patty (1976) tested a causal aspect of this correlation; she found a much higher level of performance of FOS-present female undergraduates on the Digit Span Backwards test of the Wechsler Adult Intelligence Scale when they were told that performance was primarily

[7]For Krusell's (1973) study, the interaction f for males was .47 and for females .53 (assuming equal cell sizes). Data were not available to assess effect sizes of Feather and Simon's (1973) opposite finding.

dependent on external factors (rather than internal ones, in comparison with FOS-absent females): $d = .70$. Again, this correlate of FOS is as yet inadequately tested, and requires further work to understand the partly consistent (and occasionally inconsistent) findings to date.

Age

FOS has been claimed to increase for women with age since gender-role socialization gathers momentum with age, and achievement is gender-role appropriate for females in high school and earlier but becomes less appropriate in college and beyond. There was too much variation between studies to combine FOS proportions for all the different age levels found there. Besides, the relationship between age and FOS was not tested in many studies even if the data were available. In twelve studies, age was a within-sample classification, and it was this set of studies which provided the test of the relationship between FOS and age.

For many of the studies, the linear trend for men clearly showed increases in FOS with age, but in a few others the reverse was true. For females, there were as many studies showing a decreasing trend (cf. Tresemer, 1976a).[8] The relationship between FOS and age does not seem to hold in previous research, though the cases where the trend is clear could be scrutinized more closely to discover any sort of uniqueness in the sample which led to the trend.

At this point, it would be well to point out the few studies which expanded beyond the use of the college sophomore age group, or the also easily obtained high school and elementary school classroom sample. The studies by Wood and Greenfeld (1976) and by Glancy (1970) have already been mentioned. Unger and Krooth (1974) analyzed 53 responses to a questionnaire mailed to 132 married housewives between 25 and 50 years old from the north shore of Long Island. K. Moore (1974) analyzed 576 interviews from a probability sample of the greater Detroit metropolitan area.

[8]A comparison utilizing effect sizes could have involved an effect size index computed from the test for linear trend from each study. However, the data were inadequate to compute this with enough studies to make the task worthwhile.

The only study to view FOS as a factor in a longitudinal prediction of behavior was the doctoral dissertation of Stewart (1975). In 1960, as part of the Harvard Student Study of the classes of '64, '65, and '66, 244 female freshmen from a prestigious New England women's college and 172 female freshmen from another, "more traditional," New England women's college were tested in large groups with Thematic Apperception Test (TAT) pictures. In the spring of 1974, a questionnaire was sent to all for whom the alumni offices had addresses; questionnaires were returned by half of the class from the first college and by 35% of the class from the second college. A random sample of sixty alumnae from the first college were interviewed for 15–30 min by telephone about major stress experiences in their lives. Stewart used the FOS score (from the scoring system by Horner *et al.*, 1973) as a predictor of life situation fourteen years later.

After amassing the results of tests using complex multivariate statistical models of intercorrelations and partial correlations among many variables, she concluded that this relationship was indeed found. Understanding the full story of this complicated set of intercorrelations will have to wait until this promising study has been published.

Cooperation vs. Competition

A consistent finding from the few studies that have tested this notion is that, in a "mixed-motive" situation, females with FOS will show much more cooperative behavior than females without FOS. Bongort (1974; also Malone and Mio, n.d., and Zalman, 1973) reported that women high in FOS over many trials of a Prisoner's Dilemma situation stabilized in a pattern of "mutual cooperation:" both partners receiving rewards as a result of their choices. Women low in FOS stabilized in a pattern of "mutual defection:" both partners losing points as the result of the attempts of one to double-cross the other to gain points while the "sucker" loses. Whether the relationship between FOS and cooperation is seen as "good" or "bad" depends on often unstated values about cooperation and competition. Is cooperation linked with stereotypically feminine accommodation in the same way that dissimulation and "playing dumb on dates" are? Or is cooperation a more mature interpersonal style, maximizing the outcomes for everybody, rather than losing rewards because of a stubborn refusal to compromise?

Other Correlates

Single significant correlates have not been taken too seriously here, since the room for error (Type I) is too great, particularly if the finding is sensational. For example, the finding that women with FOS have more children than women without FOS (K. Moore, 1974) has far-reaching implications. First, we need to know if it is true and to what degree, through replication. Second, we need to know just what such a relationship means—that is, does it necessarily mean that women high in achievement but frustrated by the limits on women's career realization turn to raising children as an escape?

Another example is the study by Watson (1971, also cited in Horner, 1972a, and summarized in Tresemer, 1976a) which found a positive association between degree of drug use (totalling responses for marijuana, speed, LSD, and other) and presence of FOS ($\chi^2 = 8.12$, $p < .05$, $e = .22$) among 37 female Harvard summer school students. Without more information about this relationship, it is hard to know what it means.

Other examples that demand further investigation for clarification are the study by Patty and Ferrell (1974) which found a positive association between FOS imagery and the female subjects' report of being in the premenstrual part of their menstrual cycle, and the study by Fleming (1974) which found a positive association between FOS and lower-class (vs. middle-class) socioeconomic status among black women.

Still another relationship which has been tested three times has been between FOS and coeducation. While Shinn (1973) found an increase in females' FOS scores with the change from all-female education to coeducation, and Winchel *et al.* (1974) found higher FOS scores among women in coeducational institutions, Schwenn (1970) found no relationship between FOS and past experience of coeducation in her small sample of Radcliffe undergraduates.

Several samples have been taken among black students and the claim made that FOS and "fear of success" are less likely among blacks. A look at the proportions of samples showing FOS indeed shows a lower median proportion, but the range of proportions is so scattered that this might be a hazardous conclusion at present (cf. Bright, 1970; Fleming, 1972, 1974; Fleming and Horner, 1973; Mednick, 1973; Mednick and Puryear, 1975; Puryear and Mednick, 1974; Weston and Mednick, 1970). White and black subjects need to be matched according to other characteristics such as age, class, and so forth, before these suggestive findings can be generalized.

The use of these findings for public policy decisions in these controversial areas hinges on one's view of FOS: is it bad or good for people to have it, and how much? The answer to this question is necessarily linked to an assessment of what intrapsychic and performance significance the display of FOS has for an individual.

Relationships with FOS

A construct should show what McClelland calls "relational fertility"—it should be related to some things (the theoretically right things) and not to others. More formally, the "nomological net" of propositions in which the construct is embedded must show the predicted relationships with that construct (Cronbach and Meehl, 1955). All in all, there is a relatively low degree of interrelatedness between FOS and theoretically important and related variables. Perhaps a closer look at any of these relationships would reveal that the expectation of a simple relationship with FOS has been too simplistic. For example, in the case of FOS and age, Veroff (1969) included Horner's theory of a "fear of success" in a developmental theory of achievement motivation, expecting to find a "fear of success" orientation in a "stage of social comparison," but expecting not to find it in an earlier "stage of autonomy" or a later "stage of integration." Thus, curvilinear effects might be expected over a range of ages, which has not as yet been tested. Or, in the case of FOS and ability, we would simultaneously expect FOS to be associated (a) with lower performance because FOS is an inhibiting factor, and (b) with higher performance because it is the talented and ambitious who are supposedly more likely to have FOS. Perhaps the best test would be the relationship between FOS and the residual of performance behavior once performance potential (e.g., a neutral pretest of ability such as

IQ) has been accounted for. Thus FOS would be expected to correlate with being below the average performance of those in the same ability category. These examples suggest that simple studies measuring FOS and one or two other variables are not needed at this time; what is needed are studies involving a more complicated set of partial correlations (e.g., factors or clusters) which relate FOS to important constructs while holding constant the variation in still other constructs. In many cases, this suggestion does not necessitate new studies since further work can be done with secondary data analysis of the usual quantity of unanalyzed material available from competent studies already completed.

CHAPTER 6

The Relationship of Fear of Success to Performance Behavior

A test of the relative proportions of males and female who write FOS imagery in TAT-type stories has little meaning if this writing behavior is not found to be related to a behavior theoretically embedded in a *fear* of *success*. "Validity refers to the degree to which something does what it purports to do" (Rosenthal and Rosnow, 1975, p. 68)—it is the relationship between FOS and performance that more concerns the users of projective instruments, which usually have low reliability. It has been suggested, for example, that FOS is related to performance for females and unrelated to performance for males. Thus, establishing the relationship between the FOS measure and performance is obviously a task of great importance before rates of FOS from various groups can be compared as indices of the same thing.

Most of the studies in this area, however, merely measure FOS imagery, taking it as an already proven measure of a unitary personality trait and correlating its presence with other variables of interest. Like academic achievement tests (M. Levine, 1976), FOS tests are increasingly being used as absolute criteria in themselves, and not as tests in the sense of being predictors of other behavior. Furthermore, the range of behaviors that were measured in the experimental studies was very great, preventing comparisons. In addition, the presented data were often insufficient to estimate the effect size (or even the significance level) for the effects of interest, most often due to the absence of planned comparison tests of hypothesized effects for statistically significant interactions between experimental factors of several levels.

In this chapter, I will first take a very close look at Horner's original study and then present the findings of the more recent major studies of FOS and performance behavior. The review will be summarized in the overview section "The Performance of FOS."

REANALYSIS OF THE FIRST EXPERIMENT

A thorough reanalysis of the data from Horner's original study will serve as an introduction to the issues concerning the relationship of FOS imagery to performance. It will be remembered from the general account of her study in Chapter 2 that 88 male and 90 female college undergraduates were first convened in an auditorium as part of a requirement of their psychology course to participate in an experiment. In the first session, originally thought of as the pretest or baseline session, these students worked on the Lowell Scrambled Words task, unravelling as many mixed-up letters (such as EOVL and LPAPE) as possible within a certain time limit (five pages of twenty-four words each, two minutes allowed per page). In a second session, a random third of the students worked alone with tape-recorded instructions urging them to do well on the GENERATION anagrams task (also ten minutes). The other two thirds worked either with a male or a female partner in a competitive atmosphere on the same task.

Partly based on the evidence from the stories written to the medical school cue, Horner claimed that the first session aroused anxiety, a "fear of success," in the female students because of the large-group testing atmosphere and the presence of men in the competitive setting. She transformed the females' performance scores (number of words unravelled in Session 1 or created in Session 2) to normal or z scores using the observed mean and standard deviation of the group of males in each session; then she divided the performance profiles into two kinds: (1) performed better in Session 1 than in Session 2, and (2) performed better in Session 2 than in Session 1. These results have been presented earlier.

We can, however, treat the performance in interval form and look at means and variances rather than merely at a dichotomous split as explained above. Indeed, Horner reported the results for this kind of treatment in Tables 53 and 54 of Appendix D of her thesis (Horner, 1968). These data are presented in Table 2, again using the unusual *z* scores and adding a constant of 5 to all scores.

We can proceed systematically from these data, assuming that the above findings were obtained in any of the following experimental designs:

1. To test the idea that females with FOS perform more poorly when in competition with males than when working alone, a sufficient design would have been to compare the performance scores for FOS-present females in the randomly assigned Groups 1 and 2 in Session 2 alone (a true experimental posttest-only design, Campbell and Stanley, 1963). The "arousal" setting would thus be the "mixed-sex competitive" or male–female pair condition (Group 2, Session 2).

TABLE 2
Performance Scores for Female Students With or Without FOS in Three Experimental Groups[a]

	Experimental group								
	Group 1, noncompetitive alone			Group 2, mixed-gender competitive			Group 3, same-gender competitive		
FOS	n	$\bar{X}$	s.d.	n	$\bar{X}$	s.d.	n	$\bar{X}$	s.d.
				Session 1[b]					
Present	17	4.79	1.02	19	5.25	1.12	20	4.99	0.88
Absent	13	4.91	0.72	11	4.61	1.26	10	4.69	0.93
				Session 2					
Present	17	5.33	0.80	19	5.37	0.81	20	5.22	1.10
Absent	13	4.39	0.86	11	4.88	0.76	10	4.89	0.60

[a]Adapted from Horner (1968), Tables 53 and 54 of Appendix D, based on the original scoring of 56 (62.2%) women for FOS.

[b]Originally the pretest setting, later retermed the arousal or large-group mixed-sex competitive condition; all groups were tested together.

The baseline for comparison would be the situation where one was working alone on an achievement task, presumably against one's own standards for performance and success (Group 1, Session 2). So let us for the moment forget that there were any other groups or sessions. The anagrams performance data of interest would thus be as shown in Table 3. This comparison of groups yields a statistically insignificant (n.s.) comparison between means [$t(34) = .15$] and a very "small" estimate of effect size ($d = .05$), although in the reverse of expected direction. Had the study included only these groups, a perfectly legitimate experimental design, we would have had to stop here, concluding that no "fear of success" effect existed.

2. An expanded design would include the data from the FOS-absent females as an additional baseline for comparison. That is, how two randomly chosen groups of FOS-absent females performed in these two situations would be tested against the performance profile of two randomly chosen groups of FOS-present females (viewing FOS as a fixed factor). This again is a sufficient design for the test of the notion that females with FOS perform more poorly against male competitors—but here the comparison group is somewhat different. We assume that how FOS-absent females respond in these settings is more "normal," or preferrable, and look for an interaction effect between setting and presence of FOS. The data are presented in Table 4. Again, the expected statistical significance from the test of the interaction is not found: $F(1,56) = 1.11$, though the effect size is now somewhat greater than "small" ($f = .16$), and in the expected direction. This gives us some slight support for the idea that females who show FOS respond differently to competition with a male partner. However, the question arises: is the effect of FOS a debilitated performance in the presence of men or a facilitated performance for working alone? Indeed, of the six pairs of means reported in Table 1, only the comparison of FOS-present vs. FOS-

TABLE 3

Conditions (FOS-present, females only)	n	$\bar{X}$	s.d.
Working alone	17	5.33	.80
Competition with male partner	19	5.37	.81

TABLE 4

Conditions (Females only)	n	$\bar{X}$	s.d.
Working alone			
FOS-present	17	5.33	.80
FOS-absent	13	4.39	.86
Competition with male partner			
FOS-present	19	4.37	.81
FOS-absent	11	4.88	.76

absent women in Group 1, Session 2 (the "working alone" comparison above) is statistically significant [$t(28) = 2.97$, $p < .01$, $d = 1.14$]. This implies merely that women with FOS do *better* alone, not necessarily that they perform *worse* against a male partner.

3. Since the first two randomized groups designs suggest that it is not an individual male competitor that debilitates performance for FOS-present women, perhaps it is *men in groups* that create an anxiety about doing well that debilitates striving for success. In fact, Horner abandoned her original design which involved the comparison of working alone, working against a single female partner, and working against a single male partner; she relabeled as an arousing situation what she had originally intended as her pretest, the large-group mixed-gender testing condition of Session 1. A moment's thought reveals the superiority of a *group* of men and women as a setting to test avoidance of "success" in the real-world sense. When does one compete against a single member of the other gender? Conflicts with a sibling or spouse over affection vs. achievement rewards are familiar, but this is not the occupational marketplace and, unlike psychological experiments, these relationships are more than fleeting encounters with strangers. A run-off between just two executives for a vice-presidency or between just two assistant professors for tenure is rare. I think the tendency to use the competing mixed-gender college-age pair in research on "fear of success" is not only for the convenience of the experimenter. I think it shows the tenacity of the tradition in gender-role research of two famous papers by Mirra Komarovsky (1946, 1950), demonstrating that college women "play dumb on dates." As I have explained elsewhere (Tresemer, 1975a), this research has more to say about the dating situation

than about female masochism where "success" is at stake. However, when we use a mixed-gender group as a setting to arouse competition and perhaps a "fear of success," we cannot say that it was necessarily the presence of men that caused a performance decrement for the women; it might have been the presence of men or the factor of sheer numbers.

A sufficient test of the adverse effects of *groups that include men* on FOS-present women would be a comparison of the performance levels of FOS-present women with FOS-absent women in Session 1. This is another form of a posttest-only design.

Let us pool in Table 5 all the data from Session 1, the large-group mixed-gender competitive or "arousal" condition (pooling variances and totals for presence or absence of FOS). This yields a $t(88)$ of 1.46 (n.s.) and a d of .32 (greater than "small"), in the direction opposite of that predicted. Clearly, compared with women who have not shown FOS, women with FOS are not debilitated by the presence of men.

The serious flaw in this design, however, lies in the possibility of other unmeasured mediating factors or covariates—for example, differences in initial ability, for which there was some evidence in this sample (FOS-present females somewhat more likely to have college honors status, $\chi^2 = 2.57$, $e = .03$, less than "small"). We control for these differences in the next design.

4. Since none of these designs has given us the effect we have been seeking, we turn to Horner's original comparison between working alone in Session 2 and working in a large group of men and women in Session 1. We will thereby use each of the 30 relevant subjects as her own control comparison for the test of effect, thus giving us a hedge on possible ability or other initial differences. For

TABLE 5

Conditions (Females only)	n	$\bar{X}$	s.d.
Large-group mixed-gender competitive			
FOS-present	56	5.02	.91
FOS-absent	34	4.75	.75

inferential purposes, this is not necessarily superior to the three previous "between-subjects" designs (cf. Greenwald's, 1976, paper on comparisons between the "within-subjects" and the "between-subjects" designs).

The test for similarity of correlated variances of the two performance measures from Session 1 and Session 2 showed no significant difference between the variances ($r_{DS} = .28$, n.s.). This allows us to pool the variances and compute a one-way analysis of variance on change scores[1] (cf. Kenny, 1975; also Huck and McLean, 1975). The result is a statistically significant finding: $F(1,29) = 4.20$ ($p < .05$). The effect size estimate is fairly "large:" $f = .38$. Women with FOS perform at a lower level in a large-group testing situation with men present than do women without FOS, controlling for ability differences between those groups in a neutral "working alone" setting. This is the analysis of variance solution for Horner's data, dispensing with the dichotomy of "performs better" in one situation versus another and with the unusual z score transformations used in her thesis. It is a strong confirmation of her original analysis.

"Like the Men"

However, the analysis of variance approach allows us to evaluate other aspects of this finding. For example, the performance of FOS-present females was compared with that of FOS-absent females, who were said to perform "like the men." Thus, like much of achievement motivation research, the expected baseline for anagram performance was implicitly the group of all men plus all women without FOS. Let us compare in Table 6 the relevant change score means for alone vs. large-group mixed-gender settings. The difference between the group of men without FOS and the group of women *with* FOS is of a "medium" size: $d = .40$ [even though $t(42) = 1.28$ is not statistically significant]. But the difference between the group of men without FOS and the group of women *without* FOS is *also* of a "medium" size: $d = .55$ [even though $t(38) = 1.62$ is not statistically significant].

[1]The change score is performance score in Session 1 (arousal) minus performance score in Session 2 (nonarousal), taken from the original data in Appendix F of Horner (1968). Analysis of covariance yielded nearly identical results.

TABLE 6

Conditions	n	$\bar{X}$	s.d.
Men without FOS[a]	27	−5.00	8.44
Women without FOS	13	0.00	10.67
Women with FOS	17	−8.94	12.34

[a]Only three men in this third of the subjects showed FOS and I excluded them from this analysis as exceptions since men supposedly did not as a group suffer from fear of success.

It is clear that if the achievement-related performance behavior of men is to be used as a baseline, then the group "without FOS" should be conceptualized as *with* something else. That is, the FOS dimension should be conceived of in a way analogous to the old tender–tough dimension rather than as a too tender (i.e., with FOS) vs. normal (i.e., "like the men") continuum.

FOS and Achievement

Why did we have to use an individual baseline (i.e., Session 1 performance vs. Session 2 performance for each subject) in addition to the other baselines in the first three designs above to obtain the large effect for FOS in our fourth try? Seeking an answer, I looked at the simple graphic display of change scores for the men and women with and without FOS. The distributions for the first two groups [(a) and (b) above] were scattered and platykurtic, but normal. The distribution for women with FOS [group (c) above] was distinctly bimodal, with about half ($n = 9$) of the values clustering around zero and the other half ($n = 8$) showing very large negative values (from −15 to −26 performance units). Without the high negative change scores of this second subgroup, the FOS effect would not have been found.

I wondered if there might be some differences between these two subgroups of women *within* the group of women with FOS? I compared these two clusters of FOS-present women on all the other available data from Horner's (1968) Appendix F to check for explanatory differences. On the thematic measure for need for affiliation there were no differences between these two subgroups. On the questionnaire measure of feeling of importance of doing well on these tasks there were none. On the college honors status of the females, there was a very small difference ($e = .03$), with slightly fewer honors students in the group with larger performance differences. On the Alpert–Haber Debilitating Anxiety measure of Fear of Failure there was a small difference [$t(16) = .61$, $d = .30$], with greater anxiety among those performing much worse in the large group setting. However, on the thematic measure of need for achievement (nAch),[2] there was a highly significant difference: $t(15) = 4.18$ ($p < .001$),[3] as well as a huge effect size estimate $d = 2.03$. The percentage of variance of membership in these two subgroups that was explained by nAch score was 51%, a very high figure in personality research. Resultant achievement motivation (nAch minus Fear of Failure) showed a medium effect size estimate: $e = .17$. To summarize, those women with FOS who did much worse in the large group setting (Session 1) were much lower in nAch score [$\bar{X} = 3.875$ (s.d. = 2.135) vs. $\bar{X} = 11.00$ (s.d. = 3.97)] and resultant achievement motivation than those women with FOS who did not do very differently in one situation or another. It should also be noted that anagrams performance in Session 2 for these two subgroups was not different while the differences between them occurred in the large-group setting.

Since in the sample as a whole nAch was not correlated with FOS (for Group 1 alone, $r = -.03$), we must conclude that they were independent factors operating in this study and that lack of nAch and presence of FOS were necessary *in combination* to produce the performance decrement in a large-group mixed-gender testing situation.

A two-factor unweighted-means analysis of variance on performance change scores confirms the conclusion which I obtained by working backwards from the data distributions. The means and analysis of variance are given in Table 7. The large main effect for FOS [$F(1,26) = 6.135$, $p < .05$, $d = .92$] was almost entirely due to the FOS-present–low nAch group: a planned comparison between FOS-present and FOS-absent scores among low nAch females (an average

[2]Need for achievement was measured from stories written by the students to the other five TAT-type cues.

[3]With Scheffé's correction for post-hoc comparisons, p is reduced to the .05 level.

TABLE 7
Means and Analysis of Variance of Performance Change Scores

	Conditions (Females in Group 1 only)					
	High nAch			Low nAch		
FOS-present	−3.56	(n = 9)		−16.75	(n = 8)	
FOS-absent	−2.20	(n = 5)		1.875	(n = 8)	

Summary of the analysis of variance

Source of variance	Degrees of freedom	Mean square	F test	Probability (p)	Effect size (d)
FOS(A)	1	711.48	6.135	<.05	.92
nAch (B)	1	148.21	1.28	n.s.	.42
A × B	1	531.51	4.58	<.05	1.14
Error	26	115.98			

change of −16.75 compared with an average of 1.875) yielded $F(1,26) = 12.67$, $p < .01$, $d = 1.40$. For the females high in nAch score, a planned comparison between performance for FOS-present and FOS-absent students was very "small" [−3.56 compared with −2.20, $F(1,26) = .06$, n.s., $d = .09$]. It was thus the combination of low nAch *and* FOS which made the strongest effect in this comparison between performance working alone and working in a large-group mixed-gender setting.

Some Technical Points. There are a few additional technical points about this reanalysis worthy of note.

First of all, I did not alter the p values in the above table to take into account the *a priori* versus *post-hoc* comparisons, since this preferential treatment would not have been constructive. Such adjustments can be made by the interested reader.

The effect size for the interaction is diminished in relationship to the one reported earlier ($d = 2.03$) due to the dichotomization of nAch as an independent variable and the inclusion of the women low in FOS in the design. It is still very large: $d = 1.14$.

Since the use of change or difference scores has been severely criticized by several authors (e.g., Cronbach and Furby, 1970; Cox, 1957; cf. recent review in Kenny, 1975), I checked these findings with the rival methodology: analysis of covariance. I tested the differences between the performances of the experimental groups on the task in

Session 1 (the "arousal" condition) adjusting for the baseline performance of Group 1 in Session 2 (working alone). The results were quite similar to the picture reported above: the effect sizes *(d)* were 1.06 for the FOS factor, .50 for the *n*Ach factor, and 1.00 for the interaction.

A further reanalysis by Fleming (in press) used FOS scores from a newer scoring system (Horner *et al.*, 1973) based on the stories to the neutral cues completed by these students which she had obtained from Horner. When also controlling for story length, she found the same pattern of mean performances. Effect size estimates could not, however, be computed from her reanalysis due to lack of an estimate of variance.

Finally, confining ourselves to within-subjects designs, where each person participates in all the experimental situations of interest, we can identify both an ideal and a conventional experimental design. The ideal design is to present the experimental situations (e.g., competition or working alone) in random or counterbalanced order so that practice effects from the first to the second testing are controlled. The conventional design takes the neutral or baseline or pretest measurement first, then the measure of the effects of experimental treatments, thus minimizing sensitization to the purposes of the experiment. Horner's design was neither conventional (the anxiety-arousing setting was presented first) nor ideal; these improvements have yet to be made in research addressing Horner's hypotheses.

A New Interpretation? This additional finding from Horner's data is not particularly surprising except for the fact that Horner claimed that FOS was especially debilitating to highly competent women, women who were highly achievement oriented, creative, and productive. At a time when the progress of equal rights for women has been measured by the percentage of positions of power (company presidents, management, or rank-and-file employed) held by women, Horner's claim was shocking. It meant that just those women who could be attaining such positions were suffering from internal conflicts about their potential success. The finding from the reanalysis is more pedestrian—that is, it is more culturally acceptable that women (and men) who are not particularly achievement oriented in the first place might be more vulnerable to the negative effects of FOS in an arousing testing setting. The presentation of the finding from the reanalysis would not have had such impact as Horner's presentation.

We must distinguish between *n*Ach and actual achievement. Besides the relatively crude measure of college honors status, we have no other ability indices to differentiate the women in this experiment. We really need to know a person's ability potential (e.g., from an IQ test or some other neutral test of potential) and his or her current ability profile (e.g., from current occupational or academic performance), in addition to the desires to do well (*n*Ach) and to not do well (FOS), before we can conclude who is affected by FOS and how. Considering the high caliber and thus generally high achievement motivation of the students at the University of Michigan who participated in Horner's experiment, a curvilinear effect may indeed by found—the "fear of success" effect being most prominent in neither very high nor very low achievement motivation groups but in a midrange. This is where "success" is neither assured nor impossible but at the tantalizing limit of one's reach.

An additional problem is Horner's suggestion that an unbiased measure of *n*Ach from projective materials written by women was impossible because of the confounding nature of FOS. If anything, however, there would be a positive correlation between the two scores since negative achievement-related imagery can be scored in both the FOS and *n*Ach systems (cf. Chapters 2 and 4). In Horner's sample, we have found no correlation between FOS and *n*Ach scores, and it is in the group where there is FOS imagery *without* *n*Ach imagery that the debilitation effect of public competition occurs. It is most unfortunate that there has not been a single replication of Horner's experiment which has included a measure of need for achievement.[4] This reanalysis remains speculative in its implications until more work is done.

Of course, interpretation of these new findings comes back to the central questions of this study: (1) what was the psychological significance of Session 1 and of Session 2 for these college students, how were they experienced, how could they be labeled, and how

[4]Several studies have measured the relationship between FOS and *n*Ach but did not use *n*Ach as an experimental factor to explain behavior (cf. Tresemer, 1976a). Thus, secondary analysis could be done with these studies to compare with the results found here.

generalized; and (2) what psychological meaning and what relationships to behavior does FOS imagery have in its presence or absence? The answers to these questions have so far been too facile, linked with values which have not been made clear. They continue to be questions of great importance.

Other analyses could be done with these data. If the original TAT-type protocols were available, further study could be made of the thematic differences between the two FOS-present subgroups. In addition, similar investigations could be made of the "same-sex competitive" and "mixed-sex competitive" groups which were not included here for reasons of space and not of lack of interest.

The purpose of this parade of designs has been to dramatize the different meanings of each comparison, in particular with respect to the baseline group used for comparison. Using these different comparisons is not mere play; any of the comparisons are analytically legitimate and have been used in other studies. The inference that negative thematic imagery is an indication of an underlying emotional state—a "fear"—seems justified or brazen depending upon the performance criterion chosen. In reference to this study the *National Enquirer* (1973) declared: "Women fear success, doctor says." As we begin to address the actual meaning of statements such as this through attention to the specific details of the original study, we confront the recurrent problems—success in comparison to what, which women, in comparison to whom, and how much?

REPLICATIONS OF HORNER'S ORIGINAL STUDY

There has been a curious absence of replications of Horner's final experimental design—i.e., comparing performance scores of the same subjects tested alone and in a "large-group mixed-sex competitive condition." Most studies have followed Horner's originally intended design, that is, comparing groups of subjects who had worked alone or had competed against a single male competitor or had competed against a single female competitor. Since this comparison yielded no statistically significant differences in Horner's study and was rejected in favor of the final design, the prevalence of these designs is puzzling. While 14 studies compared performance in male–female pairs with that in female–female pairs and/or alone, only five studies compared performance in mixed-gender *groups* with working *alone* (Romer, 1975b; McGuinness, 1974b; and three studies in Zanna, 1973). In only three of these studies did the same subjects work alone and in the group setting (Romer, 1975b, Experiment 3 in Zanna, 1973, and McGuinness, 1974b). In no study was need for achievement measured.

In Romer's (1975b) study, 168 male and 169 female students from the 5th, 7th, 8th, 9th, and 11th grades of the Ann Arbor public schools were tested in their classrooms in each of four experimental conditions: (1) no competition, where scores on a short verbal task were announced to individuals and not to the class; (2) competition against the whole class, where only one person in the class could be the winner and was announced after the tests were scored; (3) competition against an individual of the same gender, where each student was paired with a same-gender peer and one winner per pair was announced to the class; and (4) competition against an individual of the "opposite sex," where each student was paired with an "opposite sex peer" and one winner per pair was announced to the class. A fifth condition was noncompetitive and alone, where each student was tested in a small room by himself or herself. Condition 1 always came first while the order of conditions 2 through 5 was randomly assigned to class groups; no order effects were found. Performance was measured by two-minute work periods (less for the 11th graders) on different sets of fifteen scrambled words. Clearly, the settings most similar to Horner's were conditions 1 and 5. An analysis similar to Horner's was used; that is, on the basis of their performance, students were divided into three categories: performed better in noncompetitive alone condition; performed equally in both conditions; and performed better in noncompetitive [mixed-gender] group condition.[5] The effect size of the interaction between FOS and condition on performance was very small (and in the reverse of expected direction) for females (e = .005) as well as for males (e = .013). Of course, the argument against comparing this study with Horner's is that Romer's subjects were students in the 5th, 7th, 8th,

[5]Romer (1975b; cf. also Burghardt, 1973a, 1973b; Romer, 1975a, for further details) also called this last group "Performed better in not explicitly competitive group," noting the natural competitiveness in the junior high and high school classroom. This, of course, made the condition as defined more similar to Horner's "large-group mixed-sex competitive condition."

9th, and 11th grades, and performed for only two minutes in each condition.

In Experiment 3 reported in Zanna (1973), twenty female undergraduates from Rider College performed alone and in competition with men (mixed-gender competitive condition). The order of conditions was reversed for half of the students. The performance variable was the mean visual threshold for recognition of a list of words with a Gerbrands tachistoscope. The list was varied so that it was either easy or difficult, again the order of tasks being reversed for half of the students. An analysis of variance revealed a statistically significant main effect for task difficulty (performance was better at the easier task) and for condition order (performance on the second task was better, probably due to a practice effect). Neither the main effect for FOS, nor any interactions with FOS, were statistically significant. The effect size of the interaction between the presence of FOS and performance condition was very small for an easy task (f = .006) and for a difficult task (f = .012), both in the reverse of expected direction.[6] Again, it is clear that the unique aspects of this experiment make a direct comparison with Horner's experiment unclear, even though the intention was clearly to replicate Horner's design.

The third was a comprehensive study by McGuinness (1974b), which revealed consistent support for the hypothesis that high school juniors and seniors showing FOS (to the "medical school" cue) worked better alone than in a mixed-gender competitive group when compared to students not showing FOS. For moderately difficult and difficult tasks, this seemed to be more true of males than of females [e.g., for moderate tasks, f(males) = 1.09, very large, and f(females) = .43, medium to large]. For easy tasks, this seemed true for females (f = .29, medium) but not for males (f = .22, medium, in the reverse of expected direction).[7]

For the other two studies which measured performance working

[6]This is based on an estimate of MS_e from data available in Zanna's report (cf. Tresemer, 1976a, for details).

[7]These estimates assumed equal cell size (6 for females and 2 for males). This study is an excellent example of the importance of effect size estimates. McGuinness (1974a, 1974b) did not find statistically significant effects with her small sample of 23 male and 56 female subjects and concluded no effect. The effect sizes, however, are clearly not to be ignored, especially since they offer the only results in these five studies clearly supportive of Horner's earlier work. Even in McGuinness' study there are conflicting results from other story cues, which I have not analyzed here.

alone vs. in a mixed-gender competitive *group*, each subject did not work in both conditions, but rather the means of two separate groups were compared. These studies showed no statistically significant relationship between condition and FOS on performance for females (Experiments 1 and 2 in Zanna, 1973; data insufficient to compute effect size estimates).

It is unfortunate that Hoffman's (1974) obsessively meticulous replication of Horner's experimental situation involved only the measurement of thematic imagery (cf. Chapter 5) and did not measure a performance component. As it stands, these nearest relatives to replications of Horner's design give us an inadequate basis for deciding whether or not the FOS effect does in fact exist. Furthermore, as we move among the more distantly related cousins of Horner's original study, we continue to find the same mixed picture.

Gender Composition of Group and FOS

Several rather complicated studies included FOS as a dependent or independent variable in experimental situations that were either gender-homogeneous (i.e., all-male or all-female, a setting not used in Horner's original study) or gender-heterogeneous. House (1973) introduced 57 male and 59 female undergraduates to her experiment in groups of four males, four females, or two males and two females, as a reference group for the individual testing which comprised most of the experiment. Females high in FOS[8] in heterogeneous groups were more likely to choose the very difficult task rather than an easy or moderately difficult task in a situation where no personal experience was available but where norms for college students "of equal ability" were available (a social comparison situation). This sort of choice ensured failure at the actual task. Females high in FOS in homogeneous groups were more likely to choose the moderate challenge in the social comparison situation. Choice of the moderate challenge is, of course, the earmark of the achievement-oriented personality, and House (1973) argued that a high FOS hides a high and immeasurable need for achievement.

[8]See Tresemer (1976a) or House (1973) for a description of the differences between House's measure and Horner's.

Shinn (1973) tested 39 male and 52 female high school students while attending private coordinate boys' and girls' schools, and then retested the same students seven months later after the two schools had merged into a single coeducational institution. Thus the experimental treatment was coeducation. Using a special measure of FOS,[9] she found a significant increase in "FOS" imagery for the females in the coeducational setting ($d = 1.20$), as well as a somewhat smaller increase in "FOS" imagery for the males ($d = .55$). While "FOS" imagery and performance were not related in the gender-homogeneous settings, for the female students "FOS" and performance were negatively related in the coeducational setting: $r = -.39$. Females high in "FOS" imagery performed worse at the Lowell Scrambled Words task than women low in "FOS" imagery.

Thirty-five males were asked to leave the room by Heilbrun, Kleemeier, and Piccola (1974) while 51 female undergraduates worked on a digit–symbol task. The males returned and both groups were instructed to work on the same task, promised that a comparison of scores between genders would occur afterwards. From the analysis of many variables, the authors identified two major clusters for the females: (a) high integration of social roles, moderate masculinity, moderately contemporary attitudes toward the female role, low incidence of FOS, excellence in the all-female situation, and restricted achievement strivings among males, and (b) low integration of social roles, high masculinity, strong contemporary attitudes toward the female role, high incidence of FOS, ineffective performance on the perceptual–motor task when competing among females, and excellence with males present. In short, FOS went along with excellence in performance in the gender-heterogeneous setting, the reverse of what the theory of FOS would predict, and the reverse of the direction found in the studies by House (1973) and Shinn (1973).

Finally, two studies (Halprin, 1974; Groszko, 1974, Groszko and Morgenstern, 1972, 1974) found the interaction between FOS and gender composition of group to have no effect on performance.

[9]See Tresemer (1976a) for a description of the differences between this scoring system, the original scoring system (Horner, 1968), and that described in Horner *et al.* (1973). Shinn's construct is here labeled "FOS."

Male–Female Competitive Pairs and FOS

Another test of the "fear of success" effect construes a male–female pair as a "mixed-sex competitive condition." Again, the prediction is that females with FOS perform at a higher level working alone than females with FOS competing against a single male, as compared to females without FOS. This was Horner's originally intended design, and is tested in her data in the second alternative design in the section of this chapter on reanalysis of her study. It should be remembered that the "fear of success" effect was small in that analysis (f = .16), and Horner abandoned it for her large-group comparison. However, many authors have found it convenient to measure performance in pairs; indeed, Horner *et al.* (1973) used competitive pairs in the validation of the newer scoring system for FOS.

Studies which showed support for the interaction hypothesis were done by Althof [1973, f(females) = .37, a medium to large effect size], Makosky [1972, 1976, Parker, 1972, f(females) = .20, a medium to small effect size], Karabenick, Marshall, and Karabenick (1974, data insufficient to estimate effect size), and Fleming (1974). In Fleming's study of lower- and middle-class black women, numerous correlations were given between FOS and performance in successive two-minute time segments on the GENERATION anagrams task ranging from .11 (facilitation of performance) to −.48 (debilitation in third time segment) for 16 lower-class black women. While a few of the studies which found no support for this hypothesis presented sufficient data to compute an effect size estimate [e.g., Burghardt, 1973a, e(females) = .019, a very small effect size[10]], most studies which did not find the predicted effect did not present enough information and simply concluded "no effect" (Jackaway, 1974, and Jackaway and Teevan, 1975; Karabenick and Marshall, 1974; Major, 1975; Morgan and Mausner, 1972, 1973; Schwenn, 1970b). Though Berman (1973, Murphy-Berman, 1976) did not measure performance, she found that success over a male competitor did not provoke more anxiety for females with FOS compared to those without.

[10]Of the studies which tested this effect with males, only this study provided data adequate for a test of the debilitation effect of a female competitor: e = .006, very small.

While the interaction gives better control over the behavior of FOS-absent females, one researcher used only FOS-present females in her analysis. This is the first alternative design used in the section on reanalysis of Horner's study. Rider (1973) found that FOS-present females performed at a lower level in a noncompetitive–alone setting than when competing against a male confederate on patterns 7 through 10 of the Block Design test of the Wechsler Adult Intelligence Scale [d(females) = .57]. This is the reverse of the expected direction. Recalculating the effect size estimates for the studies cited in the previous paragraph, for which data were available, showed the following supportive results for females in this design: d = .46 (medium, Althof, 1973) and d = .13 (small, Makosky, 1972).[11]

Peplau's (1973, 1974, 1976) study of one hundred college-age dating couples in the Boston area offers an interesting twist to the test of the FOS effect on performance in male–female pairs. Half of her dating couples were assigned to a competitive condition, where they were told that their score on an intellectual task would be compared with the score of their boyfriend "to see who can do better—you or your boyfriend." Instead of comparing this with performance working alone on the same or similar tasks, she compared it with performance in a "noncompetitive" group testing session from a month earlier, using scores from this earlier session as a covariate for the mean performance scores in the arousal setting. In the competitive condition, females with FOS performed at a lower level than those without (d = .45, nearly "medium"). The results were more striking when the scores on Peplau's own measure of gender-role traditionalism were taken into account. The performance of women with FOS who expressed more traditional gender-role attitudes was worse in competition with their boyfriends than the performance of women with FOS and more liberal gender-role attitudes (d = .88, "large"). Comparing the performance of women with FOS and more traditional gender-role attitudes with the other three groups of women (with FOS and liberal attitudes, without FOS and with traditional or liberal attitudes) yielded a very large d of 1.07. This is highly confirming of Horner's notion that FOS debilitates

[11]The supportive finding for Burghardt's (1973a) study for the difference between two proportions [h(females) = .26, somewhat greater than "small"] might be confounded by an unknown order effect since the same students worked in both settings.

performance in competition with men. Since the correlation between FOS and gender-role attitudes was not found ($r = .01$, curvilinear relationships also checked), this was interpreted as the operation of two independent factors on women's performance in competition.

The central problem with this study is that the baseline was the so-called "noncompetitive" group, which in Horner's study was the arousal setting. Was this "noncompetitive" group really "neutral" where Horner's was not? Although being tested with one's boyfriend in a "not-explicitly competitive condition" (cf. Romer, 1975) might not arouse concerns about competition, it might very well arouse concerns about comparison with one's boyfriend and with the others that were present. If we look at performance scores in the "noncompetitive" session by itself, we find that the women with FOS and with traditional gender-role attitudes greatly outperformed the other three groups (namely, women with FOS and liberal attitudes, and women without FOS and with traditional or liberal attitudes): $d = 1.64$ (very large, with r^2 approaching .40). The adjustment in the analysis of covariance for this much higher performance in the scores for the competitive condition would, of course, make the score in competition seem much lower than the others. We might, therefore, have the situation where we are adjusting the performance profile in one sort of arousal setting with the performance profile of another sort of arousal setting. Should we look only at the raw unadjusted scores for competition with one's boyfriend, or only at the scores for the large-group mixed-gender "noncompetitive" setting, or at some sort of interaction? Each sort of comparison, as illustrated previously in the reanalysis of Horner's results, has a different meaning and, often, different outcomes. This study dramatizes the difficulties that arise when we rely on any one baseline or "control group" setting. The optimum setting for comparison has not yet been found, and we must seek comparisons from many points of view.

Gender-Role Appropriateness of Tasks and FOS

Since Horner hypothesized FOS would be debilitating to females because career and achievement success was viewed as unfeminine, several researchers have tested the theme of this hypothesis by testing females with and without FOS in gender-role-appropriate and gender-role-inappropriate settings. The prediction is that females with FOS would respond to a task labeled as masculine (gender-role inappropriate) in the same way as they would to a verbal cue about a woman at the top of her medical school class.

Makosky (1972, 1976; Parker, 1972) asked half of her female students to work on a "masculine" task, described as words chosen "because men typically can unscramble them better than women, probably because of the ability men have in spatial and visual organization." She also told them that "the task correlates highly with other tests of masculinity and professional ability." She asked the other half of her female students to work on a "feminine" task, described as words chosen because women do better than men due to their verbal skill, and relating to femininity and to superior homemaking ability. She found that women with FOS did worse on the masculine task, compared to the feminine task, when compared with how the women without FOS did; for those working alone d = .23, for those working against a male competitor d = .25, and for those working against a female competitor d = .29, all had nearly the same effect sizes.[12]

Hundert (1974) tested only females with FOS, finding that their performance was indeed somewhat higher in a task labeled "feminine" (data inadequate to compute effect size).

In a study by Short and Sorrentino (1974; Short, 1973; Sorrentino and Short, 1973), half of the female students received a "Test of Domestic Ability" ("female-oriented condition"), and half the "Test of Drafting Ability" ("male-oriented condition"), both of which were the same task involving rapid tracing of geometric designs. Using average number of designs attempted, females with FOS scored higher in the "male-oriented condition" than in the "female-oriented condition" (d = .46), the opposite of the predicted direction. The authors suggested that the FOS measure might be more an

[12] An interesting quirk in this study was the finding that females working on the "feminine" task rated it more "masculine" in a post-experimental questionnaire than females working on the "masculine" task. This raises questions again about just how these arousal settings are experienced. Makosky (1976) offers an explanation of this finding in terms of the cognitive dissonance of the woman working on the "masculine" task.

assessment of the students' ability, reasoning that high-ability students would perform more competently at a "male-oriented," and therefore more esteemed, task.

Using a design similar to Short and Sorrentino's, Jackaway (1974a; Jackaway and Teevan, 1975) presented a symbol coding task as a wiring pattern for a nuclear reactor ("masculine") or as a needlepoint embroidery pattern ("feminine"). FOS was a dependent variable here, found not to be different for the gender-role-appropriate or inappropriate tasks.

Patty (1973a, b, 1974) tested 325 female undergraduates in an "Intellectual" condition where the students were told that the primary focus was the relationship between creativity and intelligence (a more stereotypically masculine orientation), in a "Social skills" condition where students were told the focus was on the relationship between creativity and social skills ["ability to communicate well," and so forth, in "formal (rather noncompetitive) environments, such as clubs, families, or with the opposite sex," a more stereotypically feminine orientation], and in a "Neutral" condition where the students were told that "we are not sure what the test measures or what it is related to." FOS scores were found to increase after these experimental instructions in both the Intellectual and Social skills settings, showing that they both were arousing of FOS-related concerns. (The difference between FOS scores in these two arousal settings and the Neutral setting was large, while the difference between the two arousal settings was small, d equal to about .10.) However, no performance differences were found in the FOS by instructions interaction. Echoing the Short and Sorrentino study, Patty suggested that FOS was confounded with ability which was not controlled for in this experiment. (However, a look at the many studies which did test the relationship between FOS and ability has shown no such relationship—cf. Chapter 5.)

Berkan (1972), Robbins (1973), and Turner (1974) also found no effect in the interaction between FOS and gender-role appropriateness of task, though data were inadequate to compute effect size estimates. A problem with the designs used in these studies has been mentioned in Chapter 3. The authors assume that their "masculine" setting is equal and opposite to their "feminine" setting; that is, one setting is as "masculine" as the other is "feminine." This is never tested, partly because a test would require a rigorous definition of the generalities "masculine" and "feminine." These qualities, so basic to our folkways, are more easily assumed than measured.

Another problem with some of these studies is the assumption of a traditional gender-role orientation among men and women alike; that is, women are assumed to find the "masculine" settings not only inappropriate to the female gender role, but also inappropriate to them personally. However, Gearty and Milner (1974, 1975; also Gearty, 1973) found that 24 of 30 female undergraduates having a "feminine" academic major and 22 of 30 female undergraduates having a "masculine" academic major (mathematics, chemistry, biology, and business) showed FOS imagery (e = .006, very small effect for difference). The unmeasured variable is the actual personal disposition towards stereotypically "masculine" and "feminine" situations or tasks. Perhaps the societal stereotypes have little relevance for a personal choice of task and setting. Indeed, Peplau (1973, 1976) reports a near-zero correlation between FOS and personal attitudes concerning gender roles, and found the FOS debilitation effect to be the greatest among those with FOS *in addition to* a traditional attitude toward gender roles.

One aspect of this comparison has involved the thematic analysis of responses to verbal cues depicting stereotypically masculine kinds of success and stereotypically feminine kinds of success (Breedlove and Cicirelli, 1974; Depner and O'Leary, 1976; Hoffman, 1974; Feather, 1974; Feather and Simon, 1975; McGuinness, 1974a, b; O'Leary, 1974; O'Leary and Hammack, 1974; Turner, 1974; and others cited in Tresemer, 1976a). These studies are naturally limited by the ability to describe only one such situation. For example, O'Leary and Hammack (1975) used the "medical school" cue as the representative of "traditionally masculine competitive success," and "Susan finds that she will be graduating first in her nursing school class" as the representative of "traditionally feminine competitive success." Yet in another study, the situations would be different. For example, in Depner and O'Leary (1976), the "traditionally feminine competitive success" is represented by "Barbara has just been appointed Head of Nurses in a large metropolitan hospital." The similarity between these is perhaps due to the similarity in investigators, and indeed the cue differences between cues in the other studies which seek to measure the effects of cue material on FOS are much greater. However, a close look at even these two cues shows that, similar though they might be, they are not equal, and a reviewer would hesitate before comparing proportions of FOS imagery elicited by one cue directly with proportions elicited by the other. For this reason, I did not attempt to describe the findings of these particular studies. Their results can, however, also be summarized as mixed, since the high FOS proportions expected in the "masculine" setting do not always materialize.

Other Control Groups

Other comparisons have been made between the performance of male–female pairs vs. female–female pairs competing against each other (e.g., Althof, 1973; Berens, 1972; Burghardt, 1973; Jackaway, 1974; Karabenick, 1972; Karabenick and Marshall, 1974; Karabenick *et al.*, 1974; Makosky, 1976; Major and Sherman, 1975; Murphy-Berman, 1976; Rider, 1973), or performance after test/arousing instructions vs. task/nonarousing instructions (e.g., Robbins, 1973), or after a rigged success vs. a rigged failure (e.g., Fleming, 1974; Jackaway, 1974; Karabenick, 1972; Karabenick and Marshall, 1974; Karabenick *et al.*, 1974; Murphy-Berman, 1976; Zaro, 1972, 1975), or after a social rejection vs. a social acceptance condition (e.g., Kenkel, 1974), or after difficult vs. easy instructions (McGuinness, 1974a, b; Patty, 1974; Zanna, 1973). Of course, what the "fear of success" effect means with these different comparison or baseline groups is quite different from those comparison groups used above. For example, what can one conclude from results showing lower performance scores in female–female pairs? How often and in what kinds of situations is one in achievement-oriented competition with a single male peer or a single female peer?

The accumulated results from the comparisons between performance levels in male–female and female–female pairs as well as the results from the other additional comparisons noted above follow the pattern found with the comparison groups more closely related to Horner's original test of the FOS effect—occasional support for the FOS effect amidst findings of no effect and an occasional reversal.

Compared with the popular focus on aspects of the mixed-gender competitive condition, there has been inadequate attention to the definition and replication of the exact situational determinants in Horner's baseline or "working alone" condition. When we say that there has been a "debilitation of performance" or a "performance decrement" we imply a valuation of the two settings being compared, and attach to one the expectation or hope that performance be greater in quality and quantity. When we compare a setting called "relaxed" with one called "test" or "arousal," we expect the person to rise to the occasion in the latter—there are important consequences of one's performance not to be found in the relaxed setting. Indeed, this is how the two settings are often defined to the students in these studies. But with Horner's study, there is no relaxed, or neutral, or control group setting. The context against which a lower score in the large-group mixed-gender competitive setting is judged is itself a complicated one—students are alone in a room with a tape recorder, asked to work against their own standards of excellence. The instructions were modeled on Atkinson and Reitman's (1956) "achievement-oriented conditions." Students received an introductory statement promising three tests:

> Test 1—a test of creative ability, Test 2—a test of memory and a measure of how quickly and efficiently you can think and work, and Test 3—a test of intellectual alertness. On the basis of our information about your past performance the particular tests included in YOUR booklet were chosen so that each one of you would have a 50–50 chance of doing well in this situation. Do the very best you can on each of these tests. We are interested in seeing how well people can perform when working at maximum efficiency. . . .

and so on. Compare this with the instructions in the first session for the Scrambled Words Task:

> Task C-1 is a test of verbal ability which as you probably know is considered the best single measure of general intelligence.

Are the latter instructions, used for the arousing situation of mixed-gender large-group testing, more arousing? Should the baseline setting of working alone be considered engaged but not frantic? In which setting would it be "better" to have the higher performance?

Since the interaction between FOS and condition is the test of interest, comparability of the nonarousal situations from study to study is a key, but unfortunately often missing, factor.

The FOS Effect Without the Measurement of FOS

Several researchers have sought the FOS effect without measuring individual differences in FOS imagery. Some (e.g., Karabenick, 1972; Levine *et al.*, 1976; Martyna, 1973) have assumed that "most women fear success," and have been surprised to find that most women do not act like they fear success. Others have sought to create the conditions which would lead to a debilitation effect. For example, Jellison, Jackson-White, and Bruder (1974; also Jellison, Jackson-White, Bruder, and Martyna, 1975) told students that a second performance on an achievement test would be the basis for a psychologist's impression of the student. For half, the psychologist's attitude was described as approving high intelligence, for half as disapproving. Male and female students were tested under these conditions: half were told the psychologist was a male and half that the psychologist was a female. In all cases, students improved on a second testing when the psychologist was described as approving of intelligence while after a description of disapproval of intelligence, the students did not improve or did worse. In a second set of experiments, the students were asked to imagine that they had taken two forms of six tests and had to decide which form (an "89" or a "71" score) they would send to a psychologist who again either approved or disapproved of intelligence. One twist in this latter design replaced psychologist with "a male student they [the female students] would like to date and with whom they could have a worthwhile relationship." Still another twist asked females to choose between divulging a "91" or a "77" score, knowing that the male peer's score was "84." In all these designs, where the judge's bias was toward approval rather than disapproval of high intelligence, the higher score was more likely to be divulged.

Another example of a clever experimental design (the *sine qua non* of the modern social psychologist) is given by Fisher, O'Neal, and McDonald (1974; see also Argote, Fisher, McDonald, and O'Neal, 1976). Under the guise of an industrial problem-solving study, female students were made either to succeed or fail in competition with either a male or female partner (who was a confederate of the experimenter). They then overheard a conversation in which they were either accepted or rejected by their actor/partner and then competed on another task with a different partner (of the same gender as their first partner). This second performance measure was the number of anagrams made from the word "extemporaneous" in five minutes minus how many the partner made. This second confederate carefully modulated performance to move slowly on the task. Only the three-way interaction, for gender of competitor × performance outcome × competitor evaluation, reached statistical significance: females who competed against male partners obtained lower scores on the second performance measure when rejected following success on the industrial problems or accepted following failure on the industrial problems.

A third study (Howe and Zanna, 1975), explicitly designed to suggest an alternative to "fear of success" as an intrapsychic rather than a situational phenomenon, also shows how these ingeniously designed laboratory demonstrations are not immune to problems of their own. In groups of two males and two females (a "mixed-sex competitive" condition), undergraduates worked on an anagrams task which was given a masculine or a feminine orientation. Half way through the anagrams test, each student was told that he or she was performing better than every other student in the group. Effects on subsequent performance were not found for gender of student or for gender orientation of the task. The interaction was, however, statistically significant. When students were succeeding at a masculine task, males improved more than females in the second half; when succeeding at a feminine task, females improved more than males. This was the expected avoidance of success effect due to lower performance in a gender-role-inappropriate situation. However, when Howe and Zanna (1975) replicated this design with twice as many students, the exact opposite of the pattern was found (i.e., when succeeding at a masculine task, females improved more than males). The authors seemed to be painfully aware of the dead-end inconclusiveness stemming from reversed results.

While these ingenious experimental tests of a success avoidance effect give evidence of the importance of situational determinants in the avoidance of success, they cannot replace the FOS construct as a personality variable since they did not measure FOS. Indeed they must be seen as supportive of the general notion of success avoidance. The study by Morgan and Mausner (1972, 1973) did, however, employ a measure of FOS. Male and female high school students were divided into high-performing and low-performing groups (highest quartile and lowest quartile on the basis of performance on a Hidden Figures Test). In the experimental session, students were matched in male–female pairs of unequal ability. In the pairs in which the male was originally high performing, he continued to outperform his female partner. However, where the female was originally the higher performer, relative performance of the two members of the pair reversed fifty percent of the time, a behavioral indication of the avoidance of success. Originally high-performing females who dropped below their originally low-performing male partners emitted fewer tension-release interjections (e.g., squeals of delight) in the experimental session than the originally high-performing females who remained superior in performance. The behavioral data were unrelated to FOS. This study, including the absence of relationship to FOS, has been replicated by Coles and Mausner (1974; also Kirkpatrick, 1974).

In addition, any self-derogatory or success-avoidant effect found to be related not to FOS but to situational and personality variables that are part of the definition of FOS constitutes a disconfirmation or at least a confusion. For example, if there is a debilitation of performance after success (compared to after failure) or in a gender-role-inappropriate setting (compared to an appropriate one) that is not related to FOS, then we must conclude that FOS is not related to success or gender-role-inappropriate settings while still puzzling about what caused the avoidance of success. Several studies (including Peplau, 1973, 1976; Krusell, 1973; and the studies cited in the previous paragraph) have suggested such conclusions. A thorough analysis of this point would involve the comparison of effect sizes for the various appropriate interaction terms for the FOS and other effects, an undertaking crippled by the diversity of experimental designs in studies in this area.

Finally, Chapter 3 is full of citations of studies which document a success avoidance effect without measuring FOS. Some of the theoretical approaches there (e.g., disconfirmed expectations) could be used in this area, adding FOS as a measured variable to determine the relative size of its effect.

External Validity

A further comment can be made on this research in terms of the size of the "fear of success" effect. A suggested technique for evaluating the application of results from the experimental laboratory to large-scale observations of an entire society, that is from a microlevel to a macrolevel of data, entails comparing the effect size estimates found in the psychological lab with the effect size estimates found from sociological observations of the phenomena supposedly being paralleled in the lab. For example, Horner (1970a) states:

> The arousal of motivation to avoid success may very well account for a major part of the withdrawal of so many trained American women from the mainstream of thought and achievement. (p. 70)

Let us take several effect sizes for the low number of women in certain occupational categories as an operationalization of this idea. The obvious test is for women in medical school (Dubé, 1973, 1975): in 1963–1964, this was 2, 244/32,001 (g = .43, a very large effect)[13] and in 1974–1975, this was 9,661/53,554 (g = .28, a large effect). From Epstein (1970a, p. 7), we can compute the effect size estimates for women in selected prestigious professional occupations for 1960; for lawyers, g = .465 (extremely large effect), for engineers, g = .49 (extremely large), for scientists, g = .40 (extremely large), and for biologists, g = .22 (almost large). From the material in the annotated bibliography and analyses in Chapters 5 and 6 it is clear that effect sizes for FOS obtained in the lab are only rarely this large. Therefore, a "fear of success" in women cannot be used as a sufficient explanation for gender differences in occupational attainment. A "fear of success" might be proven to be necessary for an explanation of occupational underattainment, but only along with many

[13]This is the effect size index for proportion tested against fifty percent: g equals 50% minus actual proportion; g varies between 0 and .50. Cohen's (1969) conventions hold a small effect size at .05, medium at .15, and large at .25, levels comparable with other effect size indices given in Chapter 5 (e.g., d = .2, .5, .8).

other factors related or unrelated to the FOS factor. This technique is only intended as a rough indicator of comparability, since many other aspects must be understood and compared before these two levels of measurement can be judged isomorphic or not (Szekely, 1950). Particularly important, of course, is the verity of the operationalization for the behavior cluster of interest. That is, ten minutes working on an anagrams task is taken as "achievement behavior"; it is necessary to evaluate how much this parallels competition in first-term finals in medical school or any other macrolevel setting.

An Expectancy × Value theory approach has an explanation for a finding of no effect. In the case of a "motive to avoid success," females as a group are hypothesized to have a latent stable personality disposition to avoid an achievement goal in situations which arouse that motive. If the characteristics of a situation do not arouse that personality dynamic, there is no curtailment of approach behavior. The inference to the motive is often backward from the observed behavior: if there seems to be a performance decrement in a situation involving competition or men or achievement or performance evaluation or a combination of these, then there was a "motive to avoid success" in these subjects; if no such performance differential was observed, then the conclusion was that the "motive to avoid success" *was not aroused.* The *motive* did not combine with the right Expectancy and Incentive to become *motivation,* and/or the *motivation* was blotted out by other motivations or extrinsic factors, thus not affecting actual performance behavior. Thus, we cannot prove its nonexistence until we have exhausted every *possible* manipulation of setting with no effect. This approach is elusive and hard to grasp. While it may explain lack of findings in many cases, we cannot rely on this catchall to explain every deviation FOS has made from the predictions for a "fear of success."

This cumulative record should replace enthusiasm for any one set of results with caution. There is more unity of theme to the many diverse sources cited in Part I than in the research on Horner's construct. Each new study has some new twist of method or interpretation—and often some new fault which leads not to consolidation of knowledge about FOS but to further expansion of the inquiry without adequate foundation. We hope the studies that will be done in the future will involve the meticulously careful definition of the constructs involved and of the experimental situations in which they are hypothetically at work. The broader issues also need to be addressed: what is meant by success, and when can we infer the presence of a fear? When more attention is paid to these issues, we may begin to understand a so-called "fear of success" in terms of a larger social and psychological perspective. Until that time, we may still say that "most American women fear success,"[14] but we cannot rely on the cumulative record of research on FOS to substantiate such a statement.

NEW MEASURES OF FEAR OF SUCCESS

There have been several efforts to replace Horner's projective measure of FOS with so-called "objective" questionnaire measures, as well as with other thematic scoring systems. These shall be briefly summarized here.

Revisions of the Original Scoring System

Several researchers have made minor changes in Horner's scoring criteria, in the spirit of the clarifications elaborated in Chapter 4.[15] In the context of Horner's research, Thelma Alper (1973, 1974) has written about her own earlier work with negative or "nonsuccess" themas such as "achievement can be dangerous" in the framework of achievement motivation theory.[16]

Janet Spence (1974) clarified Horner's categories and added others (e.g., negative outcomes not explicitly linked to the achievement

[14]"[Horner's] doctoral research at the University of Michigan paved the way for subsequent studies revealing that most American women fear success," *Time* (1974, p. 50).

[15]These include Hopkins (1974), House (1973), Levine and Crumrine (1973, 1975), Major (1975; Major and Sherman, 1975), Midgley and Abrams (1974), Olsen and Willemsen (1974), Peplau (1973; cf. her Appendix C), Pleck (1974), Robison (1974), Shinn (1973), Solomon (1975), Tomlinson-Keasey (1974), Tresemer (1974b), Turner (1974), Unger and Krooth (1974), and Weston and Mednick (1970). Details of these alterations can also be found in Tresemer (1976a).

[16]She scored these themes and FOS from stories written by college students in 1964–1965, the other early data point in Table 1 along with the results of Horner's study.

situation). She used longer cues such as "Susan was married right after she graduated from college. Later when both their children were in school, Susan and her husband decided she should go ahead with her ambition to become a doctor. She was accepted at the medical school of the local university. After her first-term finals, she found herself at the top of her class." Spence tried to solve the persistent problem with projective measures of difficulty in scoring and low test–retest reliability by adding a ten-item questionnaire after the story-writing task, including "How likable do Anne's classmates consider her?" (answered on a five-point scale), and "How physically attractive is she?" (answered on a five-point scale), and "If she doesn't complete her degree, what is the most likely reason?" (answered from alternatives provided from previous stories to the Anne/medical school cue). The score for negativity of perceived consequences for the hypothetical Susan or Anne were highly related to FOS scores for over three hundred undergraduates tested by Spence. She felt this "objective" measure could be used instead of the more time-consuming thematic one, though the story-writing task would naturally be presented to elicit the imagery from which the close-ended questions would be answered. Unfortunately, the nature of the measure is revealed with questions about the likeableness and attractiveness of an achieving female. And, as pointed out before, the example of Anne at the top of her medical school class has reached the readers of many introductory psychology texts. This particular elaboration of the thematic method awaits development for less structured cue material.

Knapp (1972) devised a similar questionnaire device to accompany a story-writing exercise. For example, item 17 read like the "Anne/medical school" cue, asking questions about Anne such as: "She is

a. happy but surprised she did so well (feels luck played a part)
   YES! yes -?- no NO!
c. proud and happy primarily because she has done well in a masculine field
   YES! yes -?- no NO!
g. abnormal—probably not very feminine
   YES! yes -?- no NO!"

This particular technique is interesting, though more transparent than Spence's above.

A New Scoring System for Thematic Imagery

In a lengthy program of research, Horner, Tresemer, Berens, and Watson (1973) derived a new set of scoring categories from stories written by college undergraduates based on whether or not they showed performance decrements in a theoretically threatening situation. The major improvement in the story-writing task was the abandonment of specific cues, such as the "Anne/medical school" cue, in favor of less specific neutral and achievement-oriented cues, such as "Joan seems to be particularly pleased" or "Linda is looking into her microscope." Stories were first written in a neutral setting. Then in a second session some students were tested in a nonarousal group setting. Another group of students was tested in a competitive setting, where males and females were paired to compete on a difficult arithmetic test; the female's code number was announced as the winner in each pair, and then they competed on the GENERATION anagrams task. Forty-two thematic elements that might be indicative or counterindicative of an avoidance disposition toward excellence in achievement were scored from the stories in the first or neutral setting; these scores were used in a multiple regression analysis to predict changes in performance following success in the competition-with-a-male condition. Six categories with weighted scores accounted for 44% of the variance[17] in performance change score comparing profiles for the women in the competitive setting with that of the women in the noncompetitive or nonarousal setting. Those females who had a higher score in this new system were more likely to perform at a lower level after success against a male competitor than females with low scores on this measure of "fear of success."

The categories are briefly as follows:

1. Contingent negative consequences (+2): negative outcomes in the story plot for which the actor is made somehow responsible (therefore, contingent).

2. Noncontingent negative consequences (+2): negative outcomes which bear no relationship to any characteristic or action of the actor.

3. Interpersonal engagement (+2): people are actively involved with each other in the story.

[17] r^2 of .44 is associated with a d of nearly 1.8, very large.

4. Relief (+1): tension in story suddenly or magically alleviated without any effort on the part of the actor.

5. Absence of instrumental activity (+1): no statement of any instrumental act ("thinking" or "doing") toward attaining a goal within the story.

6. Absence of mention of other persons (−2): no character or group other than the person specified in the cue are mentioned in the story (note: this category is counterindicative of FOS).[18]

Reservations about this system are (a) it has been derived from a situation theoretically threatening for females and may not be relevant to males, (b) the arousal setting of a competitive male–female pair is quite different from the arousal setting used in Horner's original study, (c) it bears close relationship to the thematic measure for "fear of failure," the Hostile Press scoring system (correlations ranged from .41 to .58 in different groups in a study reported by Jackaway and Teevan, 1976), and (d) it does not differentiate between pure "fear of success" themes and Negative Antecedent themes (cf. Chapter 4). However, the new scoring system was applied to the stories from Horner's original study at the University of Michigan and was found to account for a large proportion of variance in the performance score (difference between working alone and in a large-group mixed-gender setting, $r^2 = .42$). A major advantage of this system for a wider range of cues is the ability to rescore projective materials from older key studies. This has been done with the women from the Harvard Student Study of the early sixties (Stewart, 1975), and could well be done with other studies in the achievement motivation area or any of the major longitudinal studies using projective tests (e.g., the Berkeley Growth Study).

Although it is unclear exactly how the original scoring system and the new one are related to each other, a very few of the studies cited earlier in this chapter used the newer scoring system and were treated under Working Assumptions 2 and 3 as if they were also measuring FOS (Fleming, 1974; Halprin, 1974; Jackaway, 1974; the replication of Morgan and Mausner, 1973, namely Coles and Mausner, 1974, and Kirkpatrick, 1974; O'Leary and Hammack, 1975; Stew-

[18]A more detailed account of this study can be found in Tresemer (1976a), though analyses are still being done with these data before the full story can be told. The scoring manual in Horner *et al.* (1973) includes detailed definitions and practice stories for training scorers.

art, 1975; and Watson, 1974). In the four studies which assessed both males and females for this new measure of "fear of success," females were consistently found to score a very little bit higher (Fleming, 1974, $d = .04$; Jackaway, 1974a, $d = .22$; Stericker, 1975, $d = .12$; and Watson, 1974, consistently small). Since the scoring categories read so much more like scoring criteria for neurotic anxiety, depression, and psychopathic character disorder (cf. General Inhibition Thema in Chapter 4), comparisons can now be made with the gender differences found in those studies.

The New Questionnaire Measures

The doctoral dissertation study of Marice Pappo (1972) has been summarized in Chapter 1, within the theoretical context of "fear of success" at the root of her measure, namely Harry Stack Sullivan's interpersonal theory of psychiatry. She defined "fear of (academic) success" as "a psychological state which results in observable paralysis, withdrawal, or retraction in the presence of a consciously understood, subjective, or objective goal which is perceived by the individual at the moment of withdrawal" (Pappo, 1972, p. 1).

Items from the questionnaire were derived from clinical case material and intuition, item analyses were performed, and then a refined version of the measure was validated. An example of an item is "When friends whose opinions I value compliment my work I feel good but uneasy." In the validation study, students high and low in "fear of (academic) success" were told they had either succeeded or not succeeded after completing the first of two reading tests. For both genders, the measure of "fear of (academic) success" predicted which students would do poorly after success feedback. Analysis of a post-experimental questionnaire revealed that students scoring highly on the measure of "fear of (academic) success" also revealed the following attitudes: self-sabotage, low self-esteem, a preoccupation with the evaluation aspects of a competitive situation, a generally competitive orientation, a tendency to repudiate one's competence, and greater attributions for success to factors outside themselves and less to their own ability.

Based in the traditional psychoanalytic view of "fear of success" and not in theories about gender-role socialization, Pappo's new questionnaire found no differences between the genders.

Pappo also found her "fear of (academic) success" measure correlated highly with two other measures: (1) the Alpert–Haber Debilitating Anxiety Scale of the Achievement Anxiety Test: $r = .57$, and (2) Sarnoff's Need to Fail scale: $r = .77$. The first scale has most routinely been used in the achievement motivation tradition as the measure of "fear of failure," thus raising the question that Pappo's scale might be another measure of "fear of failure." However, this confusion is discussed in Chapter 2: the Alpert–Haber test measures anxiety which in the achievement motivation tradition has been assumed to be the same as "fear of failure." It may be that "fear of failure" and "fear of success" cannot be differentiated in terms of the scales used to measure the first at a time when the second construct was assumed to be part of the first. Thus we cannot yet say which is a measure of "fear of failure" and which a measure of "fear of success" and which a measure of both together until there are carefully designed studies which differentiate between them in terms of performance in various settings. This point about labeling applies equally to the other new questionnaire measures described in this section.

Sarnoff's Need to Fail scale is not published and currently no reliability or validity data are available for it. At present, it is a list of items that seem to cohere about a certain theme. Thus, what his scale actually measures and what the best label for it might be are still uncertain given the high correlation with Pappo's more carefully derived scale.

Scores on Pappo's scale have been found to be uncorrelated with presence or absence of FOS imagery expressed by the same students (Curtis *et al.*, 1973, in press; Zanna, 1973).[19] In the study by Curtis *et al.* (1973), exactly half of the women who scored above the median on Pappo's instrument were judged as high in Horner's FOS.

Nina Cohen (1974) sought to improve on Pappo's measure by assessing anxiety about success independent of a specific achievement context (e.g., academic achievement). The scale purports to test "the equation of accomplishment with competitive defeat of another" which "results in fantasied retaliation by the defeated

[19]This has been found to be true in other unpublished studies (personal communications from Peter Gumpert and Phillip Shaver, June 1975).

competitor." An example of one of the 64 true–false items is "I frequently find myself not telling others about my good luck so they won't have to feel envious." A fear of success is conceived as a defense against letting go, therefore based in the anal stage of development emphasizing issues of control and fear of loss of control, self-assertion vs. submission, and shame and humiliation. The correlation between Pappo's and Cohen's scales was .74. The validating experiment involved 241 high school juniors and seniors tested in twelve-person groups. In a neutral condition, there was no difference in performance levels of those high and low in Cohen's measure of "fear of success." After a task where each group of students competed for a prize of ten dollars, the students were individually given success feedback and then paired in a "run-off for the prize" with a same-gender or cross-gender opponent. Students high in Cohen's measure of "fear of success" performed at a significantly lower level in this last situation, compared with their earlier baseline performance level. While gender of competitor had no differential effect on students low in Cohen's "fear of success," for those high in her measure performance was worse against same-gender competitors. Cohen had anticipated this, since in her theory, a fear of success is linked with recurrent Oedipal conflict, symbolically associated with a same-gender peer. This is the opposite of Horner's prediction, pointing to the different theoretical orientation of Cohen's measure. Students high in Cohen's "fear of success" also reported more difficulty concentrating and then showed a significant increment in this difficulty in the arousal setting. Those high in Cohen's "fear of success" also more often devalued their performance and attributed effective performance to luck.

It should be noted in these questionnaires couched in the psychoanalytic approach to "fear of success" that it is a different kind of success that is feared. In Horner's theory, the feared negative consequences for success are deviation from social norms and stereotypes (e.g., loss of femininity); for these new measures, the feared negative consequences are the victorious defeat over one's defenses against murderous rage or Oedipal success and the awesome retaliation which will follow. Both theoretical approaches hold the same assumptions about the nature of "success" discussed elsewhere in this book; both also combine a neurotic fear of success with fear of social boundary transgression. There are certainly similarities in the themes found in the story-writing exercise and in the questionnaire items here which suggest a high degree of overlap in these various definitions of "fear of success," but it is also no surprise that Cohen's scale has not been found to be related to Horner's FOS.[20]

At the end of Zuckerman and Wheeler's (1975) extremely critical review of Horner's thematic measure of FOS, they suggest a solution in the form of an "objective" questionnaire developed by Zuckerman and Allison (in press). The highest item–scale correlations in this 27-item questionnaire were for number 2 "Often the cost of success is greater than the reward," number 23 "I believe that successful people are often sad and lonely," and number 11 "I think 'success' has been emphasized too much in our culture." These items illustrate the emphasis on success in a general and abstract societal sense in this scale.

Unlike Pappo and Cohen, Zuckerman and Allison accept much of Horner's conceptual foundation for a "fear of success," including the prediction that females will show more "fear of success" than males. And again, the prediction is supported ($d = .32$). The correlation between Zuckerman and Allison's "fear of success" and Horner's FOS was found to be .16 for 174 males and .18 for 170 females.

In the validation study, male and female undergraduate volunteers worked at an anagrams task under either low arousing instructions ("Task") or under highly arousing instructions ("Test") in groups of twenty to thirty students. Performance was on the average higher after Test than after Task instructions. Performance was higher for those low in Zuckerman and Allison's "fear of success," a linear relationship under Test instructions and a nonlinear relationship under Task instructions. No interactions were statistically significant. Reanalysis of the data in terms of effect size indices revealed small effects: comparing the performance profile under Test and Task instructions of the students low in Zuckerman and Allison's "fear of success" with the profile for the students high in this measure of "fear of success" resulted in a d(males) of .08 and a d(females) of .22, both in the predicted direction but small.

[20]Personal communication from Peter Gumpert and Donnah Canavan-Gumpert, May 1975 (cf. also Shaver, 1976). Another explanation of this zero-order correlation is method variance, used also to explain the low correlations between thematic assessments and questionnaire measures of nAch (cf. Chapter 4).

From a post-experimental questionnaire, level of importance to succeed was rated lower by students high (vs. low) in Zuckerman and Allison's "fear of success." In general, success was more likely to be attributed to internal factors than to external factors. Zuckerman and Allison's "fear of success" was negatively related to internal attribution of success, and positively related to internal attribution of failure. In contrast, analyses of variance using Horner's FOS in place of Zuckerman and Allison's new measure showed no statistically significant main or interaction effects for the FOS factor.

This scale was not related to any other sorts of behavior or measures (e.g., "fear of failure"). While reliability criteria were adequately met, validation in the relationship to behavior was not very strong.

In embracing any of these new measures, there is a danger of repeating the misunderstandings about Horner's measure with a new instrument. It has been clearly demonstrated that the phrase "fear of success" attracts attention, but that any one scale "measures" a person's individual fear any better than another cannot at this point be known. It would be premature to switch altogether to any of the so-called "objective" questionnaire measures of "fear of success." A "true" response to "I believe successful people are often sad and lonely" has face validity for a success-avoidant orientation, and perhaps rests in an attitude scale with impressive construct validity (e.g., relationship to performance profiles). Relying on such scale scores would lead us, however, to lose sight of the important clinical dynamics (cf. Chapters 1 and 7) to be learned from projectives, important in this early stage of research to understand the exact meaning of the paradoxical phenomenon of a "fear" of "success." A questionnaire has fixed the meaning of a concept while a projective has not. The latter method is less tidy and not clearcut, but at this time so is the concept of "fear of success."

Other Systems

There are two earlier and less comprehensively studied scoring systems for "fear of success." Good and Good (1973) developed a 29-item true–false questionnaire in response to Horner's research on "fear of success" which included items such as "I am sometimes afraid to do things as well as I know that I could" and "I sometimes do less than my best so that no one will be threatened.'' Though criteria of reliability were satisfactorily established for this scale (KR-20 = .81), no relationships to other measures or to a behavioral criterion were tested. Much earlier was the simple free association measure used by Haimowitz and Haimowitz (1958) in their article on ''The evil eye: fear of success.'' They asked one hundred college freshmen to free associate to ten words or phrases. Five of these words were neutral (e.g., billboard, crayon) and five indicated ''success'' (e.g., new car, best in class, a lovely marriage, promotion). Nearly three thousand associations were made to the words. Anxiety was inferred from crossed-out or misspelled words, unpleasant or negative phrases, or complete blocking of any response. Thirteen percent of the students responded with some form of anxiety to the ''success'' words. For example, ''best in class'' (similar to ''top in medical school class'') yielded ''stupid bum,'' ''teacher's pet,'' ''no friends,'' ''show-off,'' and ''time for nothing but study.'' This scale has not been used since, and was not accompanied by any assessments of reliability or validity.[21]

OVERVIEW: THE PERFORMANCE OF FOS

To recapitulate, there have been several central questions in the investigations of fear of success. First, do females show more ''fear of success'' imagery than do males? The answer we found in Chapter 5, based on many studies, is no. Second, do males respond to a cue depicting an achieving female with more ''fear of success'' imagery than do females? No. Third, have the proportions of ''fear of success'' imagery elicited by men and women in response to verbal cues changed over the last decade? For both genders there has been a very erratic and weak trend to a slight decrease. Fourth, what are the correlates of ''fear of success?'' Almost none of the expected associates are consistently correlated, positively or negatively, including ability, gender-role identification, anxiety, and age; an association between FOS and a feeling of external vs. internal control, and

[21]Gender differences were unspecified in the article, and were lost with the original data (M. L. Haimowitz, personal communication, 1973). I am grateful to Joe Pleck for bringing this piece to my attention (J. Pleck, personal communication, 1971).

cooperative vs. competitive style, were two exceptions. Finally, what is the relationship between "fear of success" imagery and performance in different kinds of situations (e.g., female achievement behavior in competition with men)? This was the province of Chapter 6, and the conclusion was that the "fear of success" effect had not been clearly and repeatedly established. Supportive results certainly do exist, but why are these not more numerous and consistent? To top it off, numerous technical difficulties were pointed out in various contexts of these three chapters with the conceptualization and execution of studies of "fear of success."

There is another level of criticism of the current research on fear of success. It is difficult enough for the natural scientist to say, for example, using the complicated methods of his field he must tell us that using spray deodorants will result in greater risk of skin cancer to ourselves and others through depletion of the ozone layer of the atmosphere. Unexplained are those complicated methods, the assumptions about models of the earth, the effect sizes thought to be worthy of note, and so forth. Like skin cancer, people can worry about whether they have the disease of fear of success without worrying about the assumptions behind that construct and trusting that the scientist is right. A symposium at a recent annual meeting of the Massachusetts Psychological Association was entitled, "Fear of Success: Is It Curable?" Female (and male) students have expressed concern at whether they might have *it*—recognizing in themselves the common anxiety felt in testing situations, they have wondered aloud if this means they will sabotage themselves when it comes to medical school, a typical adolescent paranoia about the fateful, tragic hand lurking in them too. The response to the very idea of fear of success is interesting in and of itself, and deserves further study. The question in this context is: what sort of idea has been unleashed? Have talented women who aspire been further burdened by worry about a hidden foe within themselves?

These questions and answers bring on the final question: should "fear of success" be abandoned as a useless and perhaps destructive psychological construct? My answer is no. I find "fear of success" a marvelous term, bringing together many different sorts of observations about human nature, and stimulating the expostulations of many, where more cautious terms like "anticipatory anxiety about public success at a classroom task" would have gone unnoticed. The task now is to separate the worthwhile material from the misled and misleading. The expenditure of time and energy in the pursuit of "fear of success" proves the lasting interest of a problem shown in Part I to be as old as society. In the myths, the materials from anthropology, sociology, and depth psychology, we found a "fear of success" linked to the deepest groans of the person in the social machine. How can any one or any small set of studies in social psychology, within the rules of laboratory technique and rules of inference, grasp the existential grandeur of this pain? Voluminous though it may be, the research on fear of success is still very young. We now know what questions are not worth spending energy on—the simple sensational claims about gross gender differences and so forth. What then are the next steps for research on "fear of success"? This question stimulates another question: why were the psychoanalytic and anthropological approaches in Part I so rich and interesting and understandable concerning "fear of success" while the conventional personality/social psychological methods were so barren? A full answer to this question is the province of Part III, where a synthesis of these two approaches is mapped out. In this context, however, there are three themes concerning suggestions for future work in the next section of this chapter.

ISSUES IN FUTURE RESEARCH

In the positivist scientific model used in modern social psychology, the inference of a truth for all humans in a specified group is made from a probability statement about how the average member of that group acts when compared with the average behavior in other groups. Ideally, in this model, any test of the hypothesized truth is as good as any other test. The intention is to demonstrate this truth in such a way that any person carefully following the list of directions of the previous researcher ("replicating the experiment") can come up with the same results. When these results fail to appear the second time, or if the results appear to suggest the reverse of the originally demonstrated truth, scientists look to their list of directions (and sometimes to the credentials of the investigators), trying to find the flaw. When several competent researchers follow the list of directions closely and come up with contradictory results, the positivist scientific model reaches a dead end.

Research on "fear of success" has not been so systematic, but the results are certainly contradictory. I have avoided invidious comparisons of the quality of the studies of different authors since in my experience the true quality of a piece of research cannot be reliably determined from what is written in the paper. More important at this point is the realization that certain questions and certain experimental designs do not provide information that can be used fruitfully in the understanding of the phenomenon of fear of success. My hope is that this collection of suggestions will permit future researchers to go beyond these useless endeavors.

If the research in this area were about anything less personally involving than a "fear" of "success," the area may well have been abandoned some time ago. It is because researchers, their colleagues, and their students know well persons debilitated by anxieties upon the attainment of a long-sought desire or by concerns about the gender-role appropriateness of a career line of interest that they persist with the investigation.

Whereas Part II reveals a score of reasons why Horner's original hypothesis cannot be accepted as proven—whether it be inadequacies in experimental design, use of projective measurement, statistical technique, interpretation—a weak denotation should not becloud a strong connotation of this work. Horner has made accessible to study the idea of a "fear of success"—is this a powerful mythic conception in our culture, a folk belief of our own? Perhaps so. Undergraduate and graduate students flock with interest to this idea. Shaver (1976) describes his resistant cooperation in several undergraduate projects to study FOS, three of which were published in professional journals. Inquiry motivated by personal involvement in a strong and latent folk belief should not be scoffed at. As more sophisticated designs are employed in this inquiry, perhaps a unitary construct for FOS will emerge as a measurable personality variable which can predict future behavior.

While there are many suggestions throughout Part II concerning designs and issues in this future research, several points are briefly restated here.

To begin with, since the reanalysis at the beginning of this chapter points up a particular relationship between "need for achievement" thematic imagery, "fear of success" thematic imagery, and "achievement behavior," a careful replication of Horner's study relating themes to behavior is necessary. Variability in thematic scores, the greatest concern of researchers, is not a serious drawback for a thematic measure of FOS if such a measure is found to be related to an important kind of behavior. The absence of any such replication of Horner's controversial study in the midst of so much other experimental work on "fear of success" is puzzling and unfortunate.

A main task in future work is to relate incessantly the details of research to the many theoretical issues of the first two chapters. Three issues are given here as reminders.

Avoidance Phenomena

Relative to scales and scoring systems for approach motivation (e.g., achievement, power), such devices to measure avoidance motivation have been unsuccessful, yielding insignificant and inconsistent results. I attribute this to the nature of avoidance. While there are few ways to approach a single goal, there are many ways to avoid it. These include passive strategies—negativism, seclusiveness or insulation, regression, repression, and fantasy—and active strategies—flight, attention getting, identification, compensation, rationalization, and other kinds of counterphobic aggressive approach behaviors. Perhaps for the reason of this diversity, an idiographic (vs. nomothetic) approach should be taken to avoidance phenomena, where these behaviors are understood in concrete, individual, or unique terms. In any case, while "fear of success" might be fruitfully retained as an omnibus label for a group of anxieties, those anxieties need more specific and recognizable labels. Examples of more descriptive and cautious terms are "anticipatory anxiety about public success at a classroom task" or "distress about doing too well in comparison to others;" they are clumsy, but are more accessible to common understanding. Jumping to a more "objective" questionnaire measure of "fear of success" is premature at this point since in nearly every case the meaning of this catchy paradoxical term has been inadequately questioned and understood. This point is more fully developed in Part III of this book.

Avoidance Motivation

In the achievement motivation tradition, there is the question if "fear of success" is different from a "fear of failure." To separate these as constructs, "fear of success" must be shown to lead to a performance decrement in achievement-oriented competition where success may be an outcome; "fear of success" must not lead to performance decrements in the face of failure. A "fear of failure" could, however, lead to aggressive success striving, while for the most part the situation would be avoided in one way or another. This differentiation of course depends on *a priori* determinations of the Incentives and Expectancies of the experimental or natural situation (Atkinson, 1964), which naturally require a knowledge of the situational determinants of these behaviors which we do not at present possess.

It is unclear, however, that these constructs can be differentiated, especially considering the similarity of scoring systems for them (cf. Chapter 2). Even if we find consistent, strong results for avoidance of success, it may be difficult to add a third factor to the widely used two-factor motivational models. Dichotomous splits (either two-dimensional or bipolar) into positive motivation vs. negative motivation types (Arnold, 1962), ego-philic vs. ego-phobic orientation (Lilly, 1958), optimists vs. pessimists (Nuttin, 1967; Knapp and Green, 1964), found a translation in Heckhausen's (1967) system as success-orientation vs. failure-orientation. He paralleled these to Atkinson's "Hope of Success" vs. "Fear of Failure." Further differentiations, given the still uncertain empirical status of the operationalizations of the existing terms as well as the uncertainty concerning a new term, might unduly complicate the current system.

The possible equivalence of FOS, test anxiety, and "fear of failure" (whether measured from the scale of Mandler and Sarason, 1952; or Alpert and Haber, 1960) means an integration of all these professional literatures—a task barely begun here.

Is there a fear in "fear of success?" Such questions reflect on the whole framework of motivational theory from which the modern concept of "fear of success" was derived.

Success

"Fear of success" has been found to be highly satisfying as a term which helps to label and organize a great range of previously unconnected personal experiences. This is fundamentally due to the current ambivalence about success hidden beneath the widespread assumption that everyone (everybody else) knows what it is, and that it is everyone's goal. Indeed, the surge of research on FOS has led to more published material on reactions to *success in America* than any other segment of current sociological literature. Dissemination of the idea has opened up new controversy about the nature of success, competition, and gender-role constraints.

FOS has been referred to as FOS, FS, M_{-S}, and "fear of success," showing the different theoretical contexts into which the concept has been taken. Many refer to FOS as fear of success, indicating their belief that FOS reveals a "fear" of "success," a conclusion that is possibly premature given the lack of definitions of the term. "Fear of success" is an explanation for everything or nothing; everyone has an opinion about it. But a closer look reveals little agreement about how it is defined.

Thus, the two central questions for this field are: when does a person avoid success, and, by the way, what do you mean by success?

PART III

CONCLUSION

Part I—"Fear of Success—Facts and Theories"—presented an arrangement of diverse sources from separate areas of research and inquiry which are not elsewhere integrated nor which recognize each other. These include anthropology, sociology, mythology, and psychoanalytic theory, as well as social psychology and personality psychology. The generous leavening of passages from fiction and popular books was added because literature can sometimes strike the right tone for a fuller social psychological understanding of the human experience or an expanded self-awareness where more careful scientific statements fail. Fear of success was found to be a concept of great scope, with profound intrapsychic and interpersonal repercussions.

Part II—"Recent Research on Fear of Success"—presented the research to date done on fear of success, stimulated in most cases by Matina Horner's dissertation work of 1964. This research as a whole remains inconclusive, balanced between promising and disappointing results. It does, however, suggest in which directions such research might now proceed.

Had the research summarized in Part II been more coherent, we might have been able to sketch an overarching synthesis of fear of success in this conclusion. This is not now possible. Perhaps because of the large scope of the idea, pertinent to so many areas of human experience, the many faces of fear of success could not be integrated into a neat whole. As I have said earlier in this book, I find this multiplicity attractive and useful, though I have acted to reduce its sprawl by bringing together as much of the theory and research as possible into one place.

The conclusion, denied the place of stamp of approval on what has gone before, moves simultaneously backward to Parts I and II and forward to new perspectives on fear of success. In the first of the two concluding sections—"Nomothetic and Idiographic Approaches"—the foundations of the social psychological methods used in the study of fear of success are scrutinized and found to be at least premature and perhaps inappropriate. Parts of three cases are presented which illustrate how complex this phenomenon is, complexities which must be grasped before we use social psychological methods to study it.

The final section—"The Fear of Success"—ranges over all the general issues of Part I, asking again what is meant by fear, success, and fear of success, and going beyond the fear of success conceptually and in one's own life.

CHAPTER 7

Progress for Fear of Success

NOMOTHETIC AND IDIOGRAPHIC APPROACHES

The social and personality psychology methods used in the recent study of a "fear of success" (FOS) rely on three major approaches typical to the behavioral sciences. The first is the nomothetic approach, that is, studying human behavior by comparing the average behavior of one group (naturally occurring or experimentally created) with the average behavior of another group. The individual is not important at this stage, and may never become the unit of analysis in the scientists' search for universals of human behavior.

The second major approach is the use of operationalization, that is, the labeling of a behavior or situation in terms of a theoretically important abstract concept. For example, pushing a shock button in one study and hitting a doll in another are called "aggressive behavior." The current research on FOS operationalizes a large set of concepts including career underattainment, achievement behavior, competition, and so forth. These have been operationalized by a set of settings, e.g., sitting in a classroom of other students near a particular student whose score on an anagrams test will be compared with one's own score in about eight minutes. Thus, in Horner's study, working for ten minutes on the GENERATION anagrams task has been understood to be the same as, or to symbolize, or to substitute for "achievement." "Achievement" has in turn been variously understood to be the same as, or to symbolize, or to substitute for "doing well" in school or "doing well" in the occupational structure and many other things, dramatically illustrated by the varied uses of "fear of success" (cf. Appendix A, Tresemer, 1976a). Thus, working on anagrams in a psychological experiment has been construed as operationally identical to all these "real-world" behavioral arenas.

The third major approach involves the process of inference. The first step of inference is from the average results (e.g., on an anagrams test of those showing FOS and those not showing FOS) to the experimental settings as they were created. Thus, if we put students in exactly that same situation next time, we would expect them to act in the same way. This step of inference is aided by statistical tests based on probability levels, or by estimates of effect sizes. The second level of inference is from this particular study back to the operationalized concept, such as achievement. Several sorts of expansion are possible: (1) subjects: what these students did goes for all female psychology students, or all female students, or all women, depending on how far the interpreter is willing to operationalize; (2) behaviors: what happens for anagrams happens for all forms of achievement; and (3) settings: what happened in that auditorium with the male students on one side and the females on the other happens for all actually or potentially mixed-gender settings, especially for example in male-dominated occupations. This step is supported not by statistical evidence but by the scientist's perogative to label a setting anything he or she desires provided he or she is explicit about exactly how the situation was created. Bakan (1966) criticized these second inferential jumps as sneaky; in this case, for example, the parallel or equivalence between anagrams performance and occupational achievement has not been demonstrated.

It should be clear that the nomothetic approach, operationalization, and the two steps of inference go hand in hand in the conduct of personality and social psychological research. The argument of this chapter is that, particularly in an inquiry into "success" and "fear of success," these approaches are at this time inappropriate, or at least inadequate. While the reader may be aware of several comments made throughout Parts I and II which indicate specific reasons for this point of view, the main themes of this argument will be illustrated here.

Studies demonstrating the hegemony of conformity over social behavior—indeed conformity as a social and moral good—are endemic to social psychology. There is a coherence available in the integration of diverse theoretical languages as presented in Chapter 3, each making similar generalizations about the conformity of the individual, that is compelling. This coherence is a property of a nomothetic approach to social phenomena, the seeking of broad generalizations about human behavior, in this case influenced by traditional Parsonian social theory of the normative order of society.

Role conflict between femininity and achievement must certainly exist from the point of view of the boundary-maintenance model sketchily presented earlier in Chapter 3. Two roles with demands on behavior that clash and contradict means conflict. But, as Johnson (1975) cogently argues, this is not necessarily the case—conflict must be witnessed as part of the subjective experience of the role-bound participant. Indeed, numerous exceptions can be found to disprove the hypothesis. For example, the argument of role conflict ("femininity and achievement are two desirable but mutually exclusive ends") implies that all women in these two roles would experience conflict; but, as is clear from Part II, this is not so. On the other hand, the lack of apparent conflict for many should not lead us to reject the notion altogether since this role conflict is clearly reported by some people. How do we resolve this contradiction?

The search in social science for generalizations about all human behavior is a nomothetic approach—seeking to establish the abstract recurrent universals of behavior in order to formulate scientific laws. The contrasting approach is the idiographic, where phenomena are understood in concrete, individual, or unique terms. Use of the conventional statistical methods which conclude "true" ($p < .05$) or "false" ($p > .05$) for an observed relationship make it impossible to say a relationship is both true and not true, or how much, or for whom. There are statistical methods that can be used to validate inferences of the idiographic kind; they range from revisions of current nomothetic methods (as in the effect size indices used in Part II) to the complex correlational treatment of patterns of data for each individual proposed by Herbst (1970).

Conformity is a central issue merely by virtue of the use of a nomothetic approach to method. The creation of hypotheses about human behavior in general in itself begs the question of whether or not and to what extent one conforms to that rule. The bulk of Chapter 3 is a good example of this, ignoring "how much" any of the supporting statements was true in favor of the organization of a grand pattern of converging theories into a large theory of boundary maintenance. An idiographic approach is more concerned with the individual's subjective response to social realities. Thus the scientific law of behavior is not hypostatized (or is at least viewed more flexibly) and the individual response is not relegated to confirming the law or being an exception; rather the individual is thoroughly investigated first.

Such a subjective understanding of our fellow men and women requires personal, intimate, face-to-face encounters. Johnson (1975, p. 21) suggests study "through personal autobiographical reconstructions, through our experiences with those we know well, through others' autobiographical and fictitious representations, and then through more structured research encounters, in the area of 'they' relationships, with unknown subjects."

Returning to our recurrent example, consider the following brief soliloquies by women entering Horner's "large-group mixed-sex competitive condition" (Session 1, "arousal") to work on a word game, and later showing higher scores while working alone:

1. Yikes! Competition against men! I can't do it! I'm afraid!
2. I feel it would be more appropriate to modulate my performance in this group so that I do not appear to be exceeding the proper limits of my gender role.
3. I do not accept this programming for competition, win or lose, me against others, sink or swim.
4. I've never seen so many psych. students in one place at one time. Look at Joe with his bright purple shirt! And there's Jane flirting with Bill across the room!

There are many other possible dynamics. The point is that what looks to be the same phenomenon from the word game scores is quite likely to be from many different sources. Since in the "Anne/

medical school" cue, the success was so prominent, any sort of anxiety would likely be written and read as related to success. If the criterion behavior is not doing well in the large group, then any of these women would be labeled as fearing success. The behavior cannot, however, be taken as sufficient evidence for the pathological syndrome. An example from the arena which the laboratory is intended to operationalize is the person turning down an offer for a higher paying job; if this is all we know, we would be rash to call it "fear of success." Another example: a carpenter friend refuses to take more than $3.50 an hour even though his skills could easily fetch more. Is this a dramatic behavioral indicator of a fear of success or a needed resistance to the wild accelerations of inflationary economics?

Cases

The complexities of an individual's FOS imagery and "fear of success" behavior must be found in a closer look at individuals. Would that I had been able to grab a bunch of my student "subjects" and talk with them for hours about their experience of "success;" but, as any researcher knows, there is hardly time for the nomothetic experiment without suddenly expanding its boundaries. Following then are several examples of clients from various therapy or workshop settings whose behavior could shed some light on a "fear of success."

Ted. A workshop participant was a thirty-year-old Californian who had owned a radio-repair shop, directed a public-relations campaign for a large industry, taught at a community college, and most recently had created a small business teaching body massage techniques. He did well each of the occupations he worked at; he had recently organized the teachers of massage in that area to distinguish them from the sex parlors that also advertised for massage. Much of his extra time was spent attending other workshops which kept his bank balance close to zero. His expanding familiarity and pleasure with the new humanistic and transpersonal psychologies is shown in the following story to "George is sitting in a chair with a smile on his face:"

> The place is here, the time now. George, a seeker of truth, beauty, and wisdom, has, after hours of contemplation, solved a very complicated problem that has plagued him muchly. As the light of wisdom dawns, he smiles and eases into a serene consciousness which pervades the entire room. All those who pass by, though they will share not a single word, will be filled with a sense of George's inner joy and come away fuller and happier for the contact.

However, the stories to "Al is looking into his microscope" and "After first term finals, John finds himself at the top of his medical school class" reveal a very different sort of personality dynamic.

> Al is a kid who just got a new microscope for Xmas. There is a big decorated Xmas tree behind him and his middle class, education-conscious parents are standing by his side gleaming with pride and fantasizing how Al will grow up some day to be a world-famous scientist. Al, on the other hand, is simply digging his new toy and, in the coming years, because of his parents' constant prodding, will come to hate science, though he will get a Ph.D. in micro-biology and transmit his hatred to thousands of students of his.

> Oh, John glapes and glapes! What joy! What exhilaration! After all the years of suffering, of studying, of self-sacrifice—to have at last achieved a measure of recognition! That night he and his "gang" go out and get bombed on beer, wine, whiskey, sex, and highness. In the midst of all this, John falls into a deep remorse, for he knows how little the grades mean, how little he knows—and he commits suicide. The End!

These latter two stories would be clearly scored for FOS imagery. This case adequately illustrates the importance of presenting more than one opportunity to write stories since the first story above would not be scored for FOS.[1] However, the magical aspects in that story are seen by Ovesey (1962) as the other side of the "fear of success" coin from fantasies of destruction (found in the third story). The tension between Ted and his parents hinted at in the second story was a confessed reason for attending various psychology workshops; he had spent his adult life seeking release from his mother. At the same time the autonomy was threatening and he "just wasn't

[1]In the newer system by Horner *et al.* (1973), this story would not be scored for the infrequent counterindicative category Absence of Others, which would still leave it as a zero, a very low score.

sure" about his various career pursuits. Each time he quit a new job for something else, he would punctuate the change with a visit "home."

The bizarre third story is used as an example of "General Inhibition Thema" in Chapter 4. After writing these stories, Ted referred to this one as creating tension for him. Medical school was the last place on earth he wanted to be—his mother was a nurse! He sought to create a bizarre story and, in this venture, succeeded.

While the brevity of my acquaintance prevented the construction of a case even approaching the thoroughness found in the psychoanalytic material (cf. citations in Chapter 1), we find here the same self-conception contaminated with self-depreciation.

Ollie. In this case, a different sort of exercise provided a different sort of projective test of a "fear of success."

Ollie knew of my work on "fear of success" and asked me if I thought he had *it* (Fear of Success), and what I might tell him that might cure his ailment or alleviate his distress. He told me he had spent over a hundred dollars on books concerning concentration, developing mind power, mysticism, etc.—the study which had taken much time away from his other work, in particular from his doctoral dissertation in international relations, had led to no changes, and only increased his sense of frustration.

I talked about psychomotor theory (Pesso, 1973)—especially about how emotional behavior can muck up the pure voluntary movement of getting things done, or attaining desired goals. I explained that any purely voluntary movement, ranging from picking up a paper clip to felling a tree, involves four steps: *deciding* what the goal of the action is, *planning* exactly how to get there, *implementing* this plan, and *verifying* that the plan has been carried out satisfactorily. His openness and intense curiosity led me to ask if he would like to try an exercise.

I showed him an exercise in conscious voluntary movement, involving the action of raising an arm to a forty-five degree angle. In this case, (1) the decision is the affirmation that you will raise the arm to a forty-five degree angle and becoming aware of where that is, (2) the planning is the preparation of all the separate muscles needed to do this, (3) the implementation is the enactment of the planned script—in this exercise not quickly and without thought but very

very slowly, concentrating with eyes unfocused, feeling each part of the planned movement as consciously and willfully as possible, and (4) the verification is the assessment of completion—visually, proprioceptively, or asking others. The individual variations in this exercise are exceedingly helpful in suggesting directions in personal work or therapy.

First, Ollie set himself a referrent on the floor: "If I raise my arm to there, it will be 45 degrees." Most of the movement felt automatic to him, except the last little bit, which he experienced as requiring tremendous mental effort. He was surprised when I pointed out that he had only gone about twenty degrees—after setting the external standard, it was "out of his hands." Of course, the externalization of the goal was crucial; the incorrectness of the external standard complicated its inferiority as a criterion.

A comment he made about feeling pulled back or prevented during the last bit of the movement led to the next version of the exercise: I asked him to do it again and told him I would act as an obstacle preventing him from lifting his arm, thus putting that inhibition he had earlier experienced outside himself. I asked him to be aware of what came to mind—who or what I represented. Poised in front of his forearm, I waited while he lifted his arm, this time much more slowly. The ruffled sleeve of his shirt hardly touched my hand when he stopped, excited with emotion. He told me that his experience of the heavy pressure of my hand—an extremely exaggerated perception—was very unpleasant; I represented the void, black and empty. It was scary to him and he felt he wanted to go around it, to skirt it. I commented on how it was becoming clear to him that there were emotional issues connected with voluntary movement. I suggested that sometimes a confrontation with a void represents the profound existential meeting with the meaninglessness of life as lived, or life in general; the reliance on external standards was the inability to decide on the worthiness of any goal. He was highly responsive to this suggestion, feeling it described his situation exactly. I encouraged him to confront the void directly and suggested we try one more variation in order to terminate our minisession positively, constructively.

I told him to push again and that I would let him, after some determined effort, overcome me, whoever I was or whatever I represented. I waited, poised, for the slow movement of his arm. He lifted against my hand and slowly increased pressure. I offered solid resistance and then began to give way, groaning slightly. The movement increased and groan crescendoed quickly; I backed off as if overcome while Ollie was propelled forward several steps. He was radiating with intense feeling and in a state of awe. He reported:

> I was in a tunnel, a dark coal mine deep in the earth, on a railroad track. I could see the shiny new tracks gleaming before me, heading straight ahead, and I was going down them. Then there was an obstacle across my path—there had been a cave-in and there were rocks and debris blocking the tunnel. There were side tunnels going off to either side but I kept on this track, straight ahead. And I was pushing against it, and I felt the degree (sic) begin to move. Like I was pushing through it. And I was really *curious* about that, it made me feel real *curious*. I didn't push through, I didn't actually get through that plug blocking up the hole but it started to move. I really felt *curious* about that. Just as I pushed you away, those rocks really started to move. It's like you disappeared—you, and the room, all of it—and I was in this cave.

Our discussion revealed that the term "curious" was a weakly transformed version of feeling good, elated, etc.—terms which he did use sparingly. I reminded him who I was and labeled some details of our reality situation. He was extremely surprised when he learned of his wonderful slip—using "degree" for "debris," both obstacles to him at the present time, the latter perhaps a symbolic version of the former. He remained thrilled about having a completely different sort of experience from every other he had known, and about the feeling of nascent progress, of "things beginning to move."

His attempts to intellectualize about his experience, categorize it, and thus usher it out of consciousness, were numerous, but happily simple. He persevered on his associations to the coal mine: why a coal mine? am *I* dark, cold, and dirty like that mine? Knowing there was probably something of importance in that material but not wanting, through further questioning, to arouse defenses of such strength that his experience would be obliterated, I cautioned against overanalysis and suggested he just mull over and reexperience the beginning of movement past the obstacle he was able to accomplish on his own. I deflected every question about psychomotor, about "what caves mean," about how I "got interested in this stuff," about what I do with other people, and so on in the same way. He thanked me intermittently for seeing through his devices; his elation and aroused energy remained intact. He thanked me for what I had done many times and each time I complimented him on *his* accomplishment.

Further contacts showed a willingness and ability to understand many sorts of voluntary movement in terms of the four steps, and to perceive the symbolic aspects of his experiences with this exercise in many parts of his life.

The following is Ollie's story to the cue "After much hard work, Joe has finally gotten what he wanted:"

> Joe has just been accepted for a job he's been really hoping to get. After four years of college and a lot of work, the position he has worked for has accepted him. He had to sacrifice much of his social time during college but now he'll have a lot of free time because he won't have to work in the summer. Joe feels really great and nothing can put him in a bad mood now. He plans to go to work with a lot of enthusiasm because he knows all the hard times have paid off.

There is no clear FOS imagery here or in the other stories he wrote, even though anxiety about doing well and attaining the long-sought degree was evidenced so clearly in the motoric and emotional aspects of the arm-lifting exercise.

Likewise, in a workshop at an urban day hospital for incapacitated people, including alcoholics, schizophrenics, the marginally retarded, and others of society's rejects, all in the clutch of varying degrees of anxiety, I was surprised to find that the TAT-type stories were devoid of FOS imagery. At the same time, the stories showed a real but more complex correspondence with these peoples' current circumstances and were very helpful in arranging an appropriate therapy.

Deborah. Deborah had held a series of important secretarial and assistant positions in local government and in the legal profession, but always left after a few months. As she gained a place of increased trust and responsibility, and was nearing the possibility of a promotion, she would begin to have difficulty walking, would experience a loss of sensitivity or a tingling in her fingers and toes, and would have attacks of anger at those close to her. She knew she was afraid but didn't know of what, and always quit her job to stay at home for a while and "get myself together." On two occasions she turned down a promotion because "it just wasn't right—it was a man's job." Here we encounter the frequent overlap between a neurotic "fear of success" (fear of aggression, of separation, of Oedipal victory) and and a social boundary-maintaining "fear of success" (fear of gender-role-inappropriate pursuits).

Two days after an offer from the mayor's office to work as director's assistant in a new department for design of the city's transportation system, Deborah emptied the kitchen shelves of their dishes and smashed them against the wall one-by-one. In the following days, she began feeling a tingling sensation in her scalp, toes, and fingers, and occasionally felt that she was disappearing. She quit her job and referred herself to therapy.

I do not intend to spend too much time on the details of Deborah's fascinating case. A few of the events of her life are important because they are recognizable as extreme versions of experiences everyone has had. For example, in the course of therapy she related a pivotal event from her childhood. She told it as follows:

> You know, children like flowers and things, and when I was a child I had arranged a bunch of flowers in several pots at the front of our house. I took pride in it and after school I would move the pots around and try different arrangements and water the flowers. It really was very pretty. It was sort of for other people, you know put a little enjoyment, a little color, in their lives. One day a very nice gentleman stopped by and said he was so happy these flowers were there, and I got flustered, and hemmed and hawed and blushed and gave excuses. I couldn't accept it, I was a great success! And I couldn't accept it. It's been that way every since.

This should be a familiar form of fear of success. At some point, everyone has had difficulty in accepting even the simplest confirmations and validations for one's effort, evading the reward with "no, I didn't do that" or "it's not really that good."

Whenever Deborah told this story, she rubbed her eyes with tight fists. We discovered that she had done this also when her admirer was commenting on her flowers. She did not cry when she did this; she said she felt it was keeping her exophthalmic eyes from popping out. This gesture turned out to be very important to her therapy, relating to self-punishment as a result of Oedipal guilt over both patricidal and matricidal wishes, a reminder of Oedipus' blinding the eyes that witnessed his transgressions.

Concerning her most recent dropout from a job, Deborah explained that things were "too good—I knew something had to happen." Things really weren't that good: the job paid little, her apartment was small and far from work, her diet was progressing very slowly. However, for Deborah, life was at a point of *relative* success, and she experienced this as *too much*. The breakdown was clearly brought on by this experience of excessive success, and recognition—by the mayor's office!—of her talents. Through our work together, fear of success was the single thread which pulled together all of her recent experiences and made sense of her pain. The energy which she was able to marshal to seek reemployment was reinforced and further developed. As she was able to recognize and deal with past experiences, she was able to master her inappropriate fears of occupational attainment.

Deborah's case is a good example of clinical fear of success since it shows some of the common intrapsychic and interpersonal themes enumerated in Chapter 1, elaborated in a very personal way. In any personal work with (or personal understanding of) fear of success, the common themes are only general guides. We can now take a look at Deborah's responses to some of the evaluative measures of "fear of success" from personality research.

Deborah's story to the "Judy is sitting in a chair with a smile on her face" cue was as follows:

> She is at the movies watching Fred Astaire and Ginger Rogers dancing. The people are the audience, anonymous. She feels happy, content, simple, a part of the movie.

In response to the cue, "After much work, Jane has finally gotten what she wanted," Deborah wrote

> I really don't know Jane and cannot write a story about her.

Though we find avoidance of successes in her behavior, we find none in her stories. The kind of blocking found in the second story, more extreme in instances where the story is left completely blank, is not currently scored as FOS imagery. Such a judgment would require an altogether different level of interpretation of the thought sample represented on the page; rather than piecing together elements of a story plot, the scorer must make a guess at less certain aspects of the person's behavior.

When Deborah worked on the GENERATION anagram task, she ignored the obvious words like "on" and "at," and created a small number of remarkable anagrams including "goatee" and "tangerine." Her final score was, however, lower, suggesting the reduced productivity that should accompany a "fear of success." This kind of anagram task confuses creativity with gross output. Whittemore (1924) and Deutsch (1949) have found creativity lower and productivity higher in a competitive setting than in a cooperative one. Does use of this instrument for measuring performance indicate a preference for quantity over quality? How can we understand this woman in terms of the theory of "fear of success" as it is currently assessed and validated?

The Proper Place of Stories

A series of stories can provide supplementary and supportive material for an understanding of the individual. Any one story, however, should not be relied upon as sole evidence of the presence of a personality trait or a total life posture. For example, the following story about Anne at the top of her medical school class is an example from Horner's dissertation:

> She starts proclaiming her surprise and joy. Her fellow classmates are so disgusted with her behavior that they jump on her in a body and beat her. She is maimed for life.

This story was horribly and dramatically portrayed in an animated segment of a recent film (Radcliffe College, 1973). The woman was scrawny, pursued and beaten, in a bizarre way only possible with the fantasy camera of animation. This scene was contrasted with the image from a supposedly typical male story: a square-shouldered Horatio Alger figure with curly blonde locks waving in the breeze of his acclaim whose academic robes transform to the doctor's gown, a patriarchal image of awesome power and intelligence in service of the social good (and served by it). It is unclear that the female or male writers of these stories actually intended such scenes to happen. The standard Thematic Apperception Test (TAT) involves many stories and is most fruitfully understood in the context of the whole person. Without other information, we cannot know if the "maimed for life" story was a symbolic indication of the author's deepest fears about competition against males. Perhaps it was the most humorful or creative four-minute plot the author could think of after writing five other four-minute stories. Occasional violent thoughts are normal, and it is not always clear for what reason they occur. Though the themes expressed correspond to psychological issues discussed in Chapter 1, we must know more about the person before we conclude she'll never apply to medical school or she'll never try to do well academically or she should enter psychotherapy. The material from these stories should not be treated as literal documentary about a person's life or attitudes, or about the social condition.

Many psychologists would at this point make the practical suggestion that we simply not use these troublesome projective instruments, and switch instead to more clearly interpretable "objective" questionnaire measures. As was discussed at the end of Chapter 6, these are not really solutions to the problems revealed here. The fault is not so much in the use of projectives as in the nature of the idea "fear of success." The possession of a "score" is not the signal to relax our efforts to understand what a "fear of success" might be. Indeed, the stories help us see the psychodynamics that might involve a "fear of success" in a way disallowed by a tally from a questionnaire of simple true–false items. Such use of stories would be a return to current uses of the TAT and to the assessments of basic personality themes devised by the originator of the TAT, Henry Murray (1938).[2]

Real-life fear of success is far more serious than the level on which our measures have been working; to very many the concept has had great personal appeal, allowing them to organize previously

[2]The few clinical case studies based on Horner's theory of "fear of success" (Fodor, 1974; Porjesz, 1974) have, unfortunately, not used story-writing exercises to help elucidate the psychodynamics of the individual. Spence's (1974) revised technique of assessment potentially involves story themes as additional information.

unconnected personal experiences. When the research methods lag so far behind the richness of personal (idiographic) meaning, it is time to change the research methods.

Idiographic Approach to Avoidance Motivation

Perhaps the idiographic approach is more appropriate for an investigation of avoidance phenomena in general, especially to the extent that these phenomena are not simply cognitive (as in avoidance of a hot stove) but involve emotional reactions based on more or less varied personal histories. Indeed, as Weinstein and Platt (1973) have persuasively shown, reactions to the threat of loss (basic to avoidance of boundary transgression) take on unpredictable and idiosyncratic forms (e.g., withdrawal and passivity, escape, compliance, counterphobic approach, denial, and so on) based on the individual's unique emotional history. This individual variation disallows any generalizations of a nomothetic sort about the behavior of human beings in general or specific groups concerning situations eliciting these emotions.[3] In fact, if we gather together all of the available studies on avoidance phenomena, defensive processes, and responses to fear and anxiety, we find a great many confusing and contradictory results. The rare strikingly significant finding is often followed by a string of nonreplications.

In the context of Part I, the avoidance reaction is theoretically dependent on a conflictful interpretation of success. This involves all that is *not* simple and straightforward about "success," all that is ambivalent, especially to the extent that it conflicts with "success" in one's gender role. Indeed, the many uses of the terms "success" and "failure" have seldom been accompanied by precise operational

[3]Weinstein and Platt (1973) go so far as to say that psychoanalytic theory, inasmuch as it is primarily concerned with the emotional experiences underpinning (i.e., historically responsible for) current behavior, *cannot* be integrated with sociological (or social psychological) theory. The latter theoretical domains are concerned with organizing general explanations for group phenomena. This is exactly the idiographic/nomothetic split as we have presented it. My own view is that both are right; this is why both approaches are presented in the first three chapters. The task is to integrate them. Weinstein and Platt (1973) begin to lay the complex ground rules for how these disciplines can be made compatible (cf. also Nagel, 1961, pp. 547–551).

definition, the assumption being that they plainly define themselves. The problem of how "success" in one area may mean "failure" in another and the consequent complexity with which such a "success" must be viewed has consequently been disregarded. But it is clear that variability in individual interpretations of "success" of various sorts compounds the influence of individual, as opposed to group, factors on success avoidance. This level of analysis was only just begun in the section on "Success" in Chapter 2.

The implication of this view is that research on avoidance phenomena and conflicts concerning such difficult personal concepts as "success" can only be understood with the greatest emphasis on the individual, perhaps even at a clinical level. At this stage of knowledge perhaps we should refrain from imposing our categories on our subjects and openly observe what is occurring. Analyses of important factors in the lives of many individuals as they relate to success avoidance can then eventually be combined to provide some ideas about the individual differences that might be responsible for the success-avoidance phenomenon. The integrative effort in the early part of this work (Chapter 3) was an attempt to make this synthesis, but was not complete enough to generate adequate research designs. Indeed, the psychoanalytic (and clinical) literature is not well integrated with the social psychological (or sociological) literature on group phenomena in general. We must further develop the relationship of the relatively more idiographic understandings of avoidance phenomena (and specifically success avoidance) found in the former sources to the general social psychological models of proscribed behavioral domains and their boundaries.

THE FEAR OF SUCCESS

David McClelland, a modern theorist and researcher on achievement motivation, whose works are cited as authoritative several places in Chapters 2 and 4, used the term "fear of success" for the first time in his voluminous writings in the book *Power: The Inner Experience* (1975). There he used it twice: as a description of the conflicts between power, achievement, and femininity for white

American women as revealed in Horner's research (p. 91), and also as a label, perhaps even as a diagnosis, of an individual whose power visions he analyzed (p. 212). Let me tell the story of this individual without revealing his identity until a little later.

The man's father was a prosperous lawyer living in a wealthy Boston suburb, an integral member of an influential and established Jewish family. However, "his father he saw as someone who had been tremendously successful but who had paid in his view a terrible price in unhappiness" (McClelland, 1975, p. 212). There is little information given about his mother.

His father seemed eager to share his success with his son. "When he was in his early twenties, he was made special assistant to his father, then President of the New Haven Railroad. There he had all sorts of power over men with years of experience in railroading. The experience frightened him so much that he had to arrange quickly to get someone appointed in his place to still his anxiety" (McClelland, 1975, p. 212). Later the man distinguished himself as a professor of psychology at Harvard, where McClelland knew him. As he put it himself, "the keys of the kingdom were handed to me"—respect and notoriety in academic circles for his work financed by federal research grants, as well as personal wealth and links with prominent businessmen. He owned a Mercedes automobile, a Cessna airplane, and expensive antiques; he gave "charming" dinner parties and was sought after by many for his cogent witticisms. This life too he rejected, after a difficult personal search through experiences with hallucinogenic drugs. So he dropped out, and McClelland wondered if he did not fear success.

McClelland's diagnosis would be acceptable without question, as if taken from the first pages of the first chapter, if the story ended here. But this man returned from a pilgrimage to India as Baba Ram Dass (formerly Richard Alpert) to become a spiritual leader for thousands of Americans. Whereas before, when giving lectures, at which he was quite competent, he would get "extraordinary diarrhea and tension," now he was calm throughout his public appearances. Whereas before it was a challenge to hold any college audience for fifty minutes, now he would sit for as many as six hours answering questions of the enthralled young seekers. Whereas before he had great difficulty with writing in collaboration with other professionals, now he shared in a cooperative effort at the Lama Foundation to produce the inspiring book *Be Here Now* (Lama Foundation, 1971).

McClelland interpreted Alpert's embrace of Hinduism to be evidence in and of itself of the escape from success, success here being in the American business and academic spheres. I suggest that the current occupation of Ram Dass cannot be judged as any worse (even if no better) than the successes he rejected. The story of the end of an illustrious career through fear of success might turn into a story of the beginning of a very different success. This discussion leaves us with two important questions. First, if Baba Ram Dass did have a "fear of success," then why does he not continue to experience anxiety in his new success? That is, what is meant by "success" and "fear of success?" Second, is a "fear of success" a dead end proposition? That is, is there not sometimes a constructive sequel to a fear and avoidance of success? These questions shall be the focus of the next two sections.

The Meaning of Success

In a brilliant commentary on the idea of a fear of success in women, Sonya Rudikoff (1974; also 1975) analyzed the lives of several women she considered public examples of the amalgam between a personal vision and a social recognition of success: Martha Graham, Marie Curie, Rose Kennedy, the von Richthofen sisters, Jane Addams, Helene Deutsch, Margaret Mead, and Hannah Senesh. In a compassionate review of the details of the lives of these women—their conflicts and achievements, devotions and disappointments—she finds little use for the terms "fear of success" or "fear of failure" or "psychological barriers to success." Success was different to each of these women and was incidental to the true goals of their work.

> Clearly, then, there is too simplistic an idea of success in all the talk about women and achievement. There are surely lives which display very few of the signs of success until very late, or after life is over. There are lives of great significance which go unrecognized by peers for a very long time, there are those who achieve nothing for themselves but leave a legacy for others who come after, there are lives sacrificed for causes. (1975, p. 58)

The definitions of the terms "success" and "achievement" given by the psychologists (in Parts I and II) are much different, more narrow, more confined than those in the culture at large. Indeed, McClelland has said that had he and his associates known in the late 1940s that the psychological research being done on achievement motivation, or the need to achieve, was going to become so violently controversial, they would have labeled what they were studying "need for efficiency." Yet psychologists too take freedoms with the terms they use. Would such a label as "need for efficiency" have attracted so much comment, so many diligent researchers, or so much government support for training projects both here and abroad?

The same is true, of course, for "fear of success"—the term has that magic word "success" in it, so naturally every American has a flood of opinions about the possibility of a fear of success, who might fear success, when, and so forth. "Fear" is also a word with some magic about it, since basically we all know that "success" is good but "fear" bad. In combination, these words have the ability to encompass so much, to expand and contract in meaning and implication depending on the momentary needs of the writer. The current work is no exception, since a single definition of "success" or "fear of success" could not be found and the ambience of these terms had to be evoked repeatedly in discussions of the uses to which they have been put.

The contraction and expansion of meaning and implication is certainly unavoidable on a personal level, for how vague is Thoreau's (1854, p. 148) definition of a personal success:

> If the day and night are such that you greet them with joy, and life emits a fragrance like flowers and sweet-scented herbs, is more elastic, more starry, more immortal—that is your success. All nature is your congratulation, and you have cause momentarily to bless yourself.

Such poetry is necessary both to design one's own vision and to bring forth an understanding from reading the creative story-writing exercises of others. Fear, success, and fear of success are most importantly individual matters, and are useful for research only when defined so carefully that the term "fear of success" becomes a general category for several identifiable variables.

Beyond Fear of Success

William James (1900) defined self-esteem in ratio terms:

$$\text{Self-esteem} = \frac{\text{Success}}{\text{Pretensions}}$$

If one's success in the world be small but the pretensions (goals, expectations) smaller, then the self-esteem may still be great. The American dream demands for each the highest pretensions; life then is the bitter lesson that the hoped-for success is unattainable. Self-esteem suffers.

Thoreau (1854, p. 222) reacts: "We will not be shipwrecked on a vain reality." James, too, several pages after discussing his formula, approvingly quotes Carlyle:

> Make thy claim of wages a zero, then hast thou the world under thy feet. Well did the wisest of our time write, it is only with renunciation that life, properly speaking, can be said to begin. (James, 1900, p. 188)

Shatter the demands of a public success and seek to find your own "different drummer"—this is the message of countless wise men from our past and our present. David Riesman (1954) has encouraged the success-oriented Americans to have the "nerve of failure" or the ability to face the possibility of defeat without being morally crushed, requiring a more malleable and mature set of Pretensions. In this regard he quotes a saying of Nahman of Bratzlav (Riesman, 1954, p. 47):

> Victory cannot tolerate truth, and if that which is true is spread before your eyes, you will reject it, because you are a victor. Whoever would have truth itself, must drive hence the spirit of victory; only then may he prepare to behold the truth.

A few more examples of similar sentiment are cited in Chapter 2, but the same choice is presented in all of the great religions, much of modern philosophy, and parts of psychology. Thus, there are other often more compelling reasons than gender-role inappropriateness to avoid public success.

There is a tremendous difference between those who confront the fear of a success, than confront the success and reject it, and those who assuage their fear by avoiding these confrontations altogether.

In the example of Ram Dass, had he not confronted his fear and tried out what was anxiety-provoking as well as actively sought its antidote, he would today be a tired businessman, professor, or "dropout" burned out by his own physical and emotional tensions. Business or academic pursuits may be well suited for some who can fashion them into successes with personal meaning; the final occupation does not really matter. The obstacle in a personal sense is not the horror of a worldly success or the fall from success, but the *fear* of success. The success of Paradise was not lost to man through the original sin of ambition but gave way to an awakening of consciousness capable of bringing, in each person's life, new successes at higher levels (Suarès, 1970; Edinger, 1972). Even if a success leads to a failure, there are opportunities for growth and learning in this process unavailable to the person prevented from moving in any direction by anticipatory anxiety.

Indeed the fear of success can often be found to be linked to that personality construct the Jungians have called the shadow, a powerful feeling of inferiority or guilt in one's psyche, a dark thing often projected onto an outside object which can be combated, punished, or exterminated. Yet the shadow must be confronted within. Many brands of education and personal growth—from Outward Bound survival schools to meditation centers to styles of psychotherapy—are specifically designed to give the pupil opportunities to confront his or her own sense of limitations and surpass it.

The shadow is also expressed in the enculturated certainty that the wheel of fortune will turn and a success will be followed inexorably by a failure equal and opposite in its strength. There are certainly social psychological reasons for these expectations to be found, as enumerated especially in Chapter 3. But none of these social boundary-maintaining mechanisms should be regarded as inescapable reins on personal development. They can be overcome—first of all by recognizing one's own deeply rooted programs of failure after success. Indeed, one of the reasons so much material was packed into Part I was to reveal how widespread is this cultural programming. Awareness of these sources for our attitudes may help us overcome them.

Reprogramming with simple affirmations is a possible next step. One personal growth technique repeatedly asserts, "Good times don't have to end—things just keep getting better." Another uses the familiar "Every day in every way I'm feeling better and better and better." (Both schools claim that these affirmations are only really effective if gone over while relaxed or in "alpha" state, in contrast to the tense or "beta" state of the fears being disspelled.) Fear of success need not be treated as a permanent flaw of the personality but, in some cases, as a timely catalyst for difficult, but progressed, personal growth.

Two examples show how these personal visions have been integrated into group settings. The first involves the brand of volleyball played at Twin Oaks, a prospering community inspired by B. F. Skinner's *Walden Two* of nearly a hundred people (cf. Kinkade, 1973). Each summer night, after supper and a day's work, many will gather for volleyball outside the original farmhouse. The formations are the same and before each new server there is a rotation of place. However, at each shift, one person in the front row crosses under the net in one direction and one person crosses in the other, thereby changing teams. There are no teams, and no team competition, and one plays "against" as well as with one's teammates.

Competition is a major organizing principle of economic activity in American society. "Perfect competition" requires complete independence of units and noncommunication between them, requires that none of the units has any greater than a small fraction of the power, and requires equal knowledge of opportunities (e.g., offers to buy and sell) given by the participants in the market (Stigler, 1968). The application of "perfect competition" to human organization in the meritocracy of achievement has been criticized by many, as summarized in Chapter 2. A specific criticism is the lower quality, albeit greater quantity, produced in an atmosphere of severe competition (Allee, 1948; Deutsch, 1949; Riesman, 1954).

The second example is the Findhorn community, tantalizingly introduced by Paul Hawken (1975; and by tapes and papers available from the Findhorn Foundation, Findhorn Bay, Forres, Moray, Scotland). The central characters in the early years of this thriving community were uniform in their disregard for conventional success goals and modes of striving, in favor of complete spiritual guidance. The community is full of the refugees of abandoned positions of worldly success: corporate executives, ministers, military careermen, small businessmen, etc. At first the community became known for its lush garden grown in sand dunes on Scotland's harsh northern coast, where plants from all climates thrived in a soil nearly devoid of organic matter. The founders claimed spiritual guidance and clearly something special had been going on. The first word that comes to mind about this community is "successful," but in a way radically different from the ordinary career success so often implied by the uses of the word cited in Parts I and II. The people at Findhorn fully believe that the individual has a divine part to play in a divine plan, and that listening within rather than following externally prescribed footsteps is the way to this personal success. This may lead to difficult times and to apparently regressive actions, but it follows a call and a rhythm that is greater than the person himself or herself.[4]

As with the volleyball example, one need not vow to play the game cooperatively in order to reap the benefits of the idea. Simply knowing about an alternative to the "killer instinct of competition" (Cousy and Devaney, 1975) is quite often enough to encourage individuals to bring to consciousness unexamined allegiances and a willingness to attempt something new. Camus (1942) said as much about the tragic hero Sisyphus: the force of habit carries the stone up the mountain. When things are on the "up and up," consciousness is unnecessary. It is when Sisyphus watches the great stone bound down the mountain and as he trudges after it to begin the ordeal again that the opportunity for awakening exists, the moments for reflection, transcendence, and joy.

The perspectives described in this section must be kept in mind to balance the overemphasis in our society on achievement, leading so often to the training of status-seeking workaholics. The criteria of success need not be higher salaries, more committeeships, more countable achievements, or even higher grades in school. All of these are plausible epiphenomena of the central task of self-development through a life's work, be it leading a corporation dedicated to goals of human awakening or raising a family or following a path of guidance wherever it leads. As we begin in psychology to integrate a personal view of success with modern methods of research, we shall be also able to construct a re-vision of "fear of success."

[4]Referring to public success, around 700 B.C. the teacher Amen-em-apt said, "There is no success with God, nor is there failure with Him" (cf. Budge, 1924).

References

Abraham, K. Manifestations of the female castration complex. *International Journal of Psycho-Analysis,* 1922, **3**, 1–29.

Adams, J. S. Toward an understanding of inequity. *Journal of Abnormal and Social Psychology,* 1963, **67**, 422–436.

Adams, J. S. Inequity in social exchange. In L. Berkowitz (Ed.), *Advances in experimental social psychology* (Vol. 2). New York: Academic Press, 1965, 267–300.

Adams, J. S., and Rosenbaum, W. E. The relationship of worker productivity to cognitive dissonance about wage inequity. *Journal of Applied Psychology,* 1962, **46**, 161–164.

Adler, A. Introduction: the fundamental views of Individual Psychology. *International Journal of Individual Psychology,* 1935, **1**, 5–8.

Alexander, R. P. Omnipotence and the avoidance of pleasure: a contribution to the problem of separation anxiety. *Psychoanalytic Forum,* 1966, **1**, 278–288.

Allee, W. C. (1938) *Cooperation among animals, with human implications,* (rev. ed.). New York: Schuman, 1951.

Alper, T. G. Predicting the direction of selective recall: its relation to ego strength and n achievement. *Journal of Abnormal and Social Psychology,* 1957, **55**, 149–165.

Alper, T. G. The relationship between role-orientation and achievement motivation in college women. *Journal of Personality,* 1973, **41**, 9–31.

Alper, T. G. Achievement motivation in college women: a now-you-see-it-now-you-don't phenomenon, *American Psychologist,* 1974, **29**, 194–203.

Alper, T. G., and Greenberger, E. Relationship of picture structure to achievement motivation in college women. *Journal of Personality and Social Psychology,* 1967, **7**, 362–371.

Alper, T. G., and Korchin, S. J. Memory for socially relevant material. *Journal of Abnormal and Social Psychology,* 1952, **47**, 25–37.

Alpert, R., and Haber, R. N. Anxiety in academic achievement situations. *Journal of Abnormal and Social Psychology,* 1960, **61**, 207–215.

Althof, S. E. *The effect of competitive and noncompetitive conditions in high and low fear of success college women on verbal problem solving ability.* Unpublished master's thesis, Oklahoma State University, 1973.

Amdur, N. Dr. Richards beats Miss Beene in tennis week open, 6–0, 6–2. *New York Times,* August 22, 1976, Section 5, p. 1.

Anderson, N. H. On the quantification of Miller's conflict theory. *Psychological Review,* 1962, **69**, 400–414.

Anderson, R. C. Failure imagery in the fantasy of induced arousal. *Journal of Educational Psychology,* 1962, **53**, 293–298.

Angrist, S. S. The study of sex roles. *Journal of Social Issues,* 1969, **25**, 215–232. (Reprinted in J. M. Bardwick (Ed.), *Readings on the psychology of women.* New York: Harper and Row, 1972, 101–107.)

Argote, L. M., Fisher, J. E., McDonald, P. J., and O'Neal, E. C. Competitiveness in males and in females: situational determinants of "fear of success" behavior. *Sex Roles,* 1976, **2**, 295–303.

Argyris, C. Dangers in applying results from experimental social psychology. *American Psychologist,* 1975, **30**, 469–485.

Arieti, S. Manic-depressive psychosis. In S. Arieti (Ed.), *American handbook of psychiatry* (Vol. 1). New York: Basic, 1959, 419–454.

Arnold, M. *Story sequence analysis.* New York: Columbia University Press, 1962.

Aronfreed, J. Moral behavior and sex identity. In D. R. Miller and G. E. Swanson (Eds.), *Innter conflict and defense.* New York: Holt, 1960, 177–193.

Aronfreed, J. The origin of self-criticism. *Psychological Review,* 1964, **71**, 193–218.

Aronson, E., and Carlsmith, J. M. Performance expectancy as a determinant of actual performance. *Journal of Abnormal and Social Psychology,* 1962, **65**, 178–182.

Asch, S. E. Studies of independence and conformity: I. A minority of one against a unanimous majority. *Psychological Monographs,* 1956, **70**, whole no. 416.

Atkinson, J. W. (Ed.). *Motives in fantasy, action, and society.* Princeton: Van Nostrand, 1958.

Atkinson, J. W. *An introduction to motivation.* New York: American Book Co., 1964.

Atkinson, J. W. Comments on papers by Crandall and Veroff. In C. P. Smith (Ed.), *Achievement-related motives in children.* New York: Russell Sage, 1969, 200–206.

Atkinson, J. W., and Birch, D. *The dynamics of action.* New York: Wiley, 1970.

Atkinson, J. W., and Feather, N. T. (Eds.). *A theory of achievement motivation.* New York: Wiley, 1966.

Atkinson, J. W., and Litwin, G. H. Achievement motive and test anxiety as motives to approach success and to avoid failure. *Journal of Abnormal and Social Psychology,* 1960, **60**, 52–63.

Atkinson, J. W., and McClelland, D. C. The effect of different intensities of the hunger drive on thematic apperception. *Journal of Experimental Psychology,* 1948, **38**, 643–658.

Atkinson, J. W., and O'Connor, P. Neglected factors in studies of achievement-oriented performance: social approval as incentive and performance decrement. In J. W. Atkinson and N. T. Feather (Eds.), *A theory of achievement motivation.* New York: Wiley, 1966, 299–325.

Atkinson, J. W., and Raynor, J. O. (Eds.). *Motivation and achievement.* New York: Wiley, 1974.

Atkinson, J. W. and Reitman, W. R. Performance as a function of motive strength and expectancy of goal attainment. *Journal of Abnormal and Social Psychology,* 1956, **53**, 361–366.

Back, K. W., Bogdonoff, M. D., Shaw, D. M., and Klein, R. I. An interpretation of experimental conformity through physiological measures. *Behavioral Science,* 1963, **8**, 34–40.

Backman, C. W., and Secord, P. F. The self and role selection. In C. Gordon and K. J. Gergen (Eds.), *The self in social interaction* (Vol. 1). New York: Wiley, 1968, 289–296.

Bacon, F. (1612). Of envy. *Works* (Vol. 1). London: James Cundee, 1807, 31–40.

Bakan, D. The test of significance in psychological research. *Psychological Bulletin,* 1966, **66**, 423–437.

Banton, M. *Roles: an introduction to the study of social relations.* London: Tavistock, 1968.

Barbe, W. *The exceptional child.* New York: Center for Applied Research in Education, 1963.

Barbe, W., and Renzulli, J. S. (Eds.). *Psychology and the education of the gifted* (2nd ed.). New York: Irvington Publishers, 1975.

Bardwick, J. *Psychology of women: a study of biocultural conflicts.* New York: Harper and Row, 1971.

Bardwick, J. M., and Douvan, E. Ambivalence: the socialization of women. In V. Gornick and B. K. Moran (Eds.), *Women in sexist society.* New York: Basic, 1971, 147–159. (Reprinted in J. M. Bardwick (Ed.), *Readings on the psychology of women.* New York: Harper and Row, 1972, 52–58.)

Barker, R. G. (1942) Success and failure in the classroom. In M. L. Haimowitz and N. R. Haimowitz (Eds.), *Human development.* New York: Crowell, 1960, 543–547.

Barry, H., III, Bacon, M. K., and Child, I. L. A cross-cultural survey of some sex differences in socialization. *Journal of Abnormal and Social Psychology,* 1957, **55**, 327–332.

Baruch, G. K. *The motive to avoid success and career aspirations of 5th and 10th grade girls.* Paper presented at the annual meeting of the American Psychological Association, Montreal, August 1973.

Baruch, G. K. Sex-role stereotyping, the motive to avoid success, and parental identification. *Sex Roles,* 1975, **1**, 303–309.

Barzun, J. *The house of intellect.* New York: Harper, 1959.

Bass, B. M. Conformity, deviation, and a general theory of interpersonal behavior. In I. A. Berg and B. M. Bass (Eds.), *Conformity and deviation.* New York: Harper, 1961, 38–100.

Bates, F. L. Position, role, and status: a reformulation of concepts. *Social Forces,* 1956, **34**, 313–321.

Beck, A. T., and Hurvich, M. S. Psychological correlates of depression: frequency of "masochistic" dream content in a private practice sample. *Psychosomatic Medicine,* 1959, **21**, 50–55.

Becker, E. *Escape from evil.* New York: Free Press, 1975.

Becker, H. S. *Outsiders.* New York: Free Press, 1963.

Beecher, W., and Beecher, M. *Beyond success and failure: ways to self-reliance and maturity.* New York: Pocket, 1966.

Beisser, A. R. *The madness in sports: psychosocial observations on sports.* New York: Appleton–Century–Crofts, 1967.

Bem, D. J. *Beliefs, attitudes, and human affairs.* Belmont, California: Brooks/Cole, 1970.

Bem, D. J. Self-perception theory. In L. Berkowitz (Ed.), *Advances in experimental social psychology* (Vol. 6). New York: Academic Press, 1972, 1–62.

Bem, S. L., and Bem, D. J. Do sex-biased job advertisements discourage applicants of the opposite sex? Unpublished testimony prepared for Equal Employment Opportunities Commission, Nov. 1971.

Benedict, R. *Patterns of culture.* New York: Mentor, 1934.

Berens, A. E. *The socialization of achievement motives in boys and girls.* Unpublished doctoral dissertation, York University, Toronto, Ontario, 1972. (See also *Proceedings of the American Psychological Association,* 1972, **7**, 273–274.)

Berger, P. L., and Luckmann, T. *The social construction of reality.* New York: Doubleday, 1966.

Berkan, J. *The effect of information about sex appropriateness of tasks on the fear of success motive.* Senior essay, Yale University, 1972.

Berman, V. A. *The motive to avoid success: a test of basic assumptions* (Doctoral dissertation, Northwestern University, 1973). (University microfilms No. 74-7709)

Bernard, J. The status of women in modern patterns of culture. *The Annals of the American Academy of Political and Social Science,* 1968, **375**, 3–14.

Bernard, J. *Women and the public interest.* Chicago: Aldine, 1971.

Bernard, J. My four revolutions: an autobiographical history of the ASA. *American Journal of Sociology,* 1973, **78**, 773–791.

Bettelheim, B. *The uses of enchantment: the meaning and importance of fairy tales.* New York: Knopf, 1976.

Bickman, L., and Henchy, T. (Eds.). *Beyond the laboratory: field research in social psychology.* New York: McGraw–Hill, 1972.

Birney, R. C., Burdick, H., and Teevan, R. C. *Fear of failure.* New York: Van Nostrand–Reinhold, 1969.

Blau, P. M. *Exchange and power in social life.* New York: Wiley, 1964.

Bobbitt, R. A. The repression hypothesis studied in a situation of hypnotically induced conflict. *Journal of Abnormal and Social Psychology,* 1958, **56**, 204–212.

Bongort, K. J. *Expression of fear of success in the Prisoner's Dilemma played by male–female pairs.* Unpublished manuscript, University of Michigan, n.d. (approximately 1974).

Bramel, D. A dissonance theory approach to defensive projection. *Journal of Abnormal and Social Psychology,* 1962, **64**, 121–129.

Breedlove, C. J., and Cicirelli, V. G. Women's fear of success in relation to personal characteristics and type of occupation. *Journal of Psychology,* 1974, **86**, 181–190.

Brehm, J. W. *A theory of psychological reactance.* New York: Academic Press, 1966.

Brehm, J. W. *Responses to loss of freedom: a theory of psychological reactance.* Morristown, New Jersey: General Learning Press, 1972.

Brehm, J. W., and Cohen, A. R. *Explorations in cognitive dissonance.* New York: Wiley, 1962.

Brenner, C. (1955) *An elementary textbook of psychoanalysis.* Garden City, New York: Doubleday Anchor, 1957.

Brenton, M. *The American male.* Greenwich, Connecticut: Fawcett, 1966.

Bright, M. V. *Factors related to the traditionality or innovativeness of career choices in black college women.* Unpublished master's thesis, Howard University, 1970. Cited in Mednick, 1973.

Brock, T., Edelman, S., Edwards, D., and Schuck, J. Seven studies of performance expectancy as a determinant of actual performance. *Journal of Experimental Social Psychology,* 1965, **1**, 295–310.

Broverman, I. K., Vogel, S. R., Broverman, D. M., Clarkson, F. E., and Rosenkrantz, P. S. Sex-role stereotypes: a current appraisal. *Journal of Social Issues,* 1972, **28**, 59–78.

Brown, D. G. Sex role preference in young children. *Psychological Monographs,* 1956, **70**, whole no. 421.

Brown, D. G. Sex role development in a changing culture. *Psychological Bulletin,* 1958, **55**, 232–242.

Brown, M., Jennings, J., and Vanik, V. The motive to avoid success: a further examination. *Journal of Research in Personality,* 1974, **8**, 172–176.

Brown, N. O. *Love's body.* New York: Vintage Books, 1966.

Brown, W. A. The meaning of success in a person with a "success phobia." *Psychiatry,* 1971, **34**, 425–430.

Bruner, J. S., and Postman, L. An approach to social perception. In W. Dennis (Ed.), *Current trends in social psychology.* Pittsburgh: University of Pittsburgh Press, 1948, 70–119.

Bryon, J., III. The evil eye. *Holiday,* May 1964, pp. 58–59, 98–101, 106–109.

Buber, M. (1937) *I and Thou* (2nd ed.). New York: Scribner and Sons, 1958.

Buck, P. S. *The Kennedy Women: a personal appraisal.* New York: Cowles, 1970.

Budge, E. A. W. *The teaching of Amen-em-apt, son of Kanekht.* London: Martin Hopkinson, 1924.

Burghardt, N. R. *The motive to avoid success in school-aged males and females* (Doctoral dissertation, University of Michigan, 1973). (University Microfilms No. 75-644) (a)

Burghardt, N. R. *The motive to avoid success in school-aged males and females.* Paper presented at the annual meeting of the American Psychlogical Association, Montreal, 1973. (b)

Burhenne, D. P. *Female and male evaluations of sex-appropriate and sex-inappropriate sex-role stereotypes.* Unpublished doctoral dissertation, Ohio State University, 1972.

Burnstein, E. Fear of failure, achievement motivation, and aspiring to prestigeful occupations. *Journal of Abnormal and Social Psychology,* 1963, **67**, 189–193.

Burt, C. *The gifted child.* New York: Wiley, 1975.

Butler, S. (1890). *The notebooks of Samuel Butler* (H. Jones, Ed.). New York: Dutton, 1926.

Byrne, D. Repression–sensitization as a dimension of personality. In B. A. Maher (Ed.), *Progress in experimental personality research* (Vol. 1). New York: Academic Press, 1964, 169–220.

Campbell, D. T., and Stanley, J. C. *Experimental and quasi-experimental designs for research.* Chicago: Rand–McNally, 1963.

Camus, A. (1942). *The myth of Sisyphus, and other essays (J. O'Brien, trans.). New York: Vintage, 1955.*

Canby, V. Bergman explores the terrors of blandness. *New York Times,* April 18, 1976, Section 2, pp. 1, 15.

Carlsmith, J. M., and Aronson, E. Affectual consequences of the disconfirmation of expectancies. *American Psychologist,* 1961, **16**, 437. (Abstract)

Carlsmith, J. M., and Aronson, E. Some hedonic consequences of confirmation and disconformation of expectancies. *Journal of Abnormal and Social Psychology,* 1963, **66**, 151–156.

Cawelti, J. G. *Apostles of the self-made man.* Chicago: University of Chicago Press, 1965.

Challmon, A. The empirical nature of worry. *American Journal of Psychiatry,* 1974, **131**, 1140–1141.

Chapman, D. W., and Volkmann, J. A social determinant of the level of aspiration. *Journal of Abnormal and Social Psychology,* 1939, **34**, 225–238.

Charters, W. W., Jr., and Newcomb, T. M. Some attitudinal effects of experimentally increased salience of a membership group. In G. E. Swanson, T. M. Newcomb, and E. L. Hartley (Eds.), *Readings in social psychology* (revised ed.). New York: Holt, 1952, 415–420.

Cheek, F. E. A serendipitous finding: sex roles and schizophrenia. *Journal of Abnormal and Social Psychology*, 1964, **69**, 392–400.

Chesler, P. *Women and madness.* Garden City, New York: Doubleday, 1972.

Chevalier-Skolnikoff, S. *The female sexual response in stumptail monkeys* (Macaca Speciosa), *and its broad implications for female mammalian sexuality.* Paper presented at annual meeting of the American Anthropological Association, Nov. 1971.

Clark, R. A. The projective measurement of experimental induced levels of sexual motivation. *Journal of Experimental Psychology*, 1952, **44**, 391–399.

Clark, R. A., and McClelland, D. C. A factor analytic integration of imaginative and performance measures of the need for achievement. *Journal of General Psychology*, 1956, **55**, 73–83.

Clark, R. A., and Sensibar, M. R. The relationship between symbolic and manifest projections of sexuality with some incidental correlates. *Journal of Abnormal and Social Psychology*, 1955, **50**, 327–334. (Also in Atkinson, J. W., 1958, 117–129.)

Clark, R. A., Teevan, R., and Ricciuti, H. N. Hope of success and fear of failure as aspects of need for achievement. *Journal of Abnormal and Social Psychology*, 1956, **53**, 182–186. (Also in J. W. Atkinson, 1958, 586–595.)

Cohen, A. R. Situational structure, self-esteem, and threat-oriented reactions to power. In D. Cartwright (Ed.), *Studies in social power.* Ann Arbor, Michigan: Institute for Social Research, 1959, 35–52.

Cohen, J. The statistical power of abnormal–social psychological research. *Journal of Abnormal and Social Psychology*, 1962, **65**, 145–153.

Cohen, J. Some statistical issues in psychological research. In B. B. Wolman (Ed.), *Handbook of clinical psychology*. New York: McGraw–Hill, 1965, 95–121.

Cohen, J. *Statistical power in the behavioral sciences.* New York: Academic Press, 1969.

Cohen, L. D. Level-of-aspiration behavior and feelings of adequacy and self-acceptance. *Journal of Abnormal and Social Psychology*, 1954, **49**, 84–86.

Cohen, N. *Explorations in the fear of success.* Unpublished doctoral dissertation, Columbia University, 1974.

Cohen, Y. A. *The transition from childhood to adolescence: cross-cultural studies of initiation ceremonies, legal systems, and incest taboos.* Chicago: Aldine, 1964.

Colby, F. M. *Essays* (Vol. 2). New York: Harper, 1926.

Coleman, J. *The adolescent society.* New York: Free Press, 1961.

Coleman, N. C. *The motive to avoid success as a function of sex, intelligence, and achievement motivation.* Unpublished master's thesis, University of Oregon, 1974.

Coles, B., and Mausner, B. *Behavioral and fantasied measures of avoidance of success in men and women: a replication.* Unpublished manuscript, Beaver College, 1974.

Collins, B. E. *Public and private conformity: competing explanations by improvisation, cognitive dissonance, and attribution theories.* Andover, Massachusetts: Warner Modular Publications, 1973.

Condry, J., and Dyer, S. Fear of success: attribution of cause to the victim. *Journal of Social Issues,* in press.

Cooley, C. H. *Human nature and the social order.* New York: Scribner, 1922.

Cooper, J. Personal responsibility and dissonance: the role of foreseen consequences. *Journal of Personality and Social Psychology*, 1971, **18**, 354–363.

Costello, C. G. Ego-involvement, success and failure: a review of the literature. In H. J. Eysenck (Ed.), *Experiments in motivation.* New York: Macmillan, 1964, 161–208.

Cottrell, N. B. Performance expectancy as a determinant of actual performance: a replication with a new design. *Journal of Personality and Social Psychology*, 1965, **2**, 685–691.

Cousy, B., and Devaney, J. *The killer instinct.* New York: Random House, 1975.

Cowan, G., and Goldberg, F. J. Need achievement as a function of the race and sex of figures of selected TAT cards. *Journal of Personality and Social Psychology,* 1967, **5**, 245–249.

Cox, B., and Sargent, H. TAT responses of emotionally disturbed and emotionally stable children: clinical judgement versus normative data. *Journal of Projective Techniques,* 1950, **14**, 61–74.

Cox, D. R. The use of a concomitant variable in selecting an experimental design. *Biometrika,* 1957, **44**, 150–158.

Crandall, V. C. Sex differences in expectancy of intellectual and academic reinforcement. In C. P. Smith (Ed.), *Achievement-related motives in children.* New York: Russell Sage, 1969, 11–45.

Crandall, V. J., Katkovsky, W., and Preston, A. A. A conceptual formulation for some research on children's achievement development. *Child Development,* 1960, **31**, 787–797.

Credner, L. Safeguards. *International Journal of Individual Psychology,* 1936, **2,** 95–102.

Cronbach, L. J., and Furby, L. How we should measure "change"—or should we? *Psychological Bulletin,* 1970, **74**, 68–80.

Cronbach, L. J., and Meehl, P. E. Construct validity in psychological tests. *Psychological Bulletin,* 1955, **52**, 281–302.

Crowne, D. P., and Liverant, S. Conformity under varying conditions of personal commitment. *Journal of Abnormal and Social Psychology,* 1963, **66**, 547–555.

Crutchfield, R. C. Conformity and character. *American Psychologist,* 1955, **10**, 191–198.

Cunliff, J. Success—worm in the apple. *New York Post,* May 23, 1973, p. 38.

Currie, E. P. Crimes without criminals: witchcraft and its control in renaissance Europe. *Law and Society Review,* 1968, **3**, 7–32.

Curtis, R., Zanna, M. P., Campbell, W. *Fear of success, sex, and the perceptions and performance of law school students.* Paper presented at the annual meeting of the Eastern Psychological Association, April 1973.

Curtis, R. C., Zanna, M. P., and Campbell, W. W., Jr. Sex, fear of success, and the perceptions and performance of law school students. *American Educational Research Journal,* in press.

Davies, A. Relations among several objective measures of anxiety under different conditions of motivation. *Journal of Consulting Psychology,* 1955, **19**, 275–279.

Davis, J. A. *Great aspirations.* Chicago: Aldine, 1968.

deBeauvoir, S. *The second sex.* New York: Knopf, 1953.

Deaux, K., and Enswiller, T. Explanation of successful performance on sex-linked tasks: what is skill for the male is luck for the female. *Journal of Personality and Social Psychology,* 1974, **29**, 72–79.

deCharms, R. Affiliation motivation and productivity in small groups. *Journal of Abnormal and Social Psychology,* 1957, **55**, 222–226.

deCharms, R., and Dave, P. N. Hope of success, fear of failure, subjective probability, and risk-taking behavior. *Journal of Personality and Social Psychology,* 1965, **1**, 558–568.

Della Fave, L. R. *Success values: are they universal or class-differentiated?* Paper presented at the annual meeting of the American Sociological Association, New York, August 1973. (ERIC Reproduction Document no. ED 081 888)

Depner, C. E., and O'Leary, V. E. Understanding female careerism: fear of success and new directions. *Sex Roles,* 1976, **2,** 259–268.

de Sahagún, B. (1530). The Florentine codex: general history of the things of New Spain, Book 2 (trans. A. J. O. Anderson and C. H. Dibble). *Monographs of the School of American Research,* 1951, No. 14, Part 3.

Deutsch, H. *The psychology of women.* New York: Grune and Stratton, 1944 (2 vols.).

Deutsch, M. (1949) The effects of cooperation and competition upon group process. In D. Cartwright and A. Zander (Eds.), *Group dynamics* (2nd ed.). Evanston, Illinois: Row, Peterson, 1960, 414–448.

Deutsch, M. Field theory in social psychology. In G. Lindzey and E. Aronson (Eds.), *Handbook of social psychology* (2nd ed.) (Vol. 1). Reading, Massachusetts: Addison–Wesley, 1969, 412–487.

Deutsch, M., Krauss, R. M., and Rosenau, N. Dissonance or defensiveness? *Journal of Personality,* 1962, **30**, 16–28.

Deutsch, M., and Solomon, L. Reactions to evaluations by others as influenced by self-evaluations. *Sociometry,* 1959, **22**, 93–112.

Diamond, S., Balvin, R. S., and Diamond, F. R. *Inhibition and choice.* New York: Harper and Row, 1963.

Diggory, J. C. The components of personal despair. In E. S. Shneidman (Ed.), *Essays in self-destruction.* New York: Science House, 1967, 300–323.

Dittes, J. E., and Kelley, H. H. Effects of different conditions of acceptance upon conformity to group norms. *Journal of Abnormal and Social Psychology,* 1956, **53**, 100–107.

DiVesta, F. J., and Bossart, P. The effect of sets induced by labeling on the modification of attitude. *Journal of Personality,* 1958, **26**, 379–387.

Dodds, E. R. *The Greeks and the irrational.* Berkeley: University of California Press, 1951.

Doerr, M. (Untitled letter) *Newsweek,* 1973, **82**(26), 4.

Douglas, M. *Purity and danger: an analysis of concepts of pollution and taboo.* New York: Praeger, 1966.

Douvan, E. Social status and success strivings. *Journal of Abnormal and Social Psychology,* 1956, **52**, 219–223.

Dornbusch, S. Afterward. In E. Maccoby (Ed.), *The development of sex differences.* Stanford: Stanford University Press, 1966, 205–219.

Douvan, E. Sex differences in adolescent character processes. *Merrill–Palmer Quarterly,* 1960, **6**, 203–211. [Reprinted in J. M. Bardwick (Ed.), *Readings on the psychology of women.* New York: Harper and Row, 1972, 44–48.]

Douvan, E., and Adelson, J. *The adolescent experience.* New York: Wiley, 1966.

Dreyer, A. S. Aspiration behavior as influenced by expectation and group comparison. *Human Relations,* 1954, **7**, 175–190.

Dubé, W. F. Woman students in U.S. medical schools: past and present trends. *Journal of Medical Education,* 1973, **48**, 186–189.

Dubé, W. F. U.S. medical school enrollment, 1969–70 through 1973–74 (Datagram). *Journal of Medical Education,* 1974, **49**, 302–307.

Dubé, W. F. U.S. medical school enrollment, 1970–71 through 1974–75 (Datagram). *Journal of Medical Education,* 1975, **50**, 303–306.

Ducey, C. *Ontogenetic precursors of the achievement motive.* Unpublished manuscript, Harvard University, 1972.

Duval, S., and Wicklund, R. A. *A theory of objective self awareness.* New York: Academic Press, 1972.

Dwyer, C. A. *Children's sex-role standards and sex-role identification and their relationship to achievement.* Unpublished doctoral dissertation, University of California, Berkeley, 1972. (Abstract)

Dynes, R. R., Clarke, A. C., and Dinitz, S. Levels of occupational aspirations: some aspects of family experience as variables. *American Sociological Review,* 1956, **21**, 212–215.

Ebel, R. L. And still the dryads linger. *American Psychologist,* 1974, **29**, 485–492.

Edinger, E. *Ego and archetype: individuation and the religious function of the psyche.* New York: Putnam, 1972.

Eisenstadt, S. N. Studies in reference group behavior. 1. Reference norms and the social structure. *Human Relations,* 1954, **7**, 191–216.

Elashoff, J. D. Analysis of covariance: a delicate instrument. *American Educational Research Journal,* 1969, **6**, 383–402.

Eliade, M. *Myths, dreams, and mysteries.* New York: Harper, 1960.

Ellis, E. Social psychological correlates of upward social mobility among unmarried career women. *American Sociological Review,* 1952, **17**, 558–563.

Elworthy, F. T. *The evil eye: an account of this ancient and widespread superstition.* London: J. Murray, 1895.

Elworthy, F. T. Evil eye. In J. Hastings (Ed.), *Encyclopedia of religion and ethics* (Vol. 5). New York: Scribner and Sons, 1928, 608–615.

Emerson, R. W. (1841). Compensation. *Complete writings of Ralph Waldo Emerson.* New York: Wise, 1875, 153–164.

Emerson, R. W. (1870). Success. *Complete writings of Ralph Waldo Emerson.* New York: Wise, 1875, 706–715.

Emmerich, W., Goldman, K. S., and Shore, R. E. Differentiation and development of social norms. *Journal of Personality and Social Psychology,* 1971, **18**, 323–353.

Engel, G. L. Psychogenic pain and the pain-prone patient. *American Journal of Medicine,* 1959, **26**, 899–918.

Entwisle, D. R. To dispell fantasies about fantasy-based measures of achievement motivation. *Psychological Bulletin,* 1972, **77**, 377–391.

Entwisle, D. R., and Greenberger, E. Adolescent's views of women's work role. *American Journal of Orthopsychiatry,* 1972, **32**, 648–656.

Epstein, C. F. *Woman's place.* Berkeley: University of California Press, 1970. (a)

Epstein, C. F. Encountering the male establishment: sex-status limits on women's careers in the professions. *American Journal of Sociology,* 1970, **75**, 965–982. (b)

Epstein, C. F. Positive effects of the multiple negative explaining the success of black professional women. *American Journal of Sociology,* 1973, **78**, 912–935.

Epstein, S. Toward a unified theory of anxiety. In B. A. Maher (Ed.), *Progress in experimental personality research* (Vol. 4). New York: Academic Press, 1967, 1–89.

Erdelyi, M. H. A new look at the new look: perceptual defense and vigilance. *Psychological Review,* 1974, **81**, 1–25.

Erikson, E. H. Concluding remarks. In J. A. Mattfeld and C. G. VanAken (Eds.), *Women and the scientific professions.* Cambridge, Massachusetts: M.I.T. Press, 1965, 232–245.

Erikson, K. T. (1962) Notes on the sociology of deviance. In T. J. Scheff (Ed.), *Mental illness and social processes.* New York: Harper and Row, 1967, 294–304.

Erikson, K. T. *Wayward Puritans: a study of the sociology of deviance.* New York: Wiley, 1966.

Erikson, K. T. Patient role and social uncertainty. In E. Rubington and M. S. Weinberg (Eds.), *Deviance: the interactionist perspective.* London: Macmillan, 1968, 337–342.

Eron, L. D. A normative study of the thematic apperception test. In B. I. Murstein (Ed.), *Handbook of projective techniques.* New York: Basic, 1965, 469–507.

Etzkowitz, H. The male sister: sexual separation of labor in society. *Journal of Marriage and the Family,* 1971, **33**, 431–434.

Fadiman, J. *Motivation in children: an exploratory study.* Honors essay, Stanford University, 1960. Cited in G. S. Lesser, 1965.

Faris, R. E. L. *Social psychology.* New York: Ronald, 1952.

Feather, N. T. Valence of outcome and expectation of success in relation to task difficulty and perceived locus of control. *Journal of Personality and Social Psychology,* 1967, **7**, 372–386.

Feather, N. T. *Positive and negative reactions to male and female success and failure in relation to the perceived status and sex-typed appropriateness of occupations.* Unpublished manuscript, Flinders University, Australia, 1974.

Feather, N. T., and Raphelson, A. C. Fear of success in Australian and American student groups: motive or sex-role stereotype? *Journal of Personality,* 1974, **42**, 190–201.

Feather, N. T., and Simon, J. G. Fear of success and causal attribution for outcome. *Journal of Personality,* 1973, **41**, 525–542.

Feather, N. T., and Simon, J. G. Reactions to male and female success and failure in sex-linked occupations: impressions of personality, causal attributions, and perceived likelihood of different consequences. *Journal of Personality and Social Psychology,* 1975, **31**, 20–31.

Feldman-Summers, S., and Kiesler, S. B. Those who are number two try harder: the effect of sex on attributions of causality. *Journal of Personality and Social Psychology,* 1974, **30**, 846–855.

Fenichel, O. *The psychoanalytic theory of neurosis.* New York: Norton, 1945.

Fenz, W., and Epstein, S. Measurement of approach–avoidance conflict along a stimulus-dimension by a thematic apperception test. *Journal of Personality,* 1962, **30**, 613–632.

Feshbach, S., and Singer, R. D. The effects of fear arousal and suppression of fear upon social perception. *Journal of Abnormal and Social Psychology,* 1957, **55**, 283–288.

Festinger, L. Motivations leading to social behavior. In M. R. Jones (Ed.), *Nebraska symposium on motivation.* Lincoln: University of Nebraska Press, 1954, 191–219. (a)

Festinger, L. A theory of social comparison processes. *Human Relations,* 1954, **7**, 117–140. (b)

Festinger, L. *A theory of cognitive dissonance.* Evanston, Illinois: Row, Peterson, 1957.

Festinger, L. *Conflict, decision, and dissonance.* Stanford, California: Stanford University Press, 1964.

Field, W. F. *The effects of thematic apperception upon certain experimentally aroused needs.* Unpublished doctoral dissertation, University of Maryland, 1951. Cited in J. W. Atkinson, 1958.

Finagrette, H. *The self in transformation.* New York: Harper and Row, 1963.

Fisher, J. E., O'Neal, E. C., and McDonald, P. J. *Female competitiveness as a function of prior performance outcome, competitor's evaluation, and sex of competitor.* Paper presented at the annual meeting of the Midwestern Psychological Association, Chicago, May 1974.

Fiske, D. W. *Measuring the concepts of personality.* Chicago: Aldine, 1971.

Fitch, G. Effects of self-esteem, perceived performance, and choice on causal attribution. *Journal of Personality and Social Psychology,* 1970, **16**, 311–315.

Fleiss, J. L. *Statistical methods for rates and proportions.* New York: Wiley, 1973.

Fleming, J. *An investigation of fear of success imagery in urban Kenya.* Unpublished manuscript, Harvard University, 1972.

Fleming, J. *Approach and avoidance motivation in interpersonal competition: a study of black male and female college students.* Unpublished doctoral dissertation, Harvard University, 1974.

Fleming, J. Comment on "Do Women Fear Success?" by David Tresemer. *Signs: Journal of Women in Culture and Society,* in press.

Fleming, J., and Horner, M. *Sex and race differences in fear of success imagery.* Unpublished manuscript, Harvard University, 1973.

Fliess, R. *Ego and body ego.* New York: International Universities Press, 1961.

Flugel, J. C. *Man, morals, and society: a psychoanalytical study.* New York: International Universities Press, 1945.

Fodor, I. The phobic syndrome in women. In V. Franks and V. Burtle (Eds.), *Women in therapy: new psychotherapies for a changing society.* New York: Bruner Mazel, 1974. (a)

Fodor, I. E. Sex role conflict and symptom formation in women: can behavior therapy help? In C. M. Franks and G. T. Wilson (Eds.), *Annual review of behavior therapy, theory, and practice: 1975.* New York: Bruner Mazel, 1974. (b)

Foote, N. N. Identification as the basis for a theory of motivation. *American Sociological Review,* 1951, **16**, 14–21.

Foote, N. N., and Cottrell, L. S. *Identity and interpersonal competence.* Chicago: University of Chicago Press, 1955.

Footlick, J. K. The new campus rebels: women. *Newsweek,* Dec. 10, 1973, pp. 120–126.

Freedman, J. L., and Doob, A. N. *Deviancy: the psychology of being different.* New York: Academic Press, 1968.

French, E. G., and Lesser, G. S. Some characteristics of the achievement motive in women. *Journal of Abnormal and Social Psychology,* 1964, **68**, 119–128.

French, J. L. The gifted. In M. V. Wisland (Ed.), *Psychoeducational diagnosis of exceptional children.* Springfield, Illinois: C. C. Thomas, 1974, 306–328.

French, J. L. The highly intelligent dropout. In W. Barbe and J. S. Renzulli (Eds.), *Psychology and the education of the gifted* (2nd ed.). New York: Irvington Publishers, 1975, 431–432.

French, J. R. P., Jr., and Caplan, R. D. Organizational stress and individual strain. In A. J. Marrow (Ed.), *The failure of success.* London: Allen and Unwin, 1973, 30–66.

French, J. R. P., Jr., and Raven, B. The bases of social power. In D. Cartwright and A. Zander (Eds.), *Group Dynamics* (2nd ed.). Evanston, Illinois: Row, Peterson, 1960, 607–623.

Freud, S. (1900). *The interpretation of dreams.* New York: Wiley, 1961.

Freud, S. (1911). Formulations regarding the two principles in mental functioning. *Collected papers* (Vol. 4). London: Hogarth, 1953, 13–21.

Freud, S. (1915). Some character-types met with in psychoanalytic work. *Collected papers* (Vol. 4). London: Hogarth, 1949, 318–344.

Freud, S. (1922). *Group psychology and the analysis of the ego.* New York: Liveright, 1951.

Freud, S. (1930). *Civilization and its discontents.* (J. Strachey, Ed. and trans.). New York: Norton, 1961.

Freud, S. The psychology of women. In *New introductory lectures.* New York: Norton, 1933, 153–185.

Freud, S. *The problem of anxiety.* New York: Psychoanalytic Quarterly Press, 1936.

Friedman, M., and Rosenman, R. H. *Type A behavior and your heart.* Greenwich, Connecticut: Fawcett, 1974.

Frieze, I., and Weiner, B. Cue utilization and attributional judgments for success and failure. *Journal of Personality,* 1971, **39**, 591–605.

Fromm, E. *Escape from freedom.* New York: Farrar and Rinehart, 1941.

Fromm, E. *The fear of freedom.* London: Kegan Paul, Trench, and Trubner, 1942.

Fromm, E. Sex and character. *Psychiatry,* 1943, **6**, 21–31.

Fromm, E. *Man for himself.* New York: Holt, 1947.

Fromm, E. *The sane society.* New York: Holt, 1955.

Frye, N. *Fearful symmetry.* Princeton, New Jersey: Princeton University Press, 1947.

Frye, N. *Anatomy of criticism.* Princeton, New Jersey: Princeton University Press, 1957.

Galvin, R. Sex and success. *Time,* March 20, 1972, pp. 46–47.

Gardner, J. W. Equality and competitive performance. In *Excellence: can we be equal and excellent too?* New York: Harper and Row, 1961, 11–20.

Gearty, J. Z. *Academic major, gender of examiner, and the motive to avoid success in women.* Unpublished master's thesis, Western Carolina University, 1973.

Gearty, J. Z., and Milner, J. S. *The motive to avoid success in women.* Paper presented at the annual meeting of the Southeastern Psychological Association, Hollywood, Florida, 1974.

Gearty, J. Z., and Milner, J. S. Academic major, gender of examiner, and the motive to avoid success in women. *Journal of Clinical Psychology,* 1975, **31**, 13–14.

Gergen, K. J. Personal consistency and the presentation of self. In C. Gordon and K. J. Gergen (Eds.), *The self in social interaction* (Vol. 1). New York: Wiley, 1968, 299–308.

Gergen, K. J. *The concept of self.* New York: Holt, Rinehart, and Winston, 1971.

Getzels, J. W., and Guba, E. G. Role, role conflict, and effectiveness. *American Sociological Review,* 1954, **19**, 164–175.

Gifford, E. S., Jr. *The evil eye: studies in the folklore of vision.* New York: Macmillan, 1958.

Gjesme, T. Achievement-related motives and school performance for girls. *Journal of Personality and Social Psychology,* 1973, **26**, 131–136.

Glancy, D. J. Women in law: the dependable ones. *Harvard Law School Bulletin,* 1970, **21**, 23–33.

Glinski, R. J., Glinski, B. C., and Slatin, G. T. Nonaivety contamination in conformity experiments: sources, effects, and implications for control. *Journal of Personality and Social Psychology,* 1970, **16**, 478–485.

Goffman, E. (1957) Normal deviants. In T. J. Scheff (Ed.), *Mental illness and social processes.* New York: Harper and Row, 1967, 267–271.

Goffman, E. *Stigma: notes on the management of spoiled identity.* Englewood Cliffs, New Jersey: Prentice–Hall, 1963.

Goldberg, P. Are women prejudiced against women? *Transaction,* 1968, **5**, 28–30. (Also in D. L. Schaeffer (Ed.), *Sex differences in personality.* Belmont, California: Brooks/Cole, 1971, 62–66.)

Goldin, P. C. Experimental investigation of selective memory and the concept of repression and defense: a theoretical synthesis. *Journal of Abnormal and Social Psychology,* 1964, **69**, 365–380.

Goldstine, D. B. *The changing roles of marriage and the marriage of changing roles.* Paper presented at the annual meeting of the American Psychological Association, Montreal, 1973.

Good, L. R., and Good, K. C. An objective measure of the motive to avoid success. *Psychological Reports,* 1973, **33**, 1009–1010.

Goode, W. J. A theory of role strain. *American Sociological Review,* 1960, **25**, 483–496. (a)

Goode, W. J. Norm commitment and conformity to role-status obligations. *American Journal of Sociology,* 1960, **66**, 246–258. (b)

Gornick, V. Why women fear success. *Ms.,* Spring 1972, 50–54. (Also in F. Klagsbrun (Ed.), *The first Ms. reader.* New York: Warner, 1973, 26–35.)

Gornick, V. Why Radcliffe women are afraid of success. *New York Times Magazine,* Jan. 14, 1973, 10ff.

Gottman, J. M. *N*-of-one and *N*-of-two research in psychotherapy. *Psychological Bulletin,* 1973, **80**, 93–105.

Gottschalk, L. A., and Gleser, G. C. *The measurement of psychological states through the content analysis of verbal behavior.* Berkeley: University of California Press, 1969.

Gough, H. G. Identifying psychological feminity. *Educational and Psychological Measurement,* 1952, **12**, 427–439.

Gough, G. H. *California personality inventory manual.* Palo Alto: Consulting Psychologists Press, 1957.

Gracian, B. *The art of worldly wisdom,* 1647. Cited in Mencken, 1942.

Graham, R. B. C. *Success.* London: Duckworth, 1902.

Green, R., and Money, J. (Eds.). *Transsexualism and sex reassignment.* Baltimore: Johns Hopkins Press, 1969.

Greenwald, A. G. Consequences of prejudice against the null hypothesis. *Psychological Bulletin,* 1975, **82**, 1–20.

Greenwald, A. G. Within-subjects designs: to use or not to use? *Psychological Bulletin,* 1976, **83**, 314–320.

Groszko, M. *Sex differences in the need to achieve and fear of success* (Doctoral dissertation, Institute of Advanced Psychological Studies, Adelphi University, 1974). (University Microfilms No. 74-24, 639)

Groszko, M., and Morgenstern, R. *Institutional discrimination: the case of achievement-oriented women in higher education.* Paper presented at the annual meeting of the American Psychological Association, September 1972.

Groszko, M., and Morgenstern, R. Institutional discrimination: the case of achievement-oriented women in higher education. *International Journal of Group Tensions,* 1974, **4**, 82–92.

Hacker, H. M. The new burdens of masculinity. *Marriage and Family Living,* 1957, **19**, 227–233.

Haimowitz, M. L., and Haimowitz, N. R. (1958) The evil eye: fear of success. In M. L. Haimowitz and N. R. Haimowitz (Eds.), *Human development.* New York: Crowell, 1960, 742–754.

Hall, E. Will success spoil B. F. Skinner? *Psychology Today,* November 1972, pp. 65–72, 130.

Halpern, H. Psychodynamic and cultural determinants of work inhibition in children. *Psychoanalytic Review,* 1964, **51**, 173–189.

Halprin, R. *The motive to avoid success: personality and performance correlates in alone and group testing situations.* Unpublished honors thesis, Smith College, 1974.

Harlow, H. F. Learning set and error factor theory. In S. Koch (Ed.), *Psychology: a study of science* (Vol. 2). New York: McGraw–Hill, 1959, 492–537.
Harrison, R. Thematic apperceptive methods. In B. B. Wolman (Ed.), *Handbook of clinical psychology*. New York: McGraw–Hill, 1965, 562–620.
Hartley, R. E. Sex-role pressures and the socialization of the male child. *Psychological Reports*, 1959, **5**, 457–468.
Hartman, A. A. An experimental examination of the thematic apperceptive technique in clinical diagnosis. *Psychological Monographs*, 1949, **63**, whole no. 303.
Hartmann, H. (1939) *Ego psychology and the problem of adaptation*. New York: International Universities Press, 1958.
Hartup, W. W., Moore, S. G., and Sager, G. Avoidance of inappropriate sex-typing by young children. *Journal of Consulting Psychology*, 1963, **27**, 467–473.
Hawken, P. *The magic of Findhorn*. New York: Harper and Row, 1975.
Hays, H. R. *The dangerous sex: the myth of feminine evil*. New York: Pocket, 1964.
Haythorn, W. The influence of individual members on the characteristics of small groups. *Journal of Abnormal and Social Psychology*, 1953, **48**, 276–284.
Heckhausen, H. *Hoffnung und Furcht in der Leistungsmotivation*. Meisenheim Glan: Hain, 1963. Cited in R. C. Birney *et al.*, 1969.
Heckhausen, H. *The anatomy of achievement motivation*. New York: Academic Press, 1967.
Heckhausen, H. Achievement motive research: current problems and some contributions toward a central theory of motivation. In D. Levine (Ed.), *Nebraska symposium on motivation*. Lincoln: University of Nebraska Press, 1968, 103–167.
Heider, F. *The psychology of interpersonal relations*. New York: Wiley, 1958.
Heilbrun, A. B., Jr. Sex-role identity and achievement motivation. *Psychological Reports*, 1963, **12**, 483–490.
Heilbrun, A. B., Jr. *Aversive maternal control: a theory of schizophrenic development*. New York: Wiley, 1973.
Heilbrun, A. B., Kleemeier, C., and Piccola, G. Developmental and situational correlates of achievement behavior in college females. *Journal of Personality*, 1974, **42**, 420–436.
Henry, J. *Pathways to madness*. New York: Random House, 1971.
Herbst, P. G. *Behavioural worlds*. London: Tavistock, 1970.
Herrnstein, R. J. On the law of effect. *Journal of the Experimental Analysis of Behavior*, 1970, **13**, 243–266.
Herzog, I. *Children of working mothers*. Washington, D. C.: Children's Bureau Publication 382, 1960. Cited in Watson and Johnson, 1972.
Hesse, H. (1953) *Beneath the wheel* (Michael Roloff, trans.). New York: Farrar, Straus, and Giroux, 1968.
Hochschild, A. R. A review of sex role research. *American Journal of Sociology*, 1973, **78**, 1011–1029.
Hoffman, L. W. Early childhood experiences and women's achievement motivation. *Journal of Social Issues*, 1972, **28**, 129–156.
Hoffman, L. W. Fear of success in males and females: 1965 and 1971. *Journal of Consulting and Clinical Psychology*, 1974, **42**, 353–358.
Hollender, J. Sex differences in sources of social self-esteem. *Journal of Consulting and Clinical Psychology*, 1972, **38**, 343–347.
Hollingshead, A. B., Ellis, R., and Kirby, E. Social mobility and mental illness. *American Sociological Review*, 1954, **19**, 577–584.

Holmes, D. S. The conscious control of thematic projection. *Journal of Counseling and Clinical Psychology*, 1974, **42**, 323–329. (a)

Holmes, D. S. Investigations of repression: differential recall of material experimentally or naturally associated with ego threat. *Psychological Bulletin*, 1974, **81**, 632–653. (b)

Holmes, O. W. *Ralph Waldo Emerson*. Boston: Houghton Mifflin, 1885.

Holt, J. C. *How children fail*. New York: Putnam, 1964.

Holter, H. *Sex roles and social structure*. Oslo: Universitetsforlaget, 1970.

Homans, G. C. *The human group*. New York: Harcourt, Brace, and World, 1950.

Homans, G. C. *Social behavior: its elementary forms*. New York: Harcourt, Brace, and World, 1961.

Hopkins, L. B. *Assessment of the motive to avoid success in men and women using male and female cue characters*. Unpublished master's thesis, Temple University, 1974.

Hoppe, F. Erfolg und Misserfolg. *Psychologische Forschung*, 1930, **14**, 1–62. Cited in Lewin *et al.*, 1944.

Horner, M. S. Sex differences in achievement motivation and performance in competitive and noncompetitive situations (Doctoral dissertation, University of Michigan, 1968). *Dissertation Abstracts International*, 1969, **30**, 407B. (University Microfilms No. 69-12, 135) (Cited here as Horner, 1968)

Horner, M. S. *A psychological barrier to achievement in women: the motive to avoid success*. Paper presented at the annual conference of the Midwestern Psychological Association, May, 1968. (Reprinted in D. C. McClelland and R. S. Steele (Eds.), *Human motivation*. Morristown, New Jersey: General Learning Press, 1973, 222–230.) (b)

Horner, M. S. Fail: bright women. *Psychology Today*, November, 1969, pp. 36–38, 62. (Reprinted in E. Adams and M. L. Briscoe (Eds.), *Up against the wall, mother. . . .* Beverly Hills, California: Glencoe Press, 1971, 379–386; and in A. Theodore (Ed.), *The professional women*. Cambridge, Massachusetts: Schenkman Publishing Co., 1971, 252–259.)

Horner, M. S. Femininity and successful achievement: a basic inconsistency. In J. Bardwick *et al.* (Eds.), *Feminine personality and conflict*. Belmont, California: Brooks/Cole, 1970, 45–74. (Reprinted in M. Garskoff (Ed.), *Roles women play: readings toward women's liberation*. Belmont, California: Brooks/Cole, 1971, 97–122.) (a)

Horner, M. S. *Follow up studies on the motive to avoid success in women*. Paper presented at the annual meeting of the American Psychological Association, Miami, Sept. 1970. (b)

Horner, M. S. The psychological significance of success in competitive achievement situations: a threat as well as a promise. In H. I. Day, D. E. Berlyne, and D. E. Hunt (Eds.), *Intrinsic motivation: a new direction in education*. Toronto: Holt, Rinehart, and Winston, 1971, 46–60.

Horner, M. S. Toward an understanding of achievement-related conflicts in women. *Journal of Social Issues*, 1972, **28**, 157–176. (Reprinted as Item 608 by Warner Modular Publications, Andover, Massachusetts; in Unger, R. K., and Denmark, F. L. (Eds.), *Woman: dependent or independent variable?* New York: Psychological Dimensions, 1975, 704–722; and in Mednick, M. S. *et al.* (Eds.), *Women and achievement: social and motivational analyses*. New York: Halsted, 1975, 206–219.) (a)

Horner, M. S. Human motivation. In *Psychology today: an introduction* (2nd ed.). Del Mar, California: CRM Books, 1972, 369–385. (b)

Horner, M. S. The measurement and behavioral implications of fear of success in women. In J. W. Atkinson and J. O. Raynor (Eds.), *Motivation and achievement.* New York: Wiley, 1974, 91–117.

Horner, M. S., and Glancy, D. Unpublished report. Cited in Horner, 1970c.

Horner, M. S., Tresemer, D. W., Berens, A. E., and Watson, R. I., Jr. *Scoring manual for an empirically derived scoring system for motive to avoid success.* Paper presented at the annual meeting of the American Psychological Association, Montreal, 1973.

Horner, M. S., and Walsh, M. R. *Causes and consequences of the existence of psychological barriers to self-actualization.* Paper presented at conference of New York Academy of Science, May 12, 1972. (Reprinted as "Psychological barriers to success in women." In Ruth Kundsin (Ed.), *Women and success.* New York: Morrow, 1974, 138–144).

Horney, K. *The neurotic personality of our time.* New York: Norton, 1937.

Horney, K. *New ways in psychoanalysis.* New York: Norton, 1939.

Horrocks, J. E., and Weinberg, S. A. Psychological needs and their development during adolescence. *Journal of Psychology,* 1970, **74**, 51–69.

House, G. F. *Orientations to achievement: autonomous, social comparison, and external* (Doctoral dissertation, University of Michigan, 1973). (University Microfilms No. 73-24, 594)

Houts, P. S., and Entwisle, D. R. Academic achievement effort among females: achievement attitudes and sex-role orientation. *Journal of Counseling Psychology,* 1968, **15**, 284-286.

Howe, K. G., and Zanna, M. P. *Sex-appropriateness of the task and achievement behavior.* Paper presented at the annual meeting of the Eastern Psychological Association, New York, 1975.

Huber, R. M. *The American idea of success.* New York: McGraw–Hill, 1971.

Huck, S. W., and McLean, R. A. Using a repeated measure ANOVA to analyze the data from a pretest–posttest design: a potentially confusing task. *Psychological Bulletin,* 1975, **82**, 511–518.

Hundert, J. *Women's "motive to avoid success" in tasks defined as "masculine or feminine."* Unpublished manuscript, McMaster University, 1974.

Hyman, H. H. Reflections on reference groups. *Public Opinion Quarterly,* 1960, **24**, 383–396.

Hyman, H. H., and Singer, E. (Eds.). *Readings in reference group theory and research.* New York: Free Press, 1968.

Ichheiser, G. Ideology of success and the dilemma of education. *Ethics,* 1943, **53**, 137–141.

Jackaway, R. *Sex differences in achievement motivation, behavior, and attributions about success and failure* (Doctoral dissertation, SUNY, Albany, 1974). *Dissertation Abstracts International,* 1974, **35**(10). (University Microfilms No. 75-9264) (a)

Jackaway, R. Sex differences in the development of fear of success. *Child Study Journal,* 1974, **4**, 71–79. (b)

Jackaway, R., and Teevan, R. *Fear of failure and fear of success: two dimensions of the same motive.* Unpublished manuscript, State University of New York, New Paltz, 1975.

Jackaway, R., and Teevan, R. Fear of failure and fear of success: two dimensions of the same motive. *Sex Roles,* 1976, **2,** 283–293.

Jackson, J. A. (Ed.). *Role.* London: Cambridge University Press, 1972.

Jacobson, E. *The self and the object world.* New York: International Universities Press, 1964.

Jacques, E. *Equitable payment.* New York: Wiley, 1961.

James, W. *Psychology*. New York: Holt, 1900.

Jellison, J. M., Jackson-White, R., and Bruder, R. A. *Fear of success?—a situational approach.* Paper presented at the annual meeting of the Western Psychological Association, San Francisco, April 1974.

Jellison, J. M., Jackson-White, R., Bruder, R. A., and Martyna, W. Achievement behavior: a situational interpretation. *Sex Roles*, 1976, **1**, 369–384.

Johnson, J. *A phenomenological alternative to the analysis of sex role conflict.* Paper presented at the annual meeting of the American Sociological Association, San Francisco, 1975.

Jones, E. E., and Gerard, H. B. *Foundations of social psychology*. New York: Wiley, 1967.

Jones, E. E., and Nisbett, R. E. The actor and the observer: divergent perceptions of the causes of behavior. In E. E. Jones *et al.* (Eds.), *Attribution: perceiving the causes of behavior*. Morristown, New Jersey: General Learning Press, 1971, 79–94.

Jones, E. The problem of Paul Morphy: a contribution to the psychology of chess. *Essays in applied psychoanalysis* (Vol. 1). London: Hogarth, 1951, 165–196. (Reissued as *Psycho-myth, Psycho-history*. New York: Hillstone, 1974.)

Jonson, B. (1606). *Volpone, or the fox*. New York: Appleton–Century–Crofts, 1958.

Jordan, J. *The relationship of sex-role orientation to competitive and noncompetitive behaviors.* Unpublished doctoral dissertation, Harvard University, 1973.

Jourard, S. Some lethal aspects of the male role. In *The transparent self*. Princeton, New Jersey: Van Nostrand, 1964, 46–55.

Jung, C. G. (1943). On the psychology of the unconscious. *Collected works of C. G. Jung* (Vol. 7). Princeton, New Jersey: Princeton University Press, 1970, 3–119.

Kagan, J. Acquisition and significance of sex typing and sex role identity. In M. L. Hoffman and L. W. Hoffman (Eds.), *Review of child development research* (Vol. 1). New York: Russell Sage, 1964, 137–168.

Kagan, J., and Moss, H. *Birth to maturity*. New York: Wiley, 1962.

Kahn, R. L., Wolfe, D. M., Quinn, R. P., and Snoek, D. J. *Organizational stress: studies in role conflict and ambiguity*. New York: Wiley, 1964.

Kanouse, D. E., and Hanson, L. R., Jr. Negativity in evaluations. In E. E. Jones *et al.* (Eds.), *Attribution: perceiving the causes of behavior*. Morristown, New Jersey: General Learning Press, 1972, 47–62.

Karabenick, S. A. *The effect of sex of competitor on the performance of females following success.* Paper presented at the annual meeting of the American Psychological Association, September 1972. (*Proceedings*, 1972, **7**, 275–276.)

Karabenick, S. A., and Marshall, J. M. Performance of females as a function of fear of success, fear of failure, type of opponent, and performance-contingent feedback. *Journal of Personality*, 1974, **42**, 220–237.

Karabenick, S. A., Marshall, J. M., and Karabenick, J. D. *Effects of fear of success, fear of failure, type of opponent, and feedback on female achievement performance.* Unpublished manuscript, Eastern Michigan University, 1974.

Kassarjian, H. H. Success, failure, and personality. *Psychological Reports*, 1963, **13**, 567–574.

Katz, F. M. The meaning of success: some differences in value systems of social classes. *Journal of Social Psychology*, 1964, **62**, 141–148.

Katz, I. (1964). Experiments on Negro performance in biracial situations. In M. B. Miles and W. W. Charters, Jr. (Eds.), *Learning in social settings*. Boston: Allyn and Bacon, 1970, 225–239.

Kelley, H. H. Two functions of reference groups. In G. E. Swanson, T. M. Newcomb, and E. L. Hartley (Eds.), *Readings in social psychology*. New York: Henry Holt, 1952, 410–414.

Kelly, H. A. *Divine providence in the England of Shakespeare's histories*. Cambridge: Harvard University Press, 1970.

Kenkel, M. B. E. *The influence of social response and sex-role stereotypes on the motive to avoid success*. Unpublished master's thesis, Miami University, Oxford, Ohio, 1974.

Kenny, D. A. A quasi-experimental approach to assessing treatment effects in the nonequivalent control group design. *Psychological Bulletin*, 1975, **82**, 345–362.

Kimball, B. Case studies in educational failure during adolescence. *American Journal of Orthopsychiatry*, 1953, **23**, 406–415.

King, G. *Herodotus*. Garden City, New York: Doubleday Doran, 1929.

Kinkade, K. *A Walden Two experience: the first five years of Twin Oaks community*. New York: William Morrow and Co., 1973.

Kirkpatrick, B. *Fear of success and its relations to the depression of performance in men and women*. Unpublished undergraduate thesis, Beaver College, 1974.

Klein, M. *Envy and gratitude: a study of unconscious sources*. New York: Basic Books, 1957.

Klinger, E. Fantasy need achievement as a motivational construct. *Psychological Bulletin*, 1966, **4**, 291–308.

Klinger, E. *Structure and functions of fantasy*. New York: Wiley, 1971.

Knapp, J. J. *Fear of academic success: a comparison of academically above-average, single, male and female college students*. Unpublished master's thesis, University of Florida, 1972.

Knapp, R. H., and Green, H. B. Personality correlates of success imagery. *Journal of Social Psychology*, 1964, **62**, 93–99.

Kogan, N., and Wallach, M. *Risk taking: a study in cognition and personality*. New York: Holt, Rinehart, and Winston, 1964.

Kohlberg, L. A cognitive-developmental analysis of children's sex-role concepts and attitudes. In E. E. Maccoby (Ed.), *The development of sex differences*. Stanford, California: Stanford University Press, 1966, 82–173.

Kohlberg, L. Stage and sequence: the cognitive-developmental approach to socialization. In D. Goslin (Ed.), *Handbook of socialization theory and research*. Chicago: Rand–McNally, 1969, 347–480.

Komarovsky, M. Cultural contradictions and sex roles. *American Journal of Sociology*, 1946, **52**, 184–189. (Reprinted in J. M. Bardwick (Ed.), *Readings on the psychology of women*. New York: Harper and Row, 1972, 58–62.)

Komarovsky, M. Functional analysis of sex roles. *American Sociological Review*, 1950, **15**, 508–516. (Reprinted in R. L. Coser (Ed.), *The family*. New York: St. Martin's, 1964, 290–306.)

Korda, M. *Male chauvinism!: how it works*. New York: Random House, 1973.

Kott, J. *The eating of the gods: an interpretation of Greek tragedy*. (B. Taborski and E. J. Czerwinski, trans.). New York: Random House, 1970.

Krusell, J. L. *Attribution of responsibility for performance outcomes of males and females*. Unpublished doctoral dissertation, University of Rochester, 1973.

Laing, R. D. *Knots*. New York: Pantheon, 1970.

Lama Foundation. *Be here now*. San Cristobal, New Mexico: Lama Foundation, 1971.

Lambert, W. E., Amos, S., and Goyeche, J. R. *The effects on pain tolerance of increasing the salience of sex-group membership*. Unpublished manuscript, McGill University, Montreal, 1967.

Lambert, W. E., Libman, E., and Poser, E. G. The effect of increased salience of a membership group on pain tolerance. *Journal of Personality,* 1960, **28**, 350–357.

Lanzetta, J. T., and Hannah, J. E. Reinforcing behavior of "naive" trainers. *Journal of Personality and Social Psychology,* 1969, **11**, 245–252.

Latane, B. Studies in social comparison—introduction and overview. *Journal of Experimental Social Psychology Supplement,* 1966, **1**, 1–5.

Lavach, J. F., and Lanier, H. B. *The motive to avoid success in high achieving 7th, 8th, 9th, and 10th grade girls.* Paper presented at the annual meeting of the Eastern Psychological Association, April 1974.

Lavach, J. F., and Lanier, H. B. The motive to avoid success in 7th, 8th, 9th, and 10th grade high-achieving girls. *Journal of Educational Research,* 1975, 216–218.

Lawson, E. D., and Stagner, R. Group pressure, attitude change, and autonomic involvement. *Journal of Social Psychology,* 1957, **45**, 299–312.

Lazarus, R. S., Deese, J., and Osler, S. F. The effects of psychological stress upon performance. *Psychological Bulletin,* 1952, **49**, 293–317.

Leacock, E. B., *Teaching and learning in city schools: a comparative study.* New York: Basic Books, 1969.

Lecky, P. *Self-consistency: a theory of personality.* New York: Island Press Cooperative, 1945.

Lederer, W. *The fear of women.* New York: Harcourt Brace Jovanovich, 1968.

Lenski, G. E. *Power and privilege.* New York: McGraw–Hill, 1966.

Lesser, G. Application of Guttman's scaling method to aggressive fantasy in children. *Educational and Psychological Measurement,* 1958, **18**, 543–551.

Lesser, G. S. (1965). Achievement motivation in women. In D. C. McClelland and R. S. Steele (Eds.), *Human motivation: a book of readings.* Morristown, New Jersey: General Learning Press, 1973, 202–221.

Lesser, G. S., Krawitz, R. N., and Packard, R. Experimental arousal of achievement motivation in adolescent girls. *Journal of Abnormal and Social Psychology,* 1963, **66**, 59–66.

Letailleur, M., Morin, J., and LeBorgne, Y. Héautoscopie hétérosexuelle et schizophrénie. (The self-induced heterosexual image and schizophrenia.) *Annual Medical Psychology,* 1958, **2**, 451–461. Cited in Cheek, 1964.

Leventhal, G. S., Weiss, T., and Long, G. Equity, reciprocity, and reallocating rewards in the dyad. *Journal of Personality and Social Psychology,* 1969, **13**, 300–305.

Levin, A. J. The fiction of the death instinct. *Psychiatric Quarterly,* 1951, **25**, 257–281.

Levine, A., and Crumrine, J. *Women and the fear of success: a problem in replication.* Paper presented at the annual meeting of the American Sociological Association, August 1973 (ERIC Reproduction Document No. ED 082 101).

Levine, A., and Crumrine, J. Women and the fear of success: a problem in replication. *American Journal of Sociology,* 1975, **80**, 964–974.

Levine, M. The academic achievement test. *American Psychologist,* 1976, **31**, 228–238.

Levine, R., Reis, H., Sue, E., and Turner, G. Fear of failure in males: a more salient factor than fear of success in females? *Sex Roles,* 1976, **2**, 389–398.

Levinson, D. J. Criminality from a sense of guilt. *Journal of Personality,* 1952, **20**, 402–429.

Levi-Strauss, C. *The savage mind.* Chicago: University of Chicago Press, 1966.

Levy, B. The school's role in the sex-role stereotyping of girls: a feminist review of the literature. *Feminist Studies,* 1972, **1**, 5–23.

Levy-Bruhl, L. *Primitives and the supernatural.* New York: E. P. Dutton, 1935.

Lewin, K., Dembo, T., Festinger, L., and Sears, P. Level of aspiration. In J. McV. Hunt (Ed.), *Personality and the behavior disorders* (Vol. I). New York: Ronald, 1944, 333–378.

Lewis, W. D. Some characteristics of very superior children. *Journal of Genetic Psychology,* 1943, **62**, 301–309.

Liebling, B. A., and Shaver, P. Evaluation, self-awareness, and task performance. *Journal of Experimental Social Psychology,* 1973, **9**, 297–306.

Lief, H. I. Anxiety reaction. In A. M. Freedman and H. I. Kaplan (Eds.), *Comprehensive textbook of psychiatry.* Baltimore: Williams and Wilkins, 1967, 857–870.

Lilly, J. C. Some considerations regarding basic mechanisms of positive and negative types of motivations. *American Journal of Psychiatry,* 1958, **115**, 498–504.

Lilly, J. C. *Programming and metaprogramming in the human biocomputer.* Menlo Park, California: Portola Inst., 1970.

Linder, D. E., Cooper, J., and Jones, E. E. Decision freedom as a determinant of the role of incentive magnitude in attitude change. *Journal of Personality and Social Psychology,* 1967, **6**, 245–254.

Lindzey, G., Bradford, J., Tejessy, C., and Davids, A. Thematic Apperception Test: an interpretive lexicon for clinician and investigator. *Journal of Clinical Psychology,* 1959, monograph supplement no. 12.

Lindzey, G., and Goldberg, M. Motivational differences between males and females as measured by the Thematic Apperception Test. *Journal of Personality,* 1953, **22**, 101–107.

Lindzey, G., and Kalnins, D. Thematic Apperception Test: some evidence bearing on the "hero assumption." *Journal of Abnormal and Social Psychology,* 1958, **57**, 76–83.

Lindzey, G., and Newburg, A. S. (1954). Thematic Apperception Test: a tentative appraisal of some "signs" of anxiety. In B. I. Murstein (Ed.), *Handbook of projective techniques.* New York: Basic, 1965, 587–597.

Lindzey, G., and Silverman, M. TAT: techniques of group administration, sex differences, and the role of verbal productivity. *Journal of Personality,* 1959, **27**, 311–323.

Lockheed, M. E. Female motive to avoid success: a psychological barrier or a response to deviancy? *Sex Roles,* 1975, **1**, 41–50.

Lockheed-Katz, M. *Female motive to avoid success: a psychological barrier or a response to deviancy?* Paper presented at the annual meeting of the American Educational Research Association, Chicago, April 1974. (ERIC Reproduction Document No. ED 089 153).

Longevity of corporate executives. *Statistical Bulletin of Metropolitan Life,* February 1974, pp. 3–4.

Lorand, S. *Clinical studies in psychoanalysis.* New York: International Universities Press, 1950.

Lowin, A., and Epstein, G. F. Does expectancy determine performance? *Journal of Experimental Social Psychology,* 1965, **1**, 248–255.

Lowy, I. Stupidity as exemption. *International Journal of Individual Psychology,* 1935, **1**, 102–110.

Lynn, K. S. *The dream of success: a study of the modern American imagination.* Boston: Little Brown, 1955.

Maccoby, E. Woman's intellect. In S. M. Farber and R. H. L. Wilson (Eds.), *The potential of women.* New York: McGraw–Hill, 1963, 24–39.

Maccoby, E. E. Sex differences in intellectual functioning. In E. E. Maccoby (Ed.), *The development of sex differences.* Stanford, California: Stanford University Press, 1966, 25–55. (a)

Maccoby, E. (Ed.) *The development of sex differences.* Stanford, California: Stanford University Press, 1966. (b)

Maccoby, E. E. The meaning of being female. *Contemporary Psychology,* 1972, **17**, 369–372.

Maccoby, E. E., and Jacklin, C. N. *The psychology of sex differences.* Stanford, California: Stanford University Press, 1974.

Machiavelli, N. (1537) *The prince* (L. Ricci, trans.). New York: Mentor, 1952.

MacKinnon, R. A., and Michels, R. *The psychiatric interview in clinical practice.* Philadelphia: Saunders, 1971.

Maclagan, R. C. *Evil eye in the Western Highlands.* London: David Nutt, 1902.

MacLeish, A. *Herakles.* Boston: Houghton Mifflin, 1967.

Mahone, C. H. Fear of failure and unrealistic vocational aspiration. *Journal of Abnormal and Social Psychology,* 1960, **60**, 253–261.

Major, B. N. *Effects on females' performance of fear of success, physical attractiveness, and competitor's sex.* Unpublished master's thesis, Miami University, 1975.

Major, B. N., and Sherman, R. C. *The competitive woman: fear of success, attractiveness, and competitor sex.* Unpublished manuscript, Miami University, 1975. (Presented at the annual meeting of the American Psychological Association, 1975.)

Makosky, V. P. *Fear of success, sex-role orientation of the task, and competitive condition as variables affecting women's performance in achievement-oriented situations.* Paper presented at annual meeting of the Midwestern Psychological Association, Cleveland, May 1972 (ERIC Reproduction Document No. ED 069 999).

Makosky, V. P. Sex-role compatibility of task and of competitor, and fear of success as variables affecting women's performance. *Sex Roles,* 1976, **2**, 237–248.

Malone, M., and Reynolds, M. K. *The effects of "fear of success" in women in the prisoner's dilemma game.* Unpublished manuscript, University of Michigan, n.d.

Mandler, G., and Sarason, S. B. A study of anxiety and learning. *Journal of Abnormal and Social Psychology,* 1952, **47**, 166–173.

Maracek, J., and Mettee, D. R. Avoidance of continued success as a function of self-esteem, level of esteem certainty, and responsibility for success. *Journal of Personality and Social Psychology,* 1972, **22**, 98–107.

Marcuse, H. *Eros and civilization.* New York: Random House, 1955.

Marks, I. M. *Fears and phobias.* New York: Academic Press, 1969.

Marrow, A. J. (Ed.). *The failure of success.* London: Allen and Unwin, 1973.

Martyna, W. *The motive to avoid success and female satisfaction with performance in achievement-oriented situations.* Unpublished manuscript, University of Southern California, 1973.

Maugham, W. S. *The summing up.* New York: Literary Guild of America, 1938.

Maxwell, P. G., and Gonzalez, A. E. J. Traditional and nontraditional role choice and the need for failure among college women. *Psychological Reports,* 1972, **31**, 545–546.

May, R. *The meaning of anxiety.* New York: Ronald, 1950.

May, R. (1961). The meaning of the Oedipus myth. In R. W. Smith (Ed.), *Guilt.* Garden City, New York: Doubleday and Co., 1971, 171–183.

May, R. Sex differences in fantasy patterns. *Journal of Projective Techniques and Personality Assessment,* 1966, **30**, 576–586. (Reprinted in J. M. Bardwick (Ed.), *Readings in the psychology of women.* New York: Harper and Row, 1972, 301–307.)

McCabe, B. Will success spoil . . .? *Boston Globe,* May 30, 1976, pp. B1, B4.

McCall, G. J., and Simmons, J. L. *Identities and interactions.* New York: Free Press, 1966.

McClelland, D. C. *Personality.* New York: Sloane, 1951.

McClelland, D. C. Toward a theory of motive acquisition. *American Psychologist*, 1965, **20**, 321–333.

McClelland, D. C. Longitudinal trends in the relation of thought to action. *Journal of Consulting Psychology*, 1966, **30**, 479–483.

McClelland, D. C. *Assessing human motivation.* New York: General Learning Corp., 1971.

McClelland, D. C. *Power: the inner experience.* New York: Irvington Publishers, 1975.

McClelland, D. C., and Apicella, F. S. Reminiscence following experimentally induced failure. *Journal of Experimental Psychology*, 1947, **37**, 159–169.

McClelland, D. C., Atkinson, J. W., Clark, R. A., and Lowell, E. L. *The achievement motive.* New York: Appleton–Century–Crofts, 1953.

McClelland, D. C., Davis, W. N., Kalin, R., and Wanner, E. *The drinking man: alcohol and human motivation.* New York: Free Press, 1972.

McClelland, D. C., and Steele, R. S. *Motivation workshops.* New York: General Learning Press, 1972.

McClelland, D. C., and Watson, R. I., Jr. Power motivation and risk-taking behavior. *Journal of Personality*, 1973, **41**, 121–139.

McClelland, D. C., and Watt, N. F. Sex-role alienation in schizophrenia. *Journal of Abnormal Psychology*, 1968, **73**, 226–239.

McClelland, D. C., and Winter, D. G. *Motivating economic achievement: accelerating economic development through psychological training.* New York: Free Press, 1969.

McGuinness, E. *Success avoidance and competitive performance.* Unpublished manuscript, Rutgers University, 1974. (a)

McGuinness, E. *The effects of success avoidance, sex of competitor, and level of task difficulty on performance.* Paper presented at the annual meeting of the Eastern Psychological Association, April 1974. (b)

McKeachie, W. J., Isaacson, R. L., Milholland, J. E., and Yin, Y. G. Student achievement motives, achievement cues, and academic achievement. *Journal of Consulting and Clinical Psychology*, 1968, **32**, 26–29.

McKee, J. P., and Sherriffs, A. C. The differential evaluation of males and females. *Journal of Personality*, 1957, **25**, 356–371.

Mead, G. H. *Mind, self, and society.* Chicago: University of Chicago Press, 1934.

Mead, M. (1949) *Male and female: a study of the sexes in a changing world.* New York: Dell, 1968.

Mednick, M. T. S. *Motivational and personality factors related to career goals of black college women* (91-09-70-36). Springfield, Virginia: Manpower Administration, U.S. Dept. of Labor, 1973. (NTIS No. PB 218-969)

Mednick, M. T. S., and Puryear, G. R. Motivational and personality factors related to career goals of black college women. *Journal of Social and Behavioral Sciences*, 1975, **21**, 1–30.

Mehl, J. Uber Erfolge und Misserfolge im Leistungs und Zufallsbereich. *Zeitschrift fuer Psychologie*, 1962, **167**, 177–267. Cited in Heckhausen, 1967.

Melville, H. (1851). *Moby Dick or the whale* (C. Feidelson, Jr., Ed.). New York: Bobbs–Merrill Co., 1964.

Mencken, H. L. (Ed.). *A new dictionary of quotations on historical principles from ancient and modern sources.* New York: Knopf, 1942.

Merton, R. K. Continuities in the theory of reference groups and social structure. In R. K. Merton (Ed.), *Social theory and social structure* (3rd ed.). New York: Free Press, 1968, 335–440.

Merton, R. K., and Rossi, A. S. (1950) Contributions to the theory of reference group behavior. In R. K. Merton (Ed.), *Social theory and social structure* (3rd ed.). New York: Free Press, 1968, 279–334.

Mettee, D. R. Rejection of unexpected success as a function of the negative consequences of accepting success. *Journal of Personality and Social Psychology*, 1971, **17**, 332–341.

Mettee, D. R., Williams, A., and Reed, H. D. *Facilitating self-image enhancement and improving reading performance in young black males.* Unpublished manuscript, University of Denver, 1974.

Midgley, N., and Abrams, M. S. Fear of success and locus of control in young women. *Journal of Counseling and Clinical Psychology*, 1974, **42**, 737.

Miles, J. Sisyphus. *New Yorker*, 1958, May 31.

Miller, B. S. *Sex differences in attitudes toward achievement in adolescence.* Unpublished honors thesis, University of Michigan, 1972.

Miller, N. E. Experimental studies of conflict. In J. McV. Hunt (Ed.), *Personality and the behavior disorders.* New York: Ronald, 1944, 431–465.

Miller, N. E. Liberalization of basic S-R concepts: extensions to conflict behavior, motivation, and social learning. In S. Koch (Ed.), *Psychology: a study of a science* (Vol. 2). New York: McGraw–Hill, 1959, 196–292.

Millman, M. Observations on sex role research. *Journal of Marriage and the Family*, 1971, **33**, 772–776.

Mills, C. W. (1940). Situated actions and vocabularies of motive. In J. G. Manis and B. N. Meltzer (Eds.), *Symbolic interaction.* Boston: Allyn and Bacon, 1967, 355–366.

Milner, E. Effects of sex role and social status on the early adolescent personality. *Genetic Psychology Monographs*, 1949, **40**, 231–325.

Milner, E. *The failure of success.* New York: Exposition, 1959.

Milton, G. A. The effects of sex-role identification upon problem-solving skill. *Journal of Abnormal and Social Psychology*, 1957, **55**, 208–212.

Milton, G. A. *Five studies of the relationship between sex-role identification and achievement in problem-solving.* Technical report #3, Department of Industrial Administration, Department of Psychology, Yale University, Dec. 1958. Cited in Bem, 1970.

Milton, G. A. Sex differences in problem-solving as a function of role appropriateness of the problem content. *Psychological Reports*, 1959, **5**, 705–708.

Mischel, W. Sex-typing and socialization. In P. H. Mussen (Ed.), *Carmichael's manual of child psychology* (3rd ed.). New York: Wiley, 1970, 3–72.

Mischel, W., Ebbesen, E. B., and Zeiss, A. R. Selective attention to the self: situational and dispositional determinants. *Journal of Personality and Social Psychology*, 1973, **27**, 129–142.

Montemayor, R. *Children's performance on and attraction to an activity as a function of masculine, feminine or neutral labels and sex-role preference.* Paper presented at the annual meeting of the Eastern Psychological Association, Boston, April 1972.

Moore, K. A. *Fear of success: the distribution, correlates, reliability and consequences for fertility of fear of success among respondents in a metropolitan survey population.* Paper presented at the annual meeting of the American Psychological Association, New Orleans, 1974.

Moore, L. L. *The relationship of academic group membership to the motive to avoid success in women* (Doctoral dissertation, University of Virginia, 1971). *Dissertation Abstracts International*, 1972, **32**, 4355A. (University Microfilms No. 72-7220)

Monahan, L., Kuhn, D., and Shaver, P. Intrapsychic versus cultural explanations of the "fear of success" motive. *Journal of Personality and Social Psychology,* 1974, **29**, 60–64.

Moreland, J. R., and Liss-Levinson, N. *An evaluation of fear of success scoring.* Unpublished manuscript, Southern Illinois University, 1975.

Morgan, S. W., and Mausner, B. *Behavioral and fantasied indicators of avoidance of success in men and women.* Paper presented at the annual meeting of the Eastern Psychological Association, Boston, April 1972 (ERIC Reproduction Document No. ED 068 851).

Morgan, S. W., and Mausner, B. Behavioral and fantasied indicators of avoidance of success in men and women. *Journal of Personality,* 1973, **41**, 457–470.

Morgan, W. R., and Sawyer, J. Bargaining, expectations, and the preference for equality over equity. *Journal of Personality and Social Psychology,* 1967, **6**, 139–149.

Morrison, D. F. *Multivariate statistical methods.* New York: McGraw–Hill, 1967.

Most women fear success, doctor claims. *National Enquirer,* 1973, **47**(23), p. 32.

Mosteller, F., and Bush, R. R. Selected quantitative techniques. In G. Lindzey (Ed.), *Handbook of social psychology* (Vol. 1). Cambridge: Addison–Wesley, 1954, 289–334.

Mosteller, F., and Youtz, C. Tables of the Freeman–Tukey transformations for binomial and Poisson distributions. *Biometrika,* 1961, **48**, 433–440.

Moulton, R. W. Notes for a projective measure of fear of failure. In J. W. Atkinson (Ed.), *Motives in fantasy, action and society,* Princeton, New Jersey: Van Nostrand, 1958, 563–571.

Muhl, A. M. Why women fail. In M. Fishbein and W. A. White (Eds.), *Why men fail.* New York: Century, 1928, 283–302.

Murphy-Berman, V. Effects of success and failure on perceptions of gender identity. *Sex Roles,* 1976, **2**, 367–374.

Murray, H. A. *Explorations in personality.* New York: Oxford University Press, 1938.

Murray, H. A. *Thematic Apperception Test Manual.* Cambridge, Massachusetts: Harvard University Press, 1943.

Murray, H. Uses of the Thematic Apperception Test. *American Journal of Psychiatry,* 1951, **107**, 577–581.

Murstein, B. *Theory and research in projective techniques.* New York: Wiley, 1963.

Nagel, E. *The structure of science: problems in the logic of scientific explanation.* New York: Harcourt, Brace, and World, 1961.

Neumann, E. *The origins and history of consciousness.* Princeton: Princeton University Press, 1970.

Newland, T. E. *The gifted in socioeducational perspective.* Englewood Cliffs, New Jersey: Prentice-Hall, 1976.

Newman, J. C., Dember, C. F., and Krug, O. "He can but he won't": a psychodynamic study of so-called "gifted underachievers." *Psychoanalytic Study of the Child,* 1973, **28**, 83–130.

Nietzsche, F. W. *Beyond good and evil* (R. J. Hollingdale, Trans.). Harmondsworth: Penguin, 1973.

Nissen, H. W. Comments on Dr. Festinger's paper. In M. R. Jones (Ed.), *Nebraska symposium on motivation.* Lincoln: University of Nebraska Press, 1954, 219–223.

Norman, R. Counselor response to female clients with deviate and conforming career goals. *Journal of Counseling Psychology,* 1971, **18**, 352–357.

Nuttin, J. *Tache, réussite et échec.* Louvain: University de Louvain Press, 1953. Cited in Heckhausen, 1967.

Oakley, A. *Sex, gender, and society.* London: Temple Smith, 1972.

O'Connell, A. *Effects of manipulated status on performance, goal setting, need achievement, anxiety, and fear of success.* Paper presented at annual meeting of the Eastern Psychological Association, Washington, D.C., May 1973.

O'Connor, P., Atkinson, J. W., and Horner, M. Motivational implications of ability grouping in schools. In J. W. Atkinson and N. T. Feather (Eds.), *A theory of achievement motivation.* New York: Wiley, 1966, 231–248.

Ogilvie, B. *Negative and positive psychological factors associated with athletic competition.* Paper presented at American Academy of Orthopedic Surgeons, June, 1970.

O'Leary, V. E. *The motive to avoid success: antecedents, correlates, and arousal contexts: some speculative results.* Paper presented at the annual conference of the Michigan Psychological Association, April 1974.

O'Leary, V. E., and Hammack, B. Sex-role orientation and achievement context as determinants of the motive to avoid success. *Sex Roles,* 1975, **1**, 225–234.

Olsen, N. J., and Willemsen, E. W. *Success as deviance: project proposal.* Unpublished manuscript, University of Santa Clara, August 1974.

Onions, C. T. (Ed.). *Shorter Oxford English Dictionary* (3rd ed.). Oxford: Clarendon, 1972.

Options in Education. *Gifted children in the schools.* St. Louis: Institute for Educational Leadership, George Washington University, 1976. (Transcript for five-part radio program)

Orwell, G. (1940) Inside the whale. *A collection of essays.* Garden City, New York: Doubleday & Co., 1954, 215–256.

Ovesey, L. Masculine aspirations in women: an adaptational analysis. *Psychiatry,* 1956, **19**, 341–351.

Ovesey, L. Fear of vocational success: a phobic extension of the paranoid reaction. *Archives of General Psychiatry,* 1962, **7**, 82–93.

Papanek, H. Men, women, and work: reflections on the two-person career. *American Journal of Sociology,* 1973, **78**, 852–872.

Pappo, M. *Fear of success: a theoretical analysis and the construction and validation of a measuring instrument.* (Doctoral dissertation, Columbia University, 1972.) (University Microfilms No. 282-161)

Parker, V. J. *Fear of success, sex-role orientation of the task, and competition condition as variables affecting women's performance in achievement-oriented situations* (Doctoral dissertation, Ohio University, 1971). *Dissertation Abstracts International,* 1972, **32**, 5495B. (University Microfilms No. 72-9593)

Parsons, T. Age and sex in the social structure. *American Sociological Review,* 1942, **7**, 604–616. (Also in R. L. Coser (Ed.), *The family.* New York: St. Martin's, 1964, 251–266.)

Parsons, T., and Bales, R. F. *Family, socialization, and interaction process.* Glencoe, Illinois: Free Press, 1955.

Patty, R. A. *The arousal of the motive to avoid success in college women* (Doctoral dissertation, University of Nebraska, 1973). (University Microfilms No. 73-25, 474) (a)

Patty, R. A. *The arousal of the motive to avoid success: an extension and test of the theory.* Unpublished manuscript, University of Nebraska, 1973. (b)

Patty, R. A. *The arousal of the motive to avoid success in college women.* Paper presented at the annual meeting of the Southeastern Psychological Association, Hollywood, Florida, 1974.

Patty, R. A. The motive to avoid success and instructional set. *Sex Roles: A Journal of Research,* 1976, **2**, 81–83.

Patty, R. A., and Ferrell, M. M. A preliminary note on the motive to avoid success and the menstrual cycle. *Journal of Psychology,* 1974, **86**, 173–177.

Patty, R. A., and Shelley, H. P. *Motive to avoid success: a profile.* Paper presented at the annual meeting of the Southeastern Psychological Association, Hollywood, Florida, 1974.

Paulus, P. B., and Murdoch, P. Anticipated evaluation and audience presence in the enhancement of dominant responses. *Journal of Experimental Social Psychology,* 1971, **7**, 280–291.

Peplau, L. A. *The impact of fear of success, sex-role attitudes, and opposite-sex relationships on women's intellectual performance: an experimental study of competition in dating couples.* Unpublished doctoral dissertation, Harvard University, 1973.

Peplau, L. A. *When do women fear successful achievement?* Unpublished manuscript, University of California, Los Angeles, 1974.

Peplau, L. A. Fear of success in dating couples. *Sex Roles,* 1976, **2**, 249–258.

Perris, C., and Espvall, M. Depressive-type psychic reactions caused by success. *Psychiatria Clinica,* 1973, **6**, 346–356.

Pesso, A. *Experience in action.* New York: Free Press, 1973.

Pettigrew, T. Social evaluation theory. In D. Levine (Ed.), *Nebraska symposium on motivation.* Lincoln: University of Nebraska Press, 1967, 241–311.

Pheterson, G. I. *Female prejudice against women.* Unpublished manuscript, Connecticut College, 1969. Cited in Pheterson *et al.*, 1971.

Pheterson, G. I., Kiesler, S. B., and Goldberg, P. A. Evaluation of the performance of women as a function of their sex, achievement, and personal history. *Journal of Personality and Social Psychology,* 1971, **19**, 114–118.

Phillips, B. N. Sex, social class, and anxiety as sources of variation in school achievement. *Journal of Educational Psychology,* 1962, **53**, 316–322.

Piaget, J. *Structuralism.* New York: Basic Books, 1970.

Pierce, J. V., and Bowman, P. H. Motivational patterns of superior high school students. *Cooperative research monographs,* 1960, No. 2, 33–66 (U.S. Dept. of Health, Education, and Welfare Publication No. OE-35016). Cited by E. Lewis *Developing woman's potential.* Ames: Iowa State University Press, 1968.

Pitts, J. The hippies as contrameritocracy. *Dissent,* 1969, July–August, 326–337.

Pleck, J. *Male threat from female competence: an experimental study in college dating couples* (Doctoral dissertation, Harvard University, 1973). *Dissertation Abstracts International,* 1974, **34**, 6221B. (University Microfilms No. 74–11, 721)

Pleck, J. Male threat from female competence: an experimental study in college dating couples. *Journal of Clinical and Consulting Psychology,* in press.

Podhoretz, N. *Making it.* New York: Bantam, 1969.

Porjesz, Y. R. *The femininity-achievement conflict: an expanded formulation of the 'motive to avoid success' in females* (Doctoral dissertation, City University of New York, 1974). *Dissertation Abstracts International,* 1974, **35**, 2443B–2444B. (University Microfilms No. 74-23, 715)

Portnoy, I. The anxiety states. In S. Arieti (Ed.), *American handbook of psychiatry* (Vol. 1). New York: Basic, 1959, 307–323.

Powers, E. A., Braito, R., and Dean, D. G. *Cultural contradictions and sex roles: fact or arti-fact?* Paper presented at meeting of National Council of Family Relations, Portland, Oregon, October 1972.

Puryear, G. R., and Mednick, M. S. Black militancy, affective attachment, and the fear of success in black college women. *Journal of Consulting and Clinical Psychology,* 1974, **42**, 263–266.

Radcliffe College (Producer). *Radcliffe's Sixth President.* Cambridge, Massachusetts: Alumnae Office, Radcliffe College, 1973. (Film)

Radloff, R. Social comparison and ability evaluation. *Journal of Experimental Social Psychology Supplement,* 1966, **1**, 6–26.

Radloff, R. Affiliation and social comparison. In E. F. Borgatta and W. F. Lambert (Eds.), *Handbook of personality theory and research.* Chicago: Rand–McNally, 1968, 943–958.

Rand, P. *Achievement motivation and school performance.* Oslo, Norway: Unversitets-forlaget, 1965.

Rank, O. (1914) *The myth of the birth of the hero and other writings* (P. Freund, Ed.). New York: Vintage, 1959.

Rapaport, D. Toward a theory of thinking. In D. Rapaport (Ed.), *Organization and pathology of thought.* New York: Columbia University Press, 1951, 689–730.

Rapaport, D., Gill, M. M., and Schafer, R. *Diagnostic psychological testing* (rev. ed. by R. R. Holt). London: University of London Press, 1970.

Raphelson, A. C., and Moulton, R. W. The relationship between imaginative and direct verbal measures of test anxiety under two conditions of uncertainty. *Journal of Personality,* 1958, **26**, 556–567.

Rasmussen, G., and Zander, A. Group membership and self-evaluation. *Human Relations,* 1954, **7**, 239–251.

Ray, J. J. Projective tests *can* be made reliable: measuring need for achievement. *Journal of Personality Assessment,* 1974, **38**, 303–307.

Raynor, J. O. Relationships between achievement-related motives, future orientation, and academic performance. *Journal of Personality and Social Psychology,* 1970, **15**, 28–33.

Reed, M. R. The masculinity-femininity dimension in normal and psychotic subjects. *Journal of Abnormal and Social Psychology,* 1957, **55**, 289–294.

Reich, A. Pathologic forms of self-esteem regulation. *Psychoanalytic Study of the Child,* 1960, **15**, 215–232.

Reik, T. *Masochism in modern man.* New York: Farrar, Strauss, 1941.

Rider, E. A. *The barrier to female achievement: motive to avoid success or social proscription?* Paper presented at the annual meeting of the Washington State Psychological Association, May 1973.

Riesman, D. *Individualism reconsidered.* Glencoe, Illinois: Free Press, 1954.

Rishchin, M. (Ed.). *The American gospel of success.* Chicago: Quadrangle, 1965.

Ritzer, G. Sociology: a multiple paradigm science. *American Sociologist,* 1975, **10**, 156–167.

Robbins, L., and Robbins, E. Comment on "Toward an understanding of achievement-related conflicts in women." *Journal of Social Issues,* 1973, **29**, 133–137.

Robbins, R. B. Achievement performance and fantasy arousal in college women as a function of the motive to avoid success, problem format, and relationship to experimenter (Doctoral dissertation, Temple University, 1973). *Dissertation Abstracts International,* 1973, **34**, 2950B. (University Microfilms No. 73-30, 172)

Robison, K. A. *Fear of success and future orientation.* Paper presented at the annual meeting of the American Psychological Association, New Orleans, August 1974.

Roethlisberger, F. J., and Dickson, W. J. *Management and the worker.* Cambridge: Harvard University Press, 1939.

Rokkan, S., and Valen, H. The mobilization of the periphery. In S. Rokkan (Ed.), *Approaches to the study of political participation.* Bergen, 1962. Cited in Holter, 1970.

Romer, N. *Sex differences in the development of the motive to avoid success, sex role identity, and performance in competitive and noncompetitive conditions.* Paper presented at meeting of the American Educational Research Association, Washington, D.C., April 1975. (a)

Romer, N. The motive to avoid success and its effects on performance in school-aged males and females. *Developmental Psychology,* 1975, **11**(6), November. (b)

Rommetveit, R. *Social norms and roles.* Minneapolis: University of Minnesota Press, 1955.

Rosenbaum, J., and McAuliffe, L. *What is fear?* Englewood Cliffs, New Jersey: Prentice-Hall, 1972.

Rosenberg, B. G., and Hyde, J. S. *Female development revisited.* Paper presented at the annual meeting of the American Psychological Association, Montreal, 1973.

Rosenberg, M. J. When dissonance fails: on eliminating evaluation apprehension from attitude measurement. *Journal of Personality and Social Psychology,* 1965, **1**, 28–42.

Rosenthal, R. The Pygmalion effect lives. *Psychology Today,* 1973, **7**(4), 56–63. (a)

Rosenthal, R. On the social psychology of the self-fulfilling prophecy: further evidence for Pygmalion effects and their mediating mechanisms. In M. King (Ed.), *Reading and school achievement: cognitive and affective influences.* Eighth annual spring reading conference, Rutgers University, 1973. (Also Andover, Massachusetts: Warner Modular Publications, 1973.) (b)

Rosenthal, R., Archer, D., Koivumaki, J. H., DiMatteo, M. R., and Rogers, P. L. Assessing sensitivity to nonverbal communication: the PONS test. *Division 8 Newsletter,* Jan. 1974, 1–3.

Rosenthal, R., and Jacobson, L. *Pygmalion in the classroom.* New York: Holt, Rinehart, and Winston, 1968.

Rosenthal, R., and Rosnow, R. L. *Primer of methods for the behavioral sciences.* New York: Wiley, 1975.

Ross, M. Suicide among physicians. *Diseases of the Nervous System,* 1973, **34**, 146–150.

Rossi, A. S. Barriers to the career choice of engineering, medicine, or science among American women. In J. A. Mattfeld and C. G. Van Aken (Eds.), *Women and the scientific professions.* Cambridge, Massachusetts: M.I.T. Press, 1965, 51–127. (Reprinted in J. M. Bardwick (Ed.), *Readings on the psychology of women.* New York: Harper and Row, 1972, 72-82.)

Rossi, A. S. Transition to parenthood. *Journal of Marriage and the Family,* 1968, **30**, 26–39.

Rotter, J. B. Studies in the use and validity of the thematic apperception test with mentally retarded patients. I. Method of analysis and clinical problems. *Character and Personality,* 1940, **9**, 18–34.

Rotter, J. B. Thematic Apperception Tests: suggestions for administration and interpretation. *Journal of Personality,* 1946, **15**, 70–92.

Rotter, J. B. *Social learning and clinical psychology.* New York: Prentice-Hall, 1954.

Rotter, J. B. The role of the psychological situation in determining the direction of human behavior. In M. R. Jones (Ed.), *Nebraska Symposium on Motivation.* Lincoln: University of Nebraska Press, 1955, 245–269.

Roy, D. F. Quota restriction and goldbricking in a machine shop. *American Journal of Sociology,* 1952, **57**, 427–442.

Roy, D. F. Work satisfaction and social reward in quota achievement: an analysis of piecework incentive. *American Sociological Review,* 1953, **18**, 507–514.

Rozeboom, W. W. The fallacy of the null-hypothesis significance test. *Psychological Bulletin,* 1960, **57**, 416–428.

Rubovits, P. C., and Maehr, M. L. *The effect of the labels "gifted" and "nongifted" on teachers' interaction with Black and White students.* Unpublished manuscript, University of Illinois, 1972. Cited by Rosenthal, 1973b.

Rudikoff, S. Women and success. *Commentary,* 1974, **58**(4), 49–59.

Rudikoff, S. Women and success. *Commentary,* February 1975, pp. 7, 10–11, 14.

Ruitenbeek, H. M. *The male myth.* New York: Dell, 1967.

Russell, D. G., and Sarason, E. G. Test anxiety, sex and experimental conditions in relation to anagram solution. *Journal of Personality and Social Psychology,* 1965, **1**, 493–496.

Ruzicka, W. J. *The nightmare of success: the fallacy of the super-success dream.* Los Altos, California: Peninsula, 1973.

Ryan, F. J. An investigation of personality differences associated with competitive ability. In B. M. Wedge (Ed.), *Psychosocial problems of college men.* New Haven: Yale University Press, 1958, 113–122. (a)

Ryan, F. J. Further observations on competitive ability in athletics. In B. M. Wedge (Ed.), *Psychosocial problems of college men.* New Haven: Yale University Press, 1958, 123–139. (b)

Ryan, W. *Blaming the victim.* New York: Random House, 1971.

Samelson, F. Conforming behavior under two conditions of conflict in the cognitive field. *Journal of Abnormal and Social Psychology,* 1957, **55**, 181–187.

Sampson, E. E. Studies in status congruence. In L. Berkowitz (Ed.), *Advances in experimental social psychology* (Vol. 4). New York: Academic Press, 1969, 225–270.

Sarason, S. B., Davidson, K. S., Lighthall, F. F., Waite, R. R., and Ruebush, B. K. *Anxiety in elementary school children.* New York: Wiley, 1960.

Sarbin, T. R., and Allen, V. L. Role theory. In G. Lindzey and E. Aronson (Eds.), *Handbook of social psychology* (2nd ed.) (Vol. 1). Reading, Massachusetts: Addison–Wesley, 1969, 488–567.

Sarnoff, I. *The need to fail scale.* Unpublished questionnaire, 1967. Cited in Pappo, 1972.

Schafer, R. Ideals, the ego ideal, and the ideal self. In R. R. Holt (Ed.), *Motives and thought: psychoanalytic essays in honor of David Rapaport, Psychological Issues,* 1967, **5**, monograph 18–19, 131–174.

Schachter, S. *The psychology of affiliation: experimental studies of the sources of gregariousness.* Stanford: Stanford University Press, 1959.

Schafer, R. The psychoanalytic vision of reality. *International Journal of Psycho-Analysis,* 1970, **51**, 279–297.

Scheff, T. J. *Being mentally ill: a sociological theory.* Chicago: Aldine, 1966.

Schervish, P. G. The labeling perspective: its bias and potential in the study of political deviance. *The American Sociologist,* 1973, **8**, 47–57.

Schilder, P. *Psychoanalysis, man, and society.* New York: Norton, 1951.

Schlosberg, H. The relationship between success and the laws of conditioning. *Psychological Review,* 1937, **44**, 379–394.

Schneider, D. J. Tactical self-presentation after success and failure. *Journal of Personality and Social Psychology,* 1969, **13**, 262–268.

Schoenfeld, W. N. An experimental approach to anxiety, escape, and avoidance behavior. In P. M. Hoch and J. Zubin (Eds.), *Anxiety.* New York: Grune and Stratton, 1950, 70–99.

Schroder, H. M., and Hunt, D. E. Failure-avoidance in situational interpretation and problem solving. *Psychological Monographs,* 1957, **71**, whole no. 432.

Schuster, D. B. On the fear of success. *Psychiatric Quarterly,* 1955, **29**, 412–420.

Schwenn, M. *Arousal of the motive to avoid success at Radcliffe College.* Unpublished manuscript, Radcliffe College, 1970. Cited in Horner, 1972a. (a)

Schwenn, M. *A study of fear of success in eighteen Radcliffe undergraduates.* Unpublished manuscript, Radcliffe College, 1970. (b)

Scott, W. A. The avoidance of threatening material in imaginative behavior. *Journal of Abnormal and Social Psychology,* 1956, **52**, 338–346. (Reprinted in J. W. Atkinson (Ed.), *Motives in fantasy, action, and society.* Princeton, New Jersey: Van Nostrand, 1958, 572–585.)

Sears, P. S. Levels of aspiration in academically successful and unsuccessful children. *Journal of Abnormal and Social Psychology,* 1940, **35**, 498–536.

Sears, R. R. Initiation of the repression sequence by experienced failure. *Journal of Experimental Psychology,* 1937, **20**, 570–580.

Seeman, W., and Buck, R. On a behavioristic approach to the concept of wish-fulfillment. *Journal of Abnormal and Social Psychology,* 1952, **47**, 17–24.

Segal, B. Male nurses: a case study in contradiction and prestige loss. *Social Forces,* 1962, **41**, 31–38.

Segal, E. Slouching towards America: the prize of failure. *New Republic,* October 2, 1976, pp. 25–27.

Seligman, M. E. P. Fall into helplessness. *Psychology Today,* 1973, **7**(1), 43–48.

Seligman, M. E. P. *Learned helplessness: a laboratory analogue of depression.* Lecture, Harvard University, February 1974.

Seward, G. H. *Sex and the social order.* New York: McGraw–Hill, 1946.

Seward, G. H., and Williamson, R. *Sex roles in a changing society.* New York: Random House, 1970.

Shaver, P. Questions concerning fear of success and its conceptual relatives. *Sex Roles,* 1976, **2**, 305–320.

Sheehy, G. *Passages: predictable crises of adult life.* New York: E. P. Dutton and Co., 1976.

Sherif, M. *The psychology of social norms.* New York: Harper, 1936.

Shinn, M. *Secondary school coeducation and the fears of success and failure.* Unpublished honors thesis, Harvard University, 1973.

Shore, A. L. Confirmation of expectancy and changes in teachers' evaluations of student behaviors. *Dissertation Abstracts International,* 1969, **30**, 1878–1879.

Short, J. C. *The effect of the sex-role orientation of the situation on the arousal of the motive to avoid success.* Unpublished master's thesis, University of Western Ontario, 1973.

Short, J. A., and Sorrentino, R. M. The arousal of fear of success as a function of male vs female role orientation. *Journal of Research in Personality,* 1974, **8**, 277–290.

Signorelli, A. Statistics: tool or master of the psychologist? *American Psychologist,* 1974, **29**, 774–777.

Silverman, I. Self-esteem and differential responsiveness to success and failure. *Journal of Abnormal and Social Psychology,* 1964, **69**, 115–119.

Silverman, I. Role-related behavior of subjects in laboratory studies of attitude change. *Journal of Personality and Social Psychology*, 1968, **8**, 343–348.

Silverman, I., and Marcantonio, C. Demand characteristics vs. dissonance–reduction as determinants of failure-seeking behavior. *Journal of Personality and Social Psychology*, 1965, **2**, 882–884.

Silverstein, M. The history of a short unsuccessful academic career. *Insurgent Sociologist*, 1972, **3**, 4–19. (Reprinted as The development of an identity: power and sex roles in America. *Journal of Applied Behavioral Science*, 1972, **8**, 536–563.)

Simmel, G. The sociology of sociability. (Trans. by E. Hughes) *American Journal of Sociology*, 1949, **55**, 254–261.

Simmel, G. *Conflict and the web of group affiliation*. Glencoe, Illinois: Free Press, 1955.

Singer, J. L. *Daydreaming: an introduction to the experimental study of inner experience*. New York: Random House, 1966.

Sisk, J. P. The fear of affluence. *Commentary*, June 1974, pp. 61–68.

Siu, R. G. H. *The portable dragon: the Western man's guide to the I Ching*. Cambridge: M.I.T. Press, 1968.

Slater, P. E. On social regression. *American Sociological Review*, 1963, **28**, 339–364.

Slater, P. *The glory of Hera*. Boston: Beacon Press, 1968.

Smith, C. P., and Feld, S. How to learn the method of content analysis for *n* Achievement, *n* Affiliation, and *n* Power. In J. W. Atkinson (Ed.), *Motives in fantasy, action, and society*. Princeton: Van Nostrand, 1958, 685–818.

Smith, C. R., Williams, L., and Willis, R. H. Race, sex, and belief as determinants of friendship acceptance. *Journal of Personality and Social Psychology*, 1967, **5**, 127–137.

Smith, M. B. Competence and socialization. In J. A. Clausen (Ed.), *Socialization and society*. Boston: Little, Brown, 1968, 270–320.

Solkoff, J. Can Cesar Chavez cope with success? *New Republic*, May 22, 1976, pp. 13–17.

Solomon, L. Z. Perception of a successful person of the same sex or the opposite sex. *Journal of Social Psychology*, 1975, **95**, 133–134.

Sorrentino, R. M. *Extending theory of achievement motivation to the study of group processes—is it worth the effort?* Paper presented at the annual meeting of the American Psychological Association, New Orleans, 1974.

Sorrentino, R. M., and Short, J. A. *Performance in women as a function of fear of success and sex-role orientation*. Unpublished manuscript, University of Western Ontario, 1973.

Spence, J. T. The Thematic Apperception Test and attitudes toward achievement in women: a new look at the motive to avoid success and a new method of measurement. *Journal of Consulting and Clinical Psychology*, 1974, **42**, 427–437.

Spitzer, S. *Labeling the deviant act: toward a general theory of deviant behavior*. Paper presented at the annual meeting of the American Sociological Association, New Orleans, August 1972. (ERIC Reproduction Document no. ED 070 987).

Stake, J. E. Effects of achievement on the aspiration behavior of black and white children. *Journal of Personality and Social Psychology*, 1973, **25**, 187–191.

Stein, A. H. *Children's achievement behavior on sex-typed tasks*. Paper presented at the meeting of the Society for Research in Child Development, New York, March 1967.

Stein, A. H. The effects of sex-role standards for achievement and sex-role preference on three determinants of achievement motivation. *Developmental Psychology*, 1971, **4**, 219–231.

Stein, A. H., and Bailey, M. M. The socialization of achievement orientation in females. *Psychological Bulletin,* 1973, **80**, 345–366.

Stein, A. H., Pohly, S. R., and Mueller, E. The influence of masculine, feminine, and neutral tasks on children's achievement behavior, expectancies of success, and attainment values. *Child Development,* 1971, **42**, 195–207.

Stein, A. H., and Smithells, J. Age and sex difference in children's sex-role standards about achievement. *Developmental Psychology,* 1969, **1**, 252–259.

Steiner, C. *Scripts people live.* New York: Grove, 1974.

Steinmann, A., and Fox, D. Masculine–feminine perceptions of the female role in the U.S. *Journal of Psychology,* 1966, **64**, 265–276.

Stericker, A. *Fear-of-success in male and female college students: sex-role identification and self-esteem as factors.* Unpublished doctoral dissertation, Loyola University of Chicago, 1975.

Stevenson, B. (Ed.) *The Macmillan book of proverbs, maxims, and famous phrases.* New York: Macmillan, 1948.

Stewart, A. J. *Longitudinal prediction from personality to life outcomes among college-educated women.* Unpublished doctoral dissertation, Harvard University, 1975.

Stigler, G. J. Competition. In D. Sills (Ed.), *International Encyclopedia of the Social Sciences* (Vol. 3). New York, Macmillan, 1968, 181–186.

Stoller, R. *Sex and gender: on the development of masculinity and femininity.* New York: Jason Aronson, 1971.

Suarès, C. *The cipher of genesis: the original code of the Qabala as applied to the Scriptures.* Berkeley: Shambala Publications, 1970.

Sullivan, H. S. *The interpersonal theory of psychiatry.* New York: Norton, 1953.

Sumner, W. G. *Folkways* (rev. ed.). Boston: Ginn, 1940.

Symonds, P. M. Criteria for the selection of pictures for the investigation of adolescent phantasies. *Journal of Abnormal and Social Psychology,* 1939, **34**, 271–274.

Symonds, P. M. *Adolescent fantasy: an investigation of the picture-story method of personality study.* New York: Columbia University Press, 1949.

Symonds, P. M. *From adolescent to adult.* New York: Columbia University Press, 1961.

Szekely, L. Success, success neurosis, and the self. *British Journal of Medical Psychology,* 1950, **33**, 45–51.

Tabachnick, N. Failure and masochism. *American Journal of Psychotherapy,* 1964, **18**, 304–316.

Tangri, S. S. Determinants of occupational role innovation among college women. *Journal of Social Issues,* 1972, **28**, 177–200.

Taylor, S., and Huesmann, L. R. *Replication report: expectancy confirmed again: a computer investigation of expectancy theory.* Unpublished manuscript, Yale University, 1973.

Tedeschi, J. T., Schlenker, B. R., and Bonoma, T. V. Cognitive dissonance: private ratiocination or public spectacle? *American Psychologist,* 1971, **26**, 685–695.

Terman, L. M. The discovery and encouragement of exceptional talent. *American Psychologist,* 1954, **9**, 221–230.

Thibaut, J., and Kelley, H. H. *The social psychology of groups.* New York: Wiley, 1959.

Thoreau, H. D. (1854). *Walden and civil disobedience* (S. Paul, ed.). Boston: Houghton Mifflin, 1957.

Thorpe, R. H. Whom others envy. *Lippincott's Monthly Magazine.* Philadelphia: J. B. Lippincott, 1890, 705.

Time, July 15, 1974, p. 50.

Tolman, E. C. Principles of purposive behavior. In S. Koch (Ed.), *Psychology: a study of a science* (Vol. 2). New York: McGraw–Hill, 1959, 92–157.

Tomlinson-Keasey, C. Role variables: their influence on female motivational constructs. *Journal of Counseling Psychology,* 1974, **21**, 232–237.

Torrance, E. P. *Guiding creative talent.* Englewood Cliffs, New Jersey: Prentice-Hall, 1962.

Touhey, J. C. Effects of additional women professionals on ratings of occupational prestige and desirability. *Journal of Personality and Social Psychology,* 1974, **29**, 86–89.

Tresemer, D. Fear of success: popular but unproven. *Psychology Today,* 1974, **7**(10), 82–85. (a)

Tresemer, D. Success avoidance and gender role (Doctoral dissertation, Harvard University, 1974). *Dissertation Abstracts International,* 1975, **35**, 4263B. (University Microfilms No. 75-4933) (b)

Tresemer, D. Assumptions made about gender roles. In M. Millman and R. M. Kanter (Eds.), *Another voice: feminist perspectives on social life and social science.* New York: Doubleday, 1975. (a)

Tresemer, D. Measuring "sex differences." *Sociological Inquiry,* 1975, **45**, 29–32. (b)

Tresemer, D. Research on fear of success: full annotated bibliography. JSAS *Catalog of Selected Documents in Psychology,* 1976, **6**(2), 38, Ms. 1237. (Available in photocopy or microfiche from JSAS, American Psychological Association, 1200 17th St. NW, Washington, D.C. 20036.) (a)

Tresemer, D. Do women fear success? *Signs: Journal of Women in Culture and Society,* 1976, **1**, 863–874. (b)

Tresemer, D. The cumulative record of research on fear of success. *Sex Roles: A Journal of Research,* 1976, **2**, 217–236. (c)

Tresemer, D. Conscious voluntary movement. *Vermont Psychologist,* 1976, **2**, 12–16. (d)

Tresemer, D., and Pleck, J. Sex-role boundaries and resistance to sex-role change. *Women's Studies,* 1974, **2**, 61–78.

Triandis, H. C., and Davis, E. E. Race and belief as determinants of behavioral intentions. *Journal of Personality and Social Psychology,* 1965, **2**, 715–725.

Trollope, A. (1862). *Orley farm.* New York: Knopf, 1950.

Tseng, M. S. Achievement motivation and fear of failure as determinants of vocational choice, vocational aspiration, and perception of vocational prestige. *Journal of Counseling Psychology,* 1970, **17**, 150–156.

Tuddenham, R. D. Correlates of yielding to a distorted group norm. *Journal of Personality,* 1959, **27**, 272–284.

Tuddenham, R. D. The influence of a distorted group norm upon judgements of adults and children. *Journal of Psychology,* 1961, **52**, 231–239.

Tuddenham, R. D., Macbride, P., and Zahn, V. The influence of the sex composition of the group upon yielding to a distorted norm. *Journal of Psychology,* 1958, **46**, 243–251.

Turner, M. E. *Sex role attitudes and fear of success in relation to achievement behavior in women* (Doctoral dissertation, Fordham University, 1974). *Dissertation Abstracts International,* 1974, **35**, 2451B–2452B. (University Microfilms No. 74-25, 086)

Unger, R. K., and Krooth, D. M. *Female role perceptions and attitudes toward competence as related to activism in housewives.* Paper presented at the annual meeting of the American Psychological Association, New Orleans, 1974.

Updegraff, A. *The hills look down.* Toronto: Longmans, 194.

Vaillant, G. E. Theoretical hierarchy of adaptive ego mechanisms. *Archives of General Psychiatry,* 1971, **24**, 107–118.

Valins, S., and Nisbett, R. E. *Attribution processes in the development and treatment of emotional disorders.* Morristown, New Jersey: General Learning Press, 1971.

Veroff, J. Social comparison and the development of achievement motivation. In C. P. Smith (Ed.), *Achievement-related motives in children.* New York: Russell Sage, 1969, 46–101.

Veroff, J., and Feld, S. *Marriage and work in America.* New York: Van Nostrand–Reinhold, 1970.

Veroff, J., McClelland, L., and Marquis, K. *Measuring intellectual and achievement motivation in surveys.* Final report, Office of Educational Opportunity, U.S. Dept. of Health, Education, and Welfare, Project No. OEO-4180, 1971 (three vols.).

Veroff, J., Wilcox, S., and Atkinson, J. W. The achievement motive in high school and college age women. *Journal of Abnormal and Social Psychology,* 1953, **48**, 108–119.

Vogel, W., Raymond, S., and Lazarus, R. S. Intrinsic motivation and psychological stress. *Journal of Abnormal and Social Psychology,* 1954, **49**, 23–28.

vonFranz, M. L. *The problem of the puer aeternus.* New York: Spring Publications, 1970.

Walker, E. L., and Atkinson, J. W. The expression of fear-related motivation in thematic apperception as a function of proximity to an atomic explosion. In J. W. Atkinson (Ed.) *Motives in fantasy, action, and society.* Princeton: Van Nostrand, 1958, 143–159.

Walker, E. L., and Heyns, R. W. *An anatomy for conformity.* Englewood Cliffs, New Jersey: Prentice–Hall, 1962.

Wallin, P. Cultural contradictions and sex roles: a repeat study. *American Sociological Review,* 1950, **15**, 288–293.

Walster, E., Berscheid, E., and Walster, G. W. New directions in equity research. *Journal of Personality and Social Psychology,* 1973, **25**, 151–176.

Walter, D., Denzler, L. S., and Sarason, E. G. Anxiety and the intellectual performance of high school students. *Child Development,* 1964, **35**, 917–926.

Ward, W. D., and Sandvold, K. D. Performance expectancy as a determinant of actual performance: a partial replication. *Journal of Abnormal and Social Psychology,* 1963, **67**, 293–295.

Watson, G., and Johnson, D. *Social psychology* (2nd ed.). Philadelphia: Lippincott, 1972.

Watson, R. I., Jr. *Female and male responses to the succeeding female cue.* Unpublished paper, Harvard University, 1971.

Watson, R. I., Jr. *Motivational and sex differences in aggressive behavior.* Unpublished doctoral dissertation, Harvard University, 1974.

Weaver, D., and Brickman, P. Expectancy, feedback and disconfirmation as independent factors in outcome satisfaction. *Journal of Personality and Social Psychology,* 1974, **30**, 420–428.

Webber, R. A. *Management.* Homewood, Illinois: R. D. Irwin, 1975.

Weiner, B. *Theories of motivation: from mechanism to cognition.* Chicago: Markham, 1972.

Weiner, B., Frieze, I., Kukla, A., Reed, L., Rest, S., and Rosenbaum, R. M. Perceiving the causes of success and failure. In E. E. Jones *et al.* (Eds.), *Attribution: perceiving the causes of behavior.* Morristown, New Jersey: General Learning Press, 1972, 95–120.

Weinstein, F., and Platt, G. M. *The wish to be free: society, psyche, and value change.* Berkeley: University of California Press, 1969.

Weinstein, F., and Platt, G. M. *Psychoanalytic sociology: an essay on the interpretation of historical data and the phenomena of collective behavior.* Baltimore: Johns Hopkins University Press, 1973.

Weinstein, M. S. Achievement motivation and risk preference. *Journal of Personality and Social Psychology,* 1969, **13**, 153–172.

Weiss, R. F., and Miller, F. G. The drive theory of social facilitation. *Psychological Review,* 1971, **78**, 44–57.

Wenkam, R. (Ed.). *Maui: the last Hawaiian place.* San Francisco: Friends of the Earth, 1970.

Weston, P. J., and Mednick, M. T. Race, social class, and the motive to avoid success in women. *Journal of Cross-Cultural Psychology,* 1970, **1**, 284–291. (Reprinted in Judith Bardwick (Ed.), *Readings on the psychology of women.* New York: Harper and Row, 1972, 68–71).

Wilde, O. (1890). *The picture of Dorian Gray.* New York: Heritage Press, 1957.

Williams, T. (1945). The catastrophe of success. *The glass menagerie.* New York: New Classics, 1949, xiii–xix.

Wilsnack, S. C. Femininity by the bottle. *Psychology Today,* 1973, **6**(11), 39–43, 96.

Winchel, R., Fenner, D., and Shaver, P. Impact of coeducation on "fear of success" imagery expressed by male and female high school students. *Journal of Educational Psychology,* 1974, **66**, 726–730.

Wine, J. Test anxiety and direction of attention. *Psychological Bulletin,* 1971, **76**, 92–104.

Winer, B. J. *Statistical principles in experimental design* (2nd ed.). New York: McGraw–Hill, 1971.

Winick, C. The beige epoch: depolarization of sex roles in America. *The Annals of the American Academy of Political and Social Science,* 1968, **376**, 18–24.

Winter, D. G. *The power motive.* New York: Free Press, 1973.

Wittemore, I. C. The influence of competition on performance: an experimental study. *Journal of Abnormal and Social Psychology,* 1924, **19**, 236–253.

Witty, P. (Ed.). *The gifted child.* Boston: Heath, 1951.

Wolman, B. B. *Victims of success: emotional problems of executives.* New York: Quadrangle, 1973.

Wood, M. M., and Greenfeld, S. T. Women managers and fear of success: a study in the field. *Sex Roles,* 1976, **2**, 375–387.

Wrong, D. H. The oversocialized conception of man in modern sociology. *American Sociological Review,* 1961, **26**, 183–193.

Yarrow, L. J., and Yarrow, M. R. Personality continuity and change in the family context. In P. Worchel and D. Byrne (Eds.), *Personality change.* New York: Wiley, 1964, 489–523.

Yates, F. The analysis of contingency tables with groupings based on quantitative characteristics. *Biometrika,* 1948, **35**, 176–181.

Yerkes, R. M., and Dodson, J. D. The relation of strength of stimulus to rapidity of habit formation. *Journal of Comparative Neurology and Psychology,* 1908, **18**, 459–482.

Zalman, R. *Expression of fear of success in a mixed-sex triad game.* Unpublished honors thesis, University of Michigan, 1973.

Zanna, M. P. *Intellectual competition and the female student.* Final report to United

States Dept. of Health, Education, and Welfare Office of Education, 1973 (ERIC Reproduction Document No. ED 072 389).

Zaro, J. S. *An experimental study of role conflict in women* (Doctoral dissertation, University of Connecticut, 1971). *Dissertation Abstracts International,* 1972, **33**, 2828B. (University Microfilms No. 72-32, 173)

Zaro, J. S. *The effects of motive to avoid success on women's competitive behavior.* Unpublished manuscript, University of Washington, 1975.

Zorbaugh, H., Boardman, R. K., and Sheldon P. Some observations of highly gifted children. In P. Witty (Ed.), *The gifted child.* Boston: Heath, 1951, 86–105.

Zuckerman, M., and Allison, S. N. An objective measure of fear of success: construction and validation. *Journal of Personality Assessment,* in press.

Zuckerman, M., Allison, S. N., and Marion, S. P. *The effects of the motive to avoid success on performance and attribution of success and failure.* Unpublished manuscript, University of Rochester, New York, 1974.

Zuckerman, M., and Wheeler, L. To dispel fantasies about the fantasy-based measure of fear of success. *Psychological Bulletin,* 1975, **82**, 932–946.

Index